*Understanding
and Coping
with Real-Life Crises*

Understanding and Coping with Real-Life Crises

Glenn E. Whitlock

University of Redlands

Brooks/Cole Publishing Company
Monterey, California

A Division of Wadsworth Publishing Company, Inc.

Printed in the United States of America

10 9 8 7 6 5 4 3 2 1

Library of Congress Cataloging in Publication Data

Whitlock, Glenn E.
    Understanding and coping with real-life
crises.

    Bibliography: p. 257
    Includes index.
    1. Crisis intervention (Psychiatry) I. Title.
RC480.6.W45   362.2'2   77-16157
ISBN 0-8185-0252-5

Acquisition Editor: *Charles T. Hendrix*
Project Development Editor: *Claire Verduin*
Production Editor: *John Bergez*
Interior and Cover Design: *Katherine Minerva*
Typesetting: *Chapman's Phototypesetting, Fullerton, California*

Preface

Learning how to cope with real-life crises is a crucial concern for all of us, but most especially for those who, at one time or another, may function as crisis counselors. Constructive interventions in crises by skilled and caring persons can prevent the development of more severe emotional disturbances and enable persons to cope more adequately with future stressful situations in their lives. Consequently, crisis intervention is one important aspect of preventive psychology within the community.

When I began my study and training in crisis intervention, only limited training resources were available. Since then, I have become increasingly aware of the need for an analysis of both the different kinds of crises commonly encountered in human life and the ways in which skills can be developed for coping with them. This book is intended to meet that need and thus to increase our competence in promoting community mental health.

The practice of crisis intervention presupposes some knowledge of the theory behind crisis-counseling techniques and an understanding of the relationship of crises to the normal transitions and stresses in human life. Part 1 of this book provides the necessary theoretical background, and Part 2 discusses the various types of human crises and specific counseling interventions. Numerous examples of actual crises and counselor interventions are described; most of these have been taken from my own experience as a counselor in a variety of work settings. Part 3 briefly takes up the issue of how the work of crisis counselors may be coordinated with that of mental-health specialists as part of a comprehensive approach to community mental health.

Such a comprehensive program involves many professions and disciplines. This book is primarily intended for the many nonspecialists in the field of mental health who regularly encounter persons in the midst of crises. These nonspecialists include both the "new professionals"—mental-health workers who counsel with persons in community agencies and clinics —and professionals in other human-services disciplines, such as nurses, medical doctors, police- and fire-department personnel, clergy, social workers, probation officers, and teachers. Since the book presumes no specialized knowledge of psychology, it is suitable for use in adult education, training programs for mental-health workers and paraprofessional counselors, and inservice training programs in community agencies, as well as in university-level counseling courses.

The actual writing of this book became invested with highly personal meaning. As I reflected on the emotionally hazardous transitions of my own life, I began to move beyond the formal development of the theory and practice of crisis intervention to a more personal description of the ways in which any person may cope with the real-life stresses that most frequently give rise to crises. On both a personal and a theoretical level, I became convinced that some experience of coping adaptively in one's own life is crucial for understanding the crisis experiences of others. By relating crisis experiences to the normal events and transitions in human life, and by providing a number of experiential exercises, I hope to have provided the basis for fruitful reflection by the users of this book on the significant experiences in their own lives. This kind of self-awareness provides crisis counselors with the personal understanding that no amount of formal instruction can supply.

I would like to acknowledge the contributions of several people to the development of this book. Most importantly, I want to thank those persons who have entrusted me with their inner worlds and with their own crises. David Eitzen, William Sullivan, Carl Rogers, and Charlotte Bühler have had decisive influences upon my development as a counselor and therapist; Gerald Jacobson and Martin Strickler, as directors of the Benjamin Rush Center, were my first teachers in crisis intervention. I want to thank my colleague Frank Blume for his helpful comments in the early stages of the writing and James McFarland for reading and responding to a preliminary draft of Chapter 15.

I also wish to express my appreciation to several people who reviewed the completed manuscript: James Brine, Southern

Connecticut State College; Barbara Bunch, University of North Florida; Kenneth Butler, Director of the Hot Line Crisis Intervention Center in Goldsboro, North Carolina; Clyde Crego, University of Missouri; James Dugger, Metropolitan State College, Denver; Norman Farber, Borough of Manhattan Community College; Richard Hamersma, private practice, Chicago; John Kalafat, Florida State University; Kenneth Nickerson, Center for Counseling Services, Jacksonville, Florida; and Ronald Schmidt, American River College, Sacramento.

I am grateful to Carole and Elliott for both their patience and their impatience with Dad during this writing. I am especially grateful to Emalee for her assistance and for the real-life delivery of our beautiful serendipity, Elise Bobette, during the early writing of the book. Johnston College and the University of Redlands gave me sabbatical time in which to extend my studies and complete the writing. Finally, I express my gratitude to my publishers, in particular to Claire Verduin and John Bergez, and to Shirley Peck, Diana Hernandez, and Gretchen Turner, who typed the various drafts of this book.

Glenn E. Whitlock

Contents

18 ENDINGS AND BEGINNINGS   *254*

Understanding
and Coping
with Real-Life Crises

PART 1

Theoretical Views of Real-Life Crises and Crisis Intervention

Part 1 introduces the student to the nature and development of crises, which are viewed as normal occurrences in human life. The theory and development of crisis intervention is discussed in relation to other counseling approaches to real-life crises, with special attention being given to the universal character of crisis experiences as the factor that makes crisis intervention applicable to persons of all sociocultural groups, including the "poor treatment risks." An orientation to the practice of crisis intervention is described, together with the different levels of intervention that may be used by mental-health workers. The final chapter focuses upon the training of counselors and the actual stages of crisis intervention.

1

Human Crises

Human crises are everybody's business. Everyone experiences emotionally hazardous moments of transition or loss during a lifetime. At such times *anyone* may experience a crisis in which the momentary emotional support or intervention of another person is needed.

There are two levels of learning about crises. On one level, each person needs to recognize the possibility both of experiencing a crisis and of learning how to develop the skills necessary to cope. On another level, counselors need to be trained to intervene with persons in the midst of crises in ways that can facilitate the development of their coping skills. This book examines both the nature of crises that may happen to any individual and the ways in which counselors can be trained to intervene in the crises of others.

There are also two basic levels of training in crisis intervention. First, there is the training of mental-health specialists who are specifically trained in psychotherapy and in the understanding of the psychodynamics of human behavior. In the usual course of their work, psychotherapists counsel persons in various stages of personal crises. Because psychotherapists are specialists in the understanding of human behavior, they may be needed as consultants by others involved in mental-health work. Second, there is the type of training to which this book is directed. This second level of training involves "the new professionals"—generalists who are engaged in various kinds of mental-health counseling. These individuals may be mental-health workers in community agencies or clinics who regularly encounter persons in the midst of crises. The new professionals may also be people in other professions, such as teachers, nurses, medical doctors, police officers, or clergy, who receive specific training in dealing with personal crises encountered as a part of their work. This book is intended to help anyone who may function as a counselor to understand and to intervene appropriately in crises in ways that facilitate the development of coping skills and enable persons to reach adaptive rather than maladaptive resolutions of their crises.

Since crises can happen to anyone, the development of resources for dealing with them is everybody's business. Such development may involve establishing a twofold program of (a) training persons in health services and related professions in crisis intervention and (b) creating structures within the community that can facilitate various levels of work with persons in crises. This kind of program can utilize both the usual mental-health resources of the community and the therapeutic potential of trained personnel in such institutions as the schools and churches. It should certainly involve the elimination of the toxic influences on the emotional health of a community and the development of nurturing influences. Finally, a comprehensive program for dealing with crises must include the development of a psychology of community that facilitates and enhances the mental health of all members of the community.

THE ANATOMY OF CRISES

A crisis, as I am using the term, is not the same as an emergency. An *emergency* may be defined as an unforeseen combination of circumstances that calls for some kind of immediate action and specific treatment. There are various kinds of emergencies in which persons in particular occupations are involved, including medical and psychiatric emergencies that require the intervention of a medical doctor and specific emergencies that occur in counseling and in psychotherapy. A *crisis,* however, is described more accurately as a *decisive moment* or *turning point* that can be anticipated. It is the culminating point beyond which something crucial will happen. Thus, *crisis* has been defined medically as the point at which there is a change in the disease that indicates whether the result is to be recovery or death.

An *emotional* or *psychological* crisis generally involves a *loss* or *threat of loss* or a *radical change* in one's relationship with oneself or with some significant other person or situation —for instance, the loss of another person through death or separation. A crisis may be brought on by the injection into one's life of new and threatening people or events. It may involve a significant change in status or role relationships. Each of these situations signifies a point of possible change in the way one relates to oneself and to one's life situation.

In any such significant experience in which an individual is temporarily unable to cope, a crisis occurs. It may be that the emotional stress is too intense or that the person has insufficient time or experience to develop the requisite coping skills. The problem of the counselor is to learn the ways in which interventions may be made to facilitate the development of an individual's coping skills.

Normally, a crisis will be resolved one way or another in a relatively brief period of time. The question is whether the resolution will be adaptive or maladaptive. Someone has pointed out that the Chinese word for "crisis" consists of two characters. One character represents *danger,* and the other indicates *opportunity.* Together they represent *crisis.*

We all experience hazardous situations in life that have the potential of developing into crises. Maturational crises, for example, are related to changes that occur in everyone's developmental history. There are *contractive* crises, which include a significant diminishing of human possibilities, and *expanding* crises, which may enhance and extend human potential. There are the penultimate crises related to the loss of function in aging, and there is the ultimate crisis of dying. In all of these crises, there is both *danger* and *opportunity.* The purpose of this book is to train counselors in the dynamics of these crises and in the ways in which they can intervene with troubled persons in order to diminish the dangers and enhance the opportunities of persons in the midst of crises.

THE DEVELOPMENT OF CRISES

There are two general types of crises: *developmental,* or *maturational,* crises and *situational* crises. Specifically, crises may result from the loss of something or someone of significance, the injection of new and threatening people or events, or significant changes in role or status. In other words, whenever one's relation to oneself and to one's world is dramatically changed, there is the possibility of a crisis.

In a study of life events that lead to crises, Holmes and Rahe (1967) developed a scale of the degree of stress represented by each of the events. Table 1 is an adaptation of their scale, and it is included here to point out one way to view the development of a crisis. Holmes and Rahe established both a rank ordering of the degree of stress and a mean value for the stress potential of

Table 1. Social Readjustment Rating Scale

Rank	Life Event	Mean Value
1	Death of spouse	100
2	Divorce	73
3	Marital separation	65
4	Jail term	63
5	Death of close family member	63
6	Personal injury or illness	53
7	Marriage	50
8	Fired from work	47
9	Marital reconciliation	45
10	Retirement	45
11	Change in health of family member	44
12	Pregnancy	40
13	Sex difficulties	39
14	Gain of new family member	39
15	Business readjustment	39
16	Change in financial state	38
17	Death of close friend	37
18	Change to different line of work	36
19	Change in number of arguments with spouse	35
20	Mortgage over $10,000	31
21	Foreclosure of mortgage or loan	30
22	Change in responsibilities at work	29
23	Son or daughter leaving home	29
24	Trouble with in-laws	29
25	Outstanding personal achievement	28
26	Wife begins or stops work	26
27	Begin or end school	26
28	Change in living conditions	25
29	Revision of personal habits	24
30	Trouble with boss	23
31	Change in work hours or conditions	20
32	Change in residence	20
33	Change in schools	20
34	Change in recreation	19
35	Change in church activities	19
36	Change in social activities	18

Adapted from "The Social Readjustment Rating Scale," by T. H. Holmes and R. H. Rahe, *Journal of Psychosomatic Research*, 1967, *11*, pp. 213–218. Reprinted by permission.

each of these events. As the score of mean values mounts, the likelihood of crisis increases.

Developmental and maturational crises are related to developmental stages. Stages of growth are punctuated by dips and forward thrusts, and either type of stressful period, if combined with certain other circumstances, may develop into a crisis. Both regressive dips in development and thrusts forward into the unknown can represent serious threats to a person. It is probably only during the plateau periods between transitions that a person is free of threat. When a threat is too intense for the available coping skills, a crisis occurs. At the point of crisis, there is both a greater danger of regression to an earlier level of adjustment than there is in the usual transitions and a greater opportunity to move forward rapidly into a more mature level of development.

Caplan (1964) divides the *situational crisis* into four phases. In the first phase, there is a rise in tension and the experience of disturbing feelings, as well as some disorganization of behavior, following the impact of a stressful situation. During this phase, the individual is calling upon the usual problem-solving behavior that has worked in the past. In the second phase, if the situation has not been resolved successfully, the tension increases, and the situation becomes increasingly hazardous. In the third phase, the tension reaches a point at which additional internal and external resources are mobilized. At this stage the situation may get better. Emergency problem-solving methods may be used. The problem may be defined in a new way, or certain goals may be given up as unrealistic. In the fourth phase, major disorganization occurs if the problem continues and cannot be solved or avoided.

The most significant aspect of the development of either a situational or maturational crisis is the telescoping of the total experience. The critical period rarely extends beyond four to six weeks. Interventions during this brief period of time can facilitate major changes within the individual that may remain stable for years.

One way to characterize the development of a crisis is to think of it as a drama in three acts.[1] As Act I opens, the individual is confronted with a new and stressful situation. It is usually a situation in which social forces impinge upon an individual in such a way that his or her relations with others or

[1]Originally suggested by Granger Westberg in a lecture at the Conference on Medicine and Religion, University of California Conference Center at Arrowhead, October 1966.

self-expectations undergo significant change. Suppose, for example, that a man loses his job. In normal circumstances, such a loss might be a hazardous situation with which he could cope. However, if the circumstances of age and economic conditions are such that he also loses his self-esteem, a crisis occurs. First he may begin to experience some difficulty with eating or sleeping, and then his wife and family, and finally his friends, notice that something is seriously wrong.

The second act usually begins with the individual consulting the family doctor about problems of depression and lack of energy. If the situation seems to warrant it, a hospital check-up may be recommended.

If the check-up in the hospital does not uncover some organic pathology, Act III may open with the physician referring the patient to a psychiatrist. If depression or apathy becomes severe, the individual may be hospitalized in a psychiatric hospital.

Usually, a counselor enters this drama, if at all, sometime during Act II. The professional psychotherapist does not ordinarily see an individual in crisis until Act III, or *after* the outcome of the immediate crisis has been determined.

It is important for the new professional to intervene at the earliest possible stage of the crisis. He or she needs to enter the drama in *Act I*, when a *preventive* role can most effectively be played. The counselor should come in at least at the point at which friends become aware of the person's difficulty and concurrently with, if not before, the individual's initial contact with the family doctor. *Intervention at any of these points throughout Act I can most effectively reverse the process of the crisis.* In these periods of Act I, the person is in the process of mobilizing his or her own resources—first by himself or herself, then with the understanding and acceptance of spouse and family, and finally with the understanding and acceptance of friends.

It is during Act I that the preventive role can be most effectively exercised, usually without the intervention of a specialist. New professionals who are indigenous to the community, such as teachers or clergy, may have the first opportunity to work with persons in crisis, and they may also have more going for them because of previously established relationships. An individual in a crisis may not move beyond Act I—most dramatically, if it leads to suicide. Or a person may not be able to function in the other "acts," except to complete the drama with serious emotional disturbance or psychotic withdrawal from reality.

An example of the preventive role counselors can play may be taken from some practices of the armed services during recent wars. When personnel in the field were referred to the mental-health services, they did not immediately go into a clinic to see a psychiatrist. Instead, a technician was sent out into the field, with the result that most persons never got to the clinic, because the problem was solved in the field with the technician. The obvious application here is that a person who is able to see a counselor in Act I may never need to move to Acts II or III in the drama of a crisis. In such a situation, the counselor fulfills a crucial function in the area of preventive psychology.

Anyone who has worked in the area of community mental health is aware of the unique opportunity available to the various kinds of counselors who are indigenous to the community in which they work for reducing the incidence and severity of emotional disorders. The efforts of these counselors in helping persons to learn how to cope with their crises may prevent the development of more serious emotional problems at a later time and place. Any discussion of community mental health in general, and crisis intervention in particular, must therefore include these counselors, as well as the institutions they serve, within its scope.

A PSYCHOLOGY OF THE COMMUNITY

Crisis intervention is a significant dimension of preventive psychology and hence of a psychology *of* the community. Work with people in crises may involve people from any background or position in the community. I concluded my last book with this observation:

> Any practitioner in the area of mental health knows that the prevention of emotional pathology and the development of a sound mental health for individuals within *any* social milieu demands an integrated effort of the total community. The community can no longer charge a particular profession with the responsibility for developing the mental health of the community; nor can a specific profession lay sole claim to such a responsibility. Rather, it behooves the community as a whole to develop a psychology *of* the community that will foster the principles of sound mental health and provide the basis for the actualization of human potential [Whitlock, 1973, pp. 164–165].[2]

[2]From *Preventive Psychology and the Church*, by Glenn E. Whitlock. Copyright © MCMLXXIII, The Westminster Press. This and all other quotations from this source are reprinted by permission.

The issue of community mental health, then, involves many persons within the community. It involves not only the new professionals who have been trained in crisis intervention and the mental-health specialists who normally provide psychotherapy and mental-health consultation but also other professional persons, such as physicians, nurses, other hospital staff, clergy, police personnel, probation officers, teachers, and a variety of others. Just as this book is concerned with the emotional health of the entire community, so too an understanding of the dynamics of crises and of ways to cope with them involves *everyone* to some degree.

Interest in the area of preventive mental-health work in the community is widespread. While it may be premature to speak of the demise of the medical model in referring to the work of the psychological counselor, we are in the midst of a revolution of sorts. Several years ago M. Brewster Smith (1968) suggested in an article in *Transaction* that we are in the midst of the third revolution in the mental-health movement. The first revolution involved releasing persons from a sense of alienation from society by designating them as mentally ill rather than as lunatics possessed by demons. Persons were therefore treated in hospitals rather than put away in asylums for the insane. A second revolution resulted from the influence of dynamic psychiatry, whose chief spokesman was Freud. This revolution led to the developing practice of psychoanalysis in the treatment of persons at a level of depth.

The present revolution involves psychological counselors and the new professionals who are trained in crisis intervention, as well as others in the mental-health and allied professions. This revolution consists of discarding the constraints of the doctor-patient medical model and abandoning the idea that an emotional problem is a private matter between doctor and patient or between counselor and client. Personality disturbance is no longer a matter of private misery. Both the disturbance itself and the therapeutic efforts made to alleviate it are related to the network of relationships in which an individual is involved. This revolution in our outlook concerning mental health is especially relevant to the new professionals and others who provide direct counseling services to persons in crises.

2

Crisis Intervention Theory and Practice

Crises happen to normal people. As I am using the term, crises are primarily related not to people's characterological problems but to particular situations and experiences with which they are momentarily unable to cope by themselves. Hence, by enhancing people's ability to cope, interventions may prevent further damage to their sense of well-being and enable them to return to their family relationships or jobs or whatever circumstances they happen to face.

In addition to the provision of emotional support by the counselor and by others in the community, crisis intervention involves helping individuals to improve their relationships with others, to utilize their own personality resources in coping successfully in the here-and-now, to confront the realities of their own lives head-on, and to utilize problem solving in making their behavior more constructive. Since crises are fraught with danger, interventions may prevent the development of more serious emotional impairment. Since crises also represent potential opportunities for growth, proper interventions can enable considerable personal growth to take place in a limited period of time.

THE DEVELOPMENT OF CRISIS INTERVENTION THEORY AND PRACTICE

The pioneer work of psychiatrist Erich Lindemann on the experience of grief is one of the basic building blocks for our contemporary understanding of the dynamics of human crises and crisis resolution. Lindemann studied the grief reactions of people in Boston following the tragic Coconut Grove fire in 1942. The disaster occurred on a November evening when hundreds of college students were crowded into the Coconut Grove nightclub for a dance following a game. The highly flammable decorations caught fire, and the blaze swept rapidly through the ballroom. In the ensuing panic, young men and women were packed against blocked doors, and nearly 500 perished.

In the emotionally charged aftermath of this massive community tragedy, Lindemann (1944) worked with a multitude of bereaved persons. He observed that grief was a natural and necessary reaction to the experience of a significant loss. He further noted that those people who were involved in active "grief work" for a period of about four to six weeks generally adapted successfully to their bereavement, while others reacted to the crisis by developing psychiatric or psychosomatic illnesses or experiencing abnormally prolonged periods of grief.

Another important contribution to the early development of crisis-intervention theory concerned the needs of normal people for support in circumstances that involve acute emotional hazards. U. S. Army colonel Albert J. Glass made a study of the incidence of combat neurosis during the Second World War. The results of his study indicated that the occurrence of combat neurosis was related not so much to soldiers' previously existing personality factors as to the nature of the stress in the combat situation itself (Caplan, 1964). Even more significantly, Glass found that, to the degree that a particular soldier experienced support from his buddies and felt a sense of group cohesiveness and respect for his leaders, he tended to be free of combat neurosis. Although the intensity and duration of the particular battle or series of battles influenced the incidence of combat neurosis, they were not the most important factors.

Glass also found that work with soldiers in treatment centers as near the front as possible prevented regression and the development of more severe patterns of emotional disorder (Glass, 1954; Menninger, 1948). Focusing on both the immediacy and the situational nature of the crisis took it out of the category of a mental disease or pathology that could happen to some people but not to others. Emphasizing the individual soldier's feeling about what had happened to him and helping him to recognize his group's support restored his confidence in his own ability to function. The success of this type of approach suggested to others in the mental-health disciplines that similar interventions might be useful in crisis work with people who come into community mental-health centers.

Interest in the subject of crisis intervention was further aroused by various kinds of clinical experiences. In some instances in which patients were suffering from emotional disorders, psychiatrists discovered that significant changes in personality development occurred during fairly short periods of crisis. As Gerald Caplan (1964) has indicated, "These transitional points in their history have usually been characterized by acute psychological upset, lasting from about one to four or five weeks, which appear not to have been in themselves signs of mental disorder, but rather the manifestations of adjustment and adaptation struggles in the face of a temporarily insoluble problem" (p. 35).[1]

In 1946, Caplan and Lindemann established a community program of mental health, called the Wellesley Project. In reporting on his developing theory and practice and on the result of his experiences with the Community Mental Health Program at Harvard University, Caplan (1961) concluded that the total emotional environment of the individual must be assessed in any approach to mental health, and he suggested the concept of *crisis periods* in the development of persons.

In keeping with this analysis, Parad (1965) and others have emphasized the fundamental importance of the structure of the family and the interaction among family members in both the development and the resolution of a crisis. An assessment of the individual's social role and social network is critical to any planned intervention. Any long-lasting results evidently depend on the availability of the necessary psychosocial support from the significant other persons in the individual's environment.

Caplan (1964) has also pointed out that the history of psychiatric patients often shows that they seem to have dealt with previous crisis periods in a maladaptive manner; that is, they have emerged from their crises less healthy than they had been before. This clinical evaluation is consistent with the popular view of a crisis as a turning point in one's life development. A similar view of crisis is implied in many modern plays and novels, in which the story's outcome is determined by the choices the characters make in coping with a particular situation.

Caplan's studies of emotionally disturbed patients also showed that, despite a certain measure of stability during particular phases in their development, their personalities often changed suddenly and in unexpected ways during periods of crisis. This observation tends to confirm that *crisis periods* may

---

[1]This and all other quotations from this source from *Principles of Preventive Psychiatry*, by Gerald Caplan. Copyright © 1964 by Basic Books, Inc. and The American Orthopsychiatric Association, Inc. Reprinted by permission.

be times in which constructive changes can take place within a relatively short period. Both psychotherapists and educators have utilized this insight in many ways. Personal growth has been stimulated by exposing individuals to situations of increasing challenge and then helping them to discover constructive ways of meeting the stresses.

In 1962, the Los Angeles Psychiatric Service opened a division called the Benjamin Rush Center for Problems of Living. Its function was to offer services on a walk-in basis to persons facing problems of living, specifically including life crises. The report of its work (Jacobson, Wilner, Morley, Schneider, Strickler, and Sommer, 1965) included a description of the services. Treatment was usually provided at the time of entry at the Center and was available within less than a week at most. The understanding that people in crisis respond to immediate treatment was essential to the Center's approach. Consultations were limited to six except in unusual circumstances, when an additional six visits could be arranged. The concept that a crisis will be resolved one way or another in a period of about six weeks was the basis for this rule. In general, the Center provided early access to help on a minimum-fee basis in a context unrelated to medical diagnosis and screening.

In an early report on the work of the Center, Morley (1965) characterized the program's function by indicating that the persons using the services of the Center were not the ones who tended to go to traditional mental-health clinics. Rather, clients of the Center were seeking short-term help, and they were usually unwilling to make any long-term arrangements for counseling and psychotherapy. Indeed, they were not seeking traditional psychotherapy, and they generally lacked the verbal skills to utilize this form of help. In addition, the immediacy of access to professional assistance seemed to be a crucial reason why these people utilized the service. In general, if they had had several weeks of waiting, they probably would never have returned to the Center.

A crisis counselor considers crises to be normal experiences of normal people. Since any person may experience unusual stress in relation to events and to significant other persons, crisis periods are evaluated as essentially circumstantial rather than characterological in origin. Such an evaluation is similar to Erikson's (1950) concept of developmental crises as occasions for growth. Successfully coping with one crisis will usually enable a person to cope more skillfully in the future.

THE THEORY OF CRISIS INTERVENTION

Caplan's model for crisis theory is based upon the biological concept of *homeostasis,* which refers to the process by which the physiological equilibrium of the body is maintained. Whenever physiological equilibrium is upset by some deficiency, various functions and resources of the body tend to mobilize to compensate for the deficiency—a tendency that Walter Cannon once characterized as the "wisdom of the body."

An application of the concept of homeostasis to psychological events implies that, when a person's emotional balance is in some kind of disequilibrium, his or her emotional resources will need to be mobilized to deal with the problem. The purpose of intervention can thus be viewed as helping a person to mobilize the emotional resources necessary to cope with a situation of stress. Provided that the emotional stress is not too much greater than in previous situations and that a sufficient amount of time is available, the individual may be able to resolve the crisis satisfactorily.

Stress is present whenever circumstances compel us to dramatically change our expectations of ourselves or of our relationships with other people. Often these changes involve some kind of loss or threat of loss—for example, the loss of a significant other person through death or separation, the loss of a job with its accompanying diminishment of self-esteem, the birth of a child with a deformity, the loss of a limb, the experience of a debilitating illness, and so on. The loss or threat of loss may be associated either with the normal changes involved in the emotional development of a person or with the sudden turns of events that may occur in the life of any human being.

A crisis occurs when a person does not have the skills necessary to deal with an emotionally hazardous situation. Coping skills are necessary throughout life as an individual passes through an inevitable succession of stressful experiences. Not every such experience will result in a crisis. A bereavement experience, for example, may be handled satisfactorily because the individual has worked out ways to cope with this kind of significant loss. On the other hand, the same event may result in a crisis if the means of coping are not readily available. In this case, the emotional equilibrium of the individual is upset, and he or she will need to experiment with alternative ways of restoring it. Some bereaved persons may therefore need the assistance of a counselor in working out satisfactory ways of handling the loss they have suffered.

Gerald Jacobson and his associates at the Benjamin Rush Center have made a helpful contribution to crisis-intervention theory by distinguishing between crisis intervention and other forms of psychotherapeutic intervention. In a lecture at the South Bay Mental Health Center in Southern California, Jacobson characterized crisis-intervention theory by means of a diagram representing a person's total functioning. This diagram, together with an interpretative statement of Jacobson's position, appeared in my earlier book.[2]

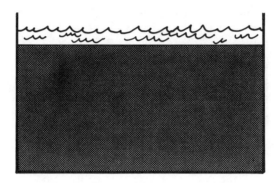

Figure 2-1.

The shaded area represents the stable or relatively stable part of a person's functioning, including his basic attitudes, values and commitment. It includes his relation to reality factors including both his inner reality (intra-psychic) and his relations with others (interpersonal). It refers to the characteristic (characterological) way a person behaves. It involves the behavior which makes a person recognizable as the same individual throughout his lifetime.

The thin fluid area on top of the solid area represents those aspects of a person's functioning which are changing from time to time. All of us are in the process of change, and the fluid area represents this part of one's functioning. In a situation of stress, a person may experience mild anxiety or depression until he develops some way of dealing with the new situation [Whitlock, 1973, pp.108–109].

In a highly stressful situation, the fluid area is enlarged, and the ratio of the fluid to the solid area is significantly changed,

[2]Figures 2-1 and 2-2 are reprinted from "Crisis Intervention," by G. Jacobson, *Pastoral Psychology*, 1970, *21* (203), 24–25. Reprinted by permission of the author.

as indicated in Figure 2-2. When this occurs, the individual encounters a crucial turning point in his or her life. If previously developed coping skills are not adequate to the new circumstances, the person will suffer considerable upset during the period of time in which he or she is experimenting with different solutions.

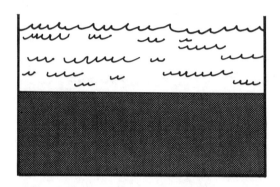

Figure 2-2.

Regardless of how it is resolved, the immediate crisis does not continue, usually, beyond four to six weeks. During this time the level of anxiety becomes increasingly high, but it usually diminishes after that period, whether the resolution is adaptive or maladaptive. In other words, if the situation is not faced realistically, a resolution is reached, but it will be a maladaptive one. The person's level of functioning will be impaired, and his or her ability to cope with future stressful situations will be less than it was prior to the crisis. An adaptive resolution, on the other hand, will help the person to deal constructively with similar stresses in the future. Thus, the question is not whether the crisis will be resolved but whether the resolution will be a constructive or a destructive one.

A crisis, then, concentrates significant learning possibilities into moments of intensity. The intensity of these moments produces the *danger* inherent in a crisis—namely, that the radical risk involved may push an individual into retreating into a maladaptive resolution. However, the insecurity of the state of disequilibrium and the sense of security that can result from a facilitating intervention may provide the unique *opportunity* a crisis affords for considerable growth within a limited period of time.

In summary, as normal persons face problems in daily life, they may experience states of tension in which emotional equilibrium is temporarily upset. If a given stressful situation is not too serious or not so very different from past situations, and if there are sufficient time and security in which to develop adequate means of coping, a crisis will not result. However, if the problem confronting an individual is unusually serious or very unlike anything he or she has ever encountered, and if sufficient time and security are not available to develop some means of coping with it, a crisis may occur, and the person may need help in coping with it.

The term *crisis* is therefore reserved for the acute disturbance resulting from an emotionally hazardous experience. A crisis usually lasts for a relatively brief period of time; in ordinary circumstances, it is resolved within a period of approximately six weeks. The physiological and/or neurological data that might account for this limit of about six weeks are not yet in; nor is the period of crisis resolution always precisely six weeks. Nevertheless, clinical evidence points to the crucial importance of this duration of time as the period in which some kind of resolution usually occurs. Obviously, not all of the pain of the crisis event is resolved during this period, but the basic dimensions of the *dangers* and *opportunities* of a crisis are determined within this approximate time frame.

Theoretical Foundations
of Crisis Intervention

Although the specific practice of crisis intervention originated in social and preventive psychiatry, it is related to the theory and practice of various professions. Social workers, clergy, doctors, nurses, police- and fire-department personnel, teachers, and others have often played valuable roles in providing people with emotional support and helping them to cope with real-life crises.

In addition to the contributions of these professionals to the practice of crisis intervention, several theoretical constructs of counseling and psychotherapy have contributed to the development of crisis counseling. Although the practice of crisis intervention is essentially eclectic, it is significantly rooted in several different theories of personality and psychotherapy. A brief survey of some of this theoretical background may put the practice of counseling, and specifically of crisis intervention, in some perspective.

PSYCHOANALYTIC FOUNDATIONS

The initial thrust in the development of depth psychology was provided by Sigmund Freud at around the turn of the century. Freud broke new ground in his approach to the emotional problems of human beings. From his observations of people in various kinds of emotional distress and of their responses to different forms of treatment, he developed the principle of *psychic causality*—that is, that present and future behavior are rooted in the life experience of an individual. Accordingly, Freud developed a method of treatment that was designed to relate past experience to present distress in such a way that his patients' understanding of the connection between the two would free them from their distress. Freud's insistence that the dynamics of present behavior must be understood in terms of the life experience of an individual made him a pioneer in the *psychodynamic* approach to the understanding of human behavior.

Later psychoanalysts have elaborated on Freud's work. In his development of ego psychology, Heinz Hartman (1964) extended Freud's work to include normal behavior and adaptation. He was concerned with the ways in which individuals relate to their culture and environment and with the strengthening of ego functioning in such adaptation. Erik Erikson (1963) has emphasized a concept of *epigenetic development* according to which a person develops through eight stages. Each stage has its own psychosocial tasks, and each one gives way to the next as these tasks are fulfilled. In postulating an orderly sequence of development, Erikson makes use of the concept of the influence of early life experience on present behavior. An important element of his theory is the importance placed upon interactions with significant other persons as factors in personal development.

CLIENT-CENTERED ROOTS OF CRISIS THERAPY

Carl Rogers, the founder of *client-centered therapy*, has acknowledged his debt to Freud and to the psychoanalytic theories of human development and psychotherapy. Although there are significant differences between client-centered therapy and crisis intervention, the client-centered approach establishes some fundamental elements of any counseling or psychotherapeutic method. Since many counseling classes have trained students in the client-centered model, it is worthwhile to note the relevance of this approach to the early stages of crisis counseling and therapy.

Rogers (1951) insists that psychotherapeutic changes occur only when certain conditions are fulfilled. (1) Significant rapport must be established between counselors (therapists) and their clients. (2) Clients must become aware of the incongruence between what they are saying and what they are doing. (3) Counselors must establish their own congruence between what they are feeling and what they are doing. (4) Counselors must have an unconditional positive regard for, and empathic understanding of, their clients; and clients must be able to identify and accept counselors' acceptance. Following these guidelines during the early stages of contact with people in crisis will facilitate the development of skills in crisis therapy.

EXISTENTIAL ROOTS OF CRISIS THERAPY

No theory of the psychodynamics of crises can ignore the existential dimension of these human experiences. Since a crisis represents a point of decision, it is essentially an existential phenomenon. Hence, the practice of crisis intervention also has an existential frame of reference. The goal of the intervention is to enhance the *opportunity* of the decisive moment and to diminish the *danger.*

Psychiatrist Viktor Frankl developed a particular application of existentialism to counseling and psychotherapy. Much of Frankl's thought stems from his experiences in a Nazi concentration camp. As we have seen, crisis theory proper first began to take shape as a result of Lindemann's observations in another extreme case of human suffering—the bereavement of an entire community following the Coconut Grove fire. Both experiences point to the importance of facing reality head-on. Lindemann's work showed that denial of reality in bereavement led to psychiatric or psychosomatic disorders, while Frankl found that denial of reality in the concentration camp resulted in death.

Three prominent themes of Frankl's work are relevant to crisis theory. They include the crucial importance of personal choice, the concept of the human "will to meaning," and the meaning of suffering.

Frankl's understanding of the nature and power of personal choice constitutes an important insight about crises. As Frankl (1959) wrote of himself and his fellow inmates in the concentration camp, "Even though conditions such as lack of sleep, insufficient food and various mental stresses may suggest that the inmates were bound to react in certain ways, in the final analysis it becomes clear that the sort of person the prisoner became was the result of an inner decision and not the result of camp influences alone" (p. 66).

Frankl's emphasis of the "will to meaning" also has implications for crisis theory. Frankl insisted that "man is neither dominated by the will-to-pleasure nor by the will-to-power, but by what I should like to call man's will-to-meaning; that is to say, his deep-seated striving and struggling for a higher and ultimate meaning to his existence" (p. 97). He therefore developed a therapeutic methodology, called *logotherapy,* to help persons experiencing a vacuum of meaning. The goal of logotherapy is to facilitate individuals' discovery that their role is to be responsible for themselves. In a similar way, the goal of crisis intervention is to assist people in crises to understand how they can become responsible. Effective intervention enables people to respond to the meaning of the alternatives available to them as they make decisions related to the resolution of their crises.

Since a crisis represents a painful set of circumstances, Frankl's understanding of the role of suffering is also relevant to crisis therapy. He used the term *medical ministry* to refer to the function of a counselor or therapist who enables an individual to accept a tragic loss and to cope with its consequences. Concerning suffering, Frankl wrote "We have not only the possibility of making life meaningful by creating and loving, but also by suffering: by the way and manner in which we face our fate, in which we take our suffering upon ourselves" (p. 105). Hence, one function of crisis therapy is to help individuals rediscover the power of their being in relation to the realities they face and to develop the skills they need to cope with those realities courageously. Crisis counselors can help their clients discover the "courage to be" Tillich (1952) talks about—the courage "in spite of" circumstances that gives a sense of authenticity and meaning.

GOALS OF CRISIS INTERVENTION

Although crisis intervention includes some elements specific to its own model, it is essentially an eclectic approach. Not only does it borrow from the theories and values of psychoanalysis, client-centered therapy, and existential psychotherapy, but it also reflects the increasingly active stance of the counselor expressed in various counseling and psychotherapeutic approaches, including the reality therapy of Glasser (1965), the gestalt therapy introduced by Perls (1969), the interpersonal "games" of transactional analysis (Berne, 1961), the behavior modification of Bandura (1969), and the eclectic contributions of Brammer and Shostrom (1968), Carkhuff (1973), and others.

The following discussion provides the methodological basis for the practice of crisis support and intervention. This methodology includes specific goals and practices that can be learned from a description of this kind, but competence in intervention ultimately depends on actual experience, coupled with professional supervision or consultation.

The new idea that is basic to crisis intervention is that a person is usually most able to make significant progress in the midst of a crisis if planned interventions can be made. The nature and purpose of these interventions must be understood by the counselor, and plans must be formulated for them.

There are two general types of interventions—*anxiety-provoking* and *anxiety-suppressive* interventions. The basic goals of both types are quite similar; however, they differ with respect to both the immediate purposes for which they are intended and the kinds of action taken by the counselor.

A primary goal of any counseling is to listen to the individual with a disciplined and empathic attitude. The possibility of such listening is facilitated both by the counselor's conceptual understanding of crises and by his or her self-understanding. Establishing a relationship of some meaning and rapport provides the foundation that will enable the counselor and the person in stress to work together. Such a foundation includes a basic trust that frees the threatened person from the fear of sharing his or her panic and encourages him or her to begin working with some hope of a resolution. There is hope simply because someone has made a commitment to listen and to work together with the client toward a resolution. Establishing rapport also enables the counselor to sort out the ways in which the individual may be able to benefit from either a provoking or suppressive type of intervention.

Anxiety-Provoking Intervention

A basic component of crisis-intervention is its *anxiety-provoking* function. One task of counselors is to identify and challenge maladaptive resolutions to emotional crises. Individuals who use denial as a means of coping ordinarily need to be challenged to examine the reality that confronts them. People who are using rigid problem-solving formulas that may have worked in the past usually need to be challenged in order to increase the options available to them in the present. Allowing maladaptive resolutions to go unchallenged may permit the formation of symptoms that require considerable psychotherapeutic work to dislodge. For example, a father received a frantic telephone call from his daughter, who was hopelessly trapped in a burning building. All she could say was "Help me Daddy! Help me Daddy!" The father took his daughter's death nobly, in the eyes of some acquaintances, but he had in fact utilized denial of his grief as a coping mechanism. The result was that, months later, whenever he picked up his phone, he heard the voice of his dead daughter crying "Help me Daddy!" A maladaptive resolution to any crisis will wreak some havoc upon the individual who succumbs to using it as the easy way out.

A *primary* goal of anxiety-provoking interventions is to assist persons in crises to look into themselves as quickly as possible. Since they may talk to someone or consult with a counselor within a period of one to three weeks after the precipitating event, it is important to confront them in ways that help them to make contact with their own feelings and behavior, including their most highly charged emotions, thoughts, purposes, and conduct. The purpose of this confrontation is to encourage them to express buried feelings as soon as possible after the event that has precipitated the crisis. Both the supporting and the confronting dimensions of these interventions play a role in enabling individuals to reestablish contact with their own intense feelings.

A *second* goal is to oppose any further regression. People in crises are at least partially immobilized by a threat, and they tend to regress. They often want counselors to free them from the conflict between facing and evading reality. Although they usually have ambivalent feelings about it, they want someone to take care of them. Anxiety-provoking interventions confront individuals with the reality of their situation and thus oppose any further regression into a pattern of dependency. It is important that counselors treat these persons as adults with normal adult problems and introduce them to some constructive action they can take as responsible individuals. In helping persons face up to their problems realistically, counselors discourage any further infantilization or dependence upon them. Gently confronting clients with the reality of their situations provokes anxiety, and counselors must then communicate the message that they will not do anything for their clients that they can do for themselves. As they are helped to resist regression, individuals can begin to regain once again some of their sense of power to influence the outcome of their crises. Self-confidence may emerge as they see cause for hope that a resolution can be worked out.

A *third* goal of counselors is to assist persons in becoming observers of themselves in the immediate situation of the crisis. The various elements of a stressful or crisis situation should be reviewed objectively with them. Learning some facts about a problem increases a person's power to deal with it. Once a situation is understood intellectually, it may no longer be as frightening as it has been. Although they are anxiety-provoking, these interventions may increase the self-confidence of individuals in relation to their particular situations and increase their interest in experimenting with ways of dealing with the stress or crisis, as well as their ability to do so.

Finally, in situations in which counselors identify the need for supportive persons, they should confront their clients with their need and assist them in discovering the people in their families and community who can meet it. A teacher or member of the clergy may provide the emotional support needed in a particular stressful or crisis situation. Since one way to avoid reality is to deny any need for help, an acknowledgement of need can constitute a first step toward dealing with a crisis and can also provide some of the means necessary for coping with it. Such support does not protect people from the reality of their situations, but it does provide the knowledge that they are not alone and can considerably reduce feelings of panic.

An illustration of the nature of anxiety-provoking interventions is provided by the case of Stephen. Stephen was a businessman of about 40 who called in desperation to ask whether I would see his wife. After I informed him that I would indeed see her if she called for an appointment, he indicated that she had moved out of their home and had asked for a divorce. Subsequently, Stephen's wife did come in for an appointment, and she related that she had finally left her husband because she could no longer tolerate his irresponsibility in his business and with their money. She made it clear that she could no longer tolerate a marriage in which her husband was alternately dependent and domineering. Stephen was domineering in insisting on particular business propositions but dependent when she had to bail him out of trouble. This had been a recurring pattern for over 15 years of their marriage, and she had finally reached the limits of her endurance. She did not want to force a move that would necessitate her two teenage children's changing schools, so she had left her husband and son and daughter in their home and had moved into a small apartment. Although she was under considerable stress, she was coping with her problem. She had made a difficult decision, but she would no longer tolerate her husband's irresponsible behavior.

Stephen called during the afternoon of his wife's appointment and wanted to know what I could do about his wife's leaving. I told him that I would be willing to talk to him, and he made an appointment. Once more, he began the session by asking what I could do about his wife's decision. Finally he began to talk about his feelings about himself. Although he occasionally retreated to his original question, in the course of our talk his feelings of panic were recognized, accepted, and clarified. He alternated between feelings of satisfaction in being accepted and feelings of conflict over exposing his emotions. Since he assumed that his wife had referred to all their conflicts, he talked about them from his perspective.

In a second session later that week, Stephen reiterated his original question. Once again I brought him back to expressing his feelings. When he seemed to be trusting that he was not alone with his problem, I confronted him gently with some of the problems he had talked about in the previous session. Although he was reluctant to accept responsibility for his decisions, some of which involved illegal transactions, he was confronted with his wife's decision as a consequence of his actions.

In the third and fourth sessions, Stephen related a pattern of behavior in which his mother had covered for his mistakes. He had not had to act responsibly, because his irresponsible actions had never been taken seriously by his mother. His wife had similarly excused his early indiscretions. When he had gone on to actually involve himself in illegal activities, his wife had become seriously alarmed and had informed him of her opposition. He now realized that he had not taken her seriously, and he was determined to do something about it.

The fifth and final session was primarily devoted to exploring some alternatives. Stephen ultimately chose to consult an attorney and to arrange a resolution of his legal predicament. He resolved to tell his wife about his decision and to accept the legal consequences. Stephen was still anxious about his wife's decision, but he seemed able to cope with it.

Although Stephen's characteristic way of responding to reality factors may necessitate some long-term psychotherapy, this limited intervention enabled him to face up to a fearful threat without evading its consequences. I have no way of knowing the outcome of his marriage problem, but the anxiety-provoking confrontation made clear to Stephen the connection between his irresponsible behavior and the nature of his relationship with his wife.

Anxiety-Suppressive Intervention

Another type of crisis counseling is *crisis support,* or the use of *anxiety-suppressive* interventions. Peter Sifneos' concept of brief anxiety-suppressive psychotherapy includes the provision of "crisis support" for persons with severe psychiatric disorders during an acutely critical time in their lives (Sifneos, 1972). Although this approach to crisis intervention is primarily intended for use by professional therapists, mental-health workers need to understand the process and, in some instances, to coordinate their crisis-intervention work with that of mental-health professionals.

The purpose of anxiety-suppressive psychotherapy is, as the name suggests, to provide the emotional support necessary to reduce the anxiety of persons and enable them to mobilize their own resources to cope with a crisis. "It attempts to eliminate as quickly as possible the factors responsible for the patient's crisis which led to his decompensation, and it helps him overcome the acutely traumatic situation in which he finds himself" (Sifneos, 1972, pp. 47–48). This methodology utilizes both emotional support and any environmental resources that can help clients to retain or regain their basic function as human beings.

An illustration of the psychodynamic process outlined by Sifneos can be drawn from an experience I had while counseling in a crisis-intervention center. Armando was a 36-year-old Guatemalan who had emigrated to the United States three years earlier. He spoke English with some difficulty and with a strong accent. For nearly three years, Armando had been working in a jewelry-repair shop. He was single and lived alone in a small room in an area in which many single men lived. Armando's employer knew him as a conscientious and productive worker and in fact helped him set up his appointment with the clinic. Although he did not know the nature of the problem, he knew Armando was very disturbed and that something was interfering with his work. In the first session, I simply let Armando tell his story.

About three weeks earlier, Armando told me, he had begun to have difficulties getting to sleep and to hear voices outside the walls of his room. These voices called him a homosexual, and they followed him out on the streets on his way to eat or to work, with what he "knew" were intentions to do him harm. Since the clinic was related to a state mental-health grant requiring diagnostic labels, I diagnosed his present state as "schizophrenic, paranoid reaction, with auditory hallucinations."

In the course of our three sessions, which took place over a period of three weeks, Armando became able to relax as he told me what had been happening to him. When he would begin to get anxious, I would reassure him by my own relaxed attitude and by words that we could work things out together. By the close of the first session, I felt that the degree of rapport we had been able to establish and the degree of paranoid responses that he still expressed made it inadvisable to refer him for a medical consultation for possible medication.

During the second session, Armando was sufficiently relaxed to relate the extent of his loneliness and to discuss the questions that he had been asking himself. He showed a decreasing degree of tension as he described the loneliness of a man encountering a culture dramatically different from his own and a language that was difficult for him to master. He told how he had felt isolated, except for occasional contact with his sister, who lived in a nearby community. His first years in the United States had been spent learning the language and the skill of watch repair. Meanwhile, his sister and her family had provided a point of contact with his family and his cultural roots. However, about a month before his first appointment at the clinic, his sister had moved to another community, depriving him of his one source of significant relationships.

This loss had been sustained just as Armando had been beginning to have the time and energy to be thinking about his relationship to the world outside himself. In talking with me, he reflected on the fact that he had not had many social contacts with women and said that he wanted to get married and have a family. Intervention involved reducing his anxiety by reassurance and by offering help in exploring alternatives to the lonely existence in which he had boxed himself. When he said that he was used to having both adults and children around his home in Guatemala, we discussed the possibility of renting a room in a family home or an apartment in an area populated with families rather than with single men—especially families from his own ethnic background. We talked about the possibility of joining an ethnic group or other organization in which he would have the opportunity of meeting women. Armando appeared relaxed and interested in exploring these alternatives.

The final session was two weeks later. Armando had called the clinic to cancel his appointment the week before because he was busy moving. He now related with some eagerness that he had not heard any voices for two weeks and that he had moved to a small apartment in an area in which families lived. His priest had provided some information about the apartment and had also invited him to drop in on an adult group at a Catholic social-service center. He had attended a meeting of the group and had already become acquainted with one of the women. He reported that he was now able to perform his work effectively and that he was once again able to get to sleep without any problem. In reality, he did not utilize this final session for anything more than a report of his change.

My point here is not that Armando developed psychother-

apeutic insights that enabled him to make significant characterological changes. No efforts were made to effect such changes,
but he was enabled to function once again as a productive human being. Although there was evidence of a psychopathology
that may call for psychotherapeutic help in the future, Armando's emotional crisis had been occasioned by a critical loss
of emotional support. The interventions of reassurance, exploration of practical alternatives, and mobilization of community
resources were intended to reduce his anxiety to the point where
he could once again handle things by himself.

The anxiety-suppressive approach represents a supportive
rather than a confronting attitude, but it still consists of interventions. In this type of approach, the *first* goal of counselors,
once they have established the necessary rapport, is simply to
let their clients tell their stories freely—if possible, with no
interruptions.

The *second* goal is to reduce anxiety by reassurance or, if
necessary, by changing the subject temporarily. The clients
should be assured of the counselors' availability to assist in
working out solutions to their difficulties. The *third* goal is to
identify the event that precipitated a particular crisis and to
eliminate the threat of that event. The *fourth* goal is to decrease
the pressures felt by the clients. This task may involve opening
up channels of communication with others in the helping
professions, such as a nurse or a member of the clergy, or it may
involve the prescription of appropriate medication by a physician to temporarily relieve emotional stress. The *fifth* goal is to
provide assistance in specific decision making. *Finally,* counselors may provide "anticipatory guidance" in order to help
clients avoid future difficulties.

CRISIS INTERVENTION AND SOCIOCULTURAL DEPRIVATION

There is more than one line of defense against the development of serious emotional problems within a community.
The first line of defense, or *primary* level of prevention, consists
of fostering a generally nurturing environment. Most of this
book is concerned with the *secondary* level of prevention, which
consists of enabling persons in temporary need to develop coping skills for dealing with particular crises. Often this kind of
assistance will prevent the development of more serious problems in the here-and-now and also enable persons to deal with
future stresses more successfully.

The medical model of psychoanalysis and psychotherapy has served the needs of the middle and upper socioeconomic classes in fulfilling the function of the secondary level of prevention, but it has not met the needs of the poor, the uneducated, and the "poor treatment risks." People in these segments of society are often the ones who have the most serious mental-health problems; yet they are also the ones who have been least served by the prevailing methods of treatment. Society has tended to handle this problem largely by committing these people to large state mental hospitals, which are essentially caretaking institutions for broken human beings. Hence, people from socioculturally deprived backgrounds have been limited, for the most part, to three options for coping with stressful or crisis situations: they can fall back to a position of apathetic dependence on welfare, they can exercise their hostile aggression outwardly through crime, or they can turn their hostility on themselves, resulting in depression or the development of physical and emotional disorders.

The methodology of crisis intervention is applicable to the problems resulting from sociocultural deprivation. Intervention involves both giving support and calling on the personality resources of individuals to forestall the ego-weakening effect of long-term dependence on therapists. Both anxiety-provoking and anxiety-suppressive interventions treat individuals as normal people with normal problems. They involve confronting persons with responsibility for themselves and emphasizing development of the means for coping directly with the here-and-now. The psychodynamic insight concerning the importance of facing up to reality directly plays a large role, even if persons may need assistance in developing coping skills. Interventions are unapologetically designed to provide individuals with information that will enable them to increasingly assume control over their problems. The goal of intervention is to assist them in working out alternative ways of coping rather than to assess the psychodynamics of their personality structures.

In a paper on sociocultural and psychodynamic considerations in crisis-treatment strategy, Gerald Jacobson noted that "lower-class persons are less likely than those higher on the social scale to be accepted onto out-patient rolls, less likely actually to receive treatment beyond diagnostic work-up and less likely to stick it out through the prescribed and anticipated frequency and duration of treatment" (Jacobson, 1965, p. 210). There are some logistic reasons why socioculturally deprived persons do not utilize counseling and psychotherapeutic services, even when economic factors are eliminated by the availability of free clinic treatment. Nevertheless, the chief factors are cultural and psychological, and they affect both counselors and potential clients. Peace Corps volunteers have experienced culture shock when they have encountered the differences between themselves and the people with whom they worked. A similar phenomenon can occur when counselors work with people from backgrounds that are markedly different from their own.

People seeking psychotherapeutic help tend to see themselves as playing a dependent or "child" role in relation to the counselor. In addition, to the degree that their psychological defenses are not functioning in a way that provides some security and comfort, they tend to see themselves as frightened or "bad" children. This tendency can be aggravated when counselor and client come from different socioeconomic backgrounds. In Jacobson's words:

> Consider now what happens when a patient does in fact fail to establish a satisfactory therapeutic relationship. Regardless of how realistic the reason for such a turn of events, the patient may perceive the situation unconsciously as the feared rejection of his "bad child" self by the punishing "parent." This tendency will be aggravated if the therapist himself consciously or unconsciously looks at the patient as inferior, as may occur if the patient comes from a lower social class. . . . A further obstacle arises when the patient realizes that he has to search within himself for the cause of his problems. His culture has not yet taught him that one can look within oneself for psychological causes without having this mean that one is blameworthy or "out of his mind." It is not surprising then that communication between patient and therapist often breaks down early in their contact [pp. 213–214].

Thus, there are significant reasons why people from socioculturally deprived backgrounds have difficulty in utilizing the usual psychotherapeutic resources. However, there is at least one way in which crisis-oriented counseling is unique in this respect: the *universality* of crisis experiences can maximize the basis for cooperation even between people of widely different backgrounds. This point has been noted by Jacobson in the observation that a crisis is ultimately rooted in early-childhood experiences that "precede the differentiation of individuals into cultural and social subgroups" (p. 214). Indeed, he has suggested that defense mechanisms akin to those used in crises may be largely responsible for such cultural differentiation. In any event, the development of crises and the process of exploring ways of coping with them are experiences that cut across sociocultural differences. The history of the Benjamin Rush Center has substantiated the point that such differences do not alter the process of crisis counseling to any significant degree.

The significance of sociocultural differences between the persons seeking assistance and those giving it is diminished in crisis counseling for several reasons. First, the intervention is, of its nature, a short-term one. The brevity of the helping process reduces the risk individuals take in exposing themselves to alien attitudes and behavior. Second, the circumscribed scope of this support or intervention provides additional security. The nature of the contract between the persons involved is clear-cut. It does not involve the risk of exposing characteristic patterns of responses to counselors who may have significantly different ways of living.

Third, crisis therapy focuses on areas where coping mechanisms have already failed. The exploration of the reasons for this failure and of alternate ways of coping is a highly specific goal. Fourth, crisis counseling can usually be handled by mental-health workers. These new professionals may be leaders indigenous to the community or persons who have experienced similar crises in their own lives. Personal experience may provide the necessary rapport with the individuals in crisis and also demonstrates the possibility of developing the coping skills needed to survive. Finally, the need for immediate help is met by the ready access of mental-health workers on a walk-in basis.

The function of crisis intervention is to assist persons in facing their reality head-on. By doing so, crisis counseling and therapy can provide significant prevention of future self-defeating behavior, encouraging a "flight into reality" instead of a defensive "flight from reality." Thus, the effects of crisis counseling may extend far beyond the immediate critical situation. Enabling people with normal crises to face them realistically and to develop means of coping increases the possibility of their own survival as effective human beings and augments both their potential and the mental-health potential of their community.

The Practice
of Crisis Intervention

Crisis intervention may be defined as any action that is intended to influence the course of a crisis in which another individual is involved. As we have seen, the purpose of intervention is to help the individual discover an adaptive means of coping with a particular crisis.

The actual practice of crisis intervention involves a general understanding of the nature of crises and an application of this understanding to specific stressful situations. The form interventions take depends not only on the needs of the individual in crisis but also on the training and skill of the counselor. As discussed later in this chapter, there are at least three levels of crisis counseling that may be utilized by mental-health workers and by others in the helping professions.

ORIENTATION TO THE PRACTICE OF CRISIS INTERVENTION

If we look at our own personal histories or at the history of institutions, we can note that times of crisis are often times of rapid growth and development. A familiar cliché is that a crisis will either "make or break" a person. The different ways in which counselors can intervene in real-life crises to enhance the growth of persons and the effectiveness of their coping skills are the subject of this chapter.

One of the first steps counselors must take is to learn about themselves. To work with people in crises, counselors need to have recognized and learned how to cope with stressful experiences in their own lives. Counselors who have taken this step will understand that crises can happen to any person, and they will perceive themselves as fellow sufferers rather than as authorities who have all the answers. Counselors may indeed have some knowledge of the general emotional terrain of crisis experiences, but each person's questions are unique to that person. However similar the *processes* of working toward resolutions of crises may be, generalized answers are simply irrelevant to individual needs.

A superficial view of crisis counseling may confuse the concept of planned interventions with that of giving advice. Troubled persons often ask for answers to their dilemmas. They may even plead for answers. Yet they may not need ready-made answers so much as they need to be *heard*—to be *understood*. If a person has not been really heard, the counselor will have little to offer. Giving easy answers to someone's troubled questions is an inappropriate counseling response and is usually a useless endeavor. Indeed, counselors who are seduced into giving answers to genuine dilemmas are often met with the "yes, but" game. In this game, the client begs for an answer but when one is provided, always rejects it as impossible. The "yes, but" game is a dependency game that can never be resolved. Counselors who say, in effect, "If I were you. . . " simply evade the fact that, if they really were that person, they would be doing exactly what he or she is already doing.

Of course, some clients may actually take a counselor's advice. If they do, they rob themselves of the chance to resolve their crises with their own inner resources. This failure to work with their own crises may deprive them of a significant use of power. The immobilization of people in the midst of crises is expressive of a loss of power within themselves. They are temporarily unable to respond—to be *response-able*. If they learn how to cope instead of relying on another person to resolve their predicament, they can rediscover their potency to respond to themselves and to others and regain a sense of power over their own destinies.

One function of crisis counselors, therefore, is to help reverse the slide into powerlessness experienced by persons in crises. Recovery of personal power depends on the utilization of inner resources, which in many instances needs to be facilitated by the intervention of another person. A person who suffers a serious deprivation of social or emotional support, such as the loss of a spouse, may be temporarily immobilized and may need a supportive relationship in order to function at any level. A crisis counselor can provide that temporary support, but never by encouraging regressive or dependent behavior that robs the person of his or her own power to cope. The counselor's aim is rather to provide the security immobilized individuals need to recover their own power in problem solving and to summon the courage to reach out to significant other people for a continuing sense of support.

A MODEL OF INTERVENTION

A crisis provides both a *danger* and an *opportunity*. The nature of a crisis has been characterized by the stance of a sprinter. While he is standing in a firm position with his legs apart and planted firmly on the ground, it is difficult to topple him. This stance represents the position of a person who is coping satisfactorily and is in a state of equilibrium. At the point of his beginning to run, however, he is in a state of physical disequilibrium. He perches on the toe of one foot as he rocks forward to the point where the other foot and leg will take over. At this moment of precarious balance, he can be knocked over easily. This stance represents the position of a person in a crisis situation. The individual may be knocked over easily, which is the *danger*, but he or she also has the *opportunity* of moving forward rapidly. It is at this moment of precarious and painful disequilibrium that the intervention of a counselor can significantly affect the outcome for the better.

In this model of crisis intervention, the factor of time is crucial. The outcome of a crisis is not determined simply by previous experiences, although successful coping in an earlier situation may enhance one's coping skills. The outcome may be more crucially influenced by unique psychological and situational factors. Moreover, the resolution of the crisis and the new equilibrium that results may be more adequate than what had previously been achieved, and the new methods of coping that are discovered may be more adaptive than any previously developed coping skills in meeting future stressful situations. In other words, a person who resolves a crisis successfully will tend to be more healthy emotionally than he or she was before the crisis occurred. Thus, according to crisis theory and practice, at a moment of crisis a minimum of action provides a maximum possibility of change. The recognition that intervention at a point early in a crisis can have a decisive influence on its outcome and that significant progress can be made during the approximately six-week duration of most crises is an important contribution of the crisis-intervention approach to mental-health care.

LEVELS OF CRISIS INTERVENTION

1. The Supportive (Nonspecific) Level of Intervention

Any time someone provides emotional support for another human being, he or she is intervening at some level. Mental-health workers, social workers, nurses, medical doctors, police officers, and others in the helping disciplines often have the opportunity of providing emotional support to individuals in stressful or crisis situations.

The *supportive* role is a nonspecific form of intervention. It consists of careful and active listening. In a time of considerable depersonalization at all levels of human encounter, the art of listening has been largely ignored or lost; yet it is basic to any meaningful encounter and absolutely fundamental to all counseling. Disciplined listening enables a person to genuinely hear another person. This kind of listening requires a sense of inward quietness and relaxed attention. A person who is attending to his or her own restless thoughts and fears is unable to listen effectively to someone else.

The intervention of attentive listening gives a feeling of support, which in turn can help generate both the courage to deal with a crisis and the hope of influencing its outcome. This basic demonstration of caring reassures individuals that they are not entirely alone in their crises and thus enables them to mobilize their own inner resources.

2. Environmental Manipulation

Environmental manipulation can be helpful in various kinds of counseling situations, including crisis counseling. This level of intervention involves either removing some hazard from an individual's environment (for instance, an impulsive person who has experienced suicidal feelings may be encouraged to remove a loaded gun from his home) or else removing the individual from a hazardous environment (for instance, an individual on drugs may move to a rehabilitation center or to a therapeutic community such as Synanon). A change in environment is not, in itself, a solution; however, by eliminating a toxic influence or supplying a nurturing influence, it may provide the feelings of security necessary for significant personal development.

Manipulation of the environment may also include equipping individuals with the skills they need to make significant changes. Providing occupational training to unskilled workers, for example, may enable them to escape an otherwise inevitable poverty. Career assessment and development can help persons understand their strengths and use them to secure jobs in which their potential can be more fully realized. Such manipulation of environmental factors will not guarantee the resolution of any crisis. However, it may provide individuals with a sense of power in relation to their circumstances and hence provide the emotional foundation for a constructive resolution.

3. The Generic Level of Intervention

While the first two levels of crisis intervention follow some of the general guidelines for any kind of individual counseling, the generic model has been developed specifically in relation to crisis intervention. This third level of intervention always utilizes the first level of supportive listening and often includes some form of environmental manipulation as well.

The theoretical issues relevant to the generic level of intervention have been developed by Dr. Jacobson and his associates (Jacobson, Strickler, and Morley, 1968). They have made a helpful differentiation between this approach and the individually tailored approach used by the trained psychotherapist. Since no special training in the understanding of the psychodynamics of personality is required for this type of intervention, its use is especially relevant for persons not specifically trained as mental-health specialists.

The specific thesis of this approach is that, in crises involving some significant loss, there are common and identifiable patterns of response. In crises such as bereavement or divorce, for example, certain patterns of response ordinarily occur. This approach is particularly well documented in the work of Lindemann (1944) on bereavement. He discovered that a bereaved person goes through a well-defined process of so-called "grief work" in adapting to the death of a loved one.

Since there is no need to assess the psychodynamics of individual personalities in this type of counseling, the focus of generic intervention is on the course that a particular kind of crisis characteristically follows. Hence, intervention consists of specific measures designed to be effective for a target group as a whole. Although counselors should be sensitive to the highly idiosyncratic ways in which people experience their crises, they do not need to be trained in the diagnosis of personality dynamics in order to choose the proper way to intervene.

Counselors using the generic approach choose an appropriate kind of intervention, therefore, primarily on the basis of the characteristic course of a particular type of crisis. As always, their aim is to help persons in crises achieve an adaptive rather than a maladaptive resolution. Their approach includes, *first,* the general supportive measures of any good counseling. Careful listening evidences their concern and helps to give individuals a sense of hope that their crises will pass. Moreover, such listening is an encouragement to express feelings, many of which have been buried and unavailable to conscious awareness.

Second, counselors try to assist persons to look directly into themselves and to make contact with their most highly charged emotions, thoughts, purposes, and conduct. To help them in becoming observers of themselves, especially in relation to the here-and-now of their crises, counselors review the present circumstances objectively with each individual. This review is not necessarily made all at once. No one is strong enough to deal with all the aspects of a crisis at one time. Rather, clients are assisted to confront the reality of their crises gradually and in manageable doses. In the course of these reviews, counselors may also assist individuals to learn certain facts that may help them regain some hope of influencing the outcome of their crises.

Third, counselors assist individuals to work out adaptive resolutions. Acceptance of a crisis as something that could happen to any normal person encourages clients to discover adaptive ways of coping. Counselors assist individuals to experiment with alternative methods of coping and support the efforts they make toward adaptive behavior. These efforts may include learning more facts about their situations. While resisting regression and dependency, counselors help their clients to examine these facts and explore what constructive actions might be taken. In other words, the counselors should not do anything for persons in crises that they can do for themselves.

Fourth, counselors may choose to intervene through some form of environmental manipulation. Clients may be encouraged to explore such possibilities as changing jobs, moving, going to school, or otherwise experimenting with changes in their social or physical surroundings. Environmental manipulation may also include helping a client to develop an interpersonal network of supportive relationships.

A *fifth* type of intervention in the generic approach to crisis resolution has been called "anticipatory guidance." Since counselors know the general course of particular crises, some responses can be anticipated. As Dr. Jacobson once pointed out, anticipatory guidance is like seeing a cliff ahead and directing the individual's attention to it. Of course, there are those who will deny that any such danger exists, perhaps going right to the edge before they recognize the danger, and some people will be overwhelmed despite the counselor's warning. The function of counselors is simply to stand by and be available whenever any of these responses occur. Their availability and offers of support will enable individuals to call for help more readily in coping with their feelings and with the sense of falling or being overwhelmed.

The generic approach to crisis intervention may be illustrated by the following bereavement experience. Thelma's husband died suddenly at the age of 45. A medical doctor, he suffered a heart attack at the peak of his professional achievement. Thelma was 38 years old and totally unprepared for this tragedy. She had a son in high school, a daughter in junior high school, and another daughter in the third grade.

Thelma came in for counseling during the third week following her husband's death. She had been referred by her minister, who had become concerned about her seclusion and her depressed state of mind. She had stayed at home and had been unavailable to her friends. Although she had been willing to talk to the minister, he noted that she never mentioned her dead husband. She was helping to care for the children, but they tended to help each other and did not need a great deal of physical care.

Thelma appeared to be somewhat reluctant to talk, but she was concerned about her sleeplessness and her depression. Since I was entirely new to her, I encouraged her to talk about herself and her family. For the first time since her husband's death, she began to talk about him and about her difficulty in accepting her feelings about his death, By this time, she was no longer denying the fact of his death, but she didn't know what to do with her angry feelings. Everyone expected her to be mature about this tragedy. She had always been a highly competent woman who had handled the affairs of her family and of the Women's Club of which she had been president. Her friends were used to talking with her about their problems, and the family had depended upon her. When she had finally accepted the fact of her husband's death, she became aware of her anger toward the medical association and the hospital over the work load her husband had been carrying.

She talked about her anger, and these feelings were simply accepted. As she pursued the expression of her feelings, she began to cry for the first time since the funeral. Except for moments by herself, she had only cried in a highly controlled way at the funeral. Now she began to cry uncontrollably, and her entire body shook. After she had cried for several minutes, she sat quietly for a time. Then she talked a little more about her husband and ended the session by making an appointment for later in the week.

In the second session, Thelma talked about her husband and the things they had done together. Once again she expressed feelings of anger, this time directed toward her husband because he had not taken care of himself and had been away from his family too much of the time. She began to blame him directly because he had accepted such a heavy work load, while at the same time she felt guilty for blaming him. She continued to be actively verbal and dependent. Her angry and lonely feelings and her expression of dependence were accepted, and another appointment was set for the next week.

In the third session, Thelma complained about being alone and about all the estate problems she had to face. Although she was used to handling household problems by herself, her husband had always managed the finances, and she was unprepared to cope with her new financial responsibilities. Once these problems had been clarified, it became evident to her that she needed to consult with her attorney and to seek some professional assistance with the finances. This decision brought some relief and a sense of hope about resolving some of the financial problems.

In the fourth session, Thelma reported on her talk with her attorney and then began to talk about some of the stress she and her husband had experienced in their marriage, including quarrels about his demanding work load. She had attempted to work out a life of her own some time after the birth of their third child. During this period she had enrolled in adult-education programs and had had a brief affair with one of her instructors. Although her husband had never learned about the affair, and although it had happened nearly two years before, she had continued to feel guilty about it. She began to talk about her feelings of guilt, which I again simply accepted. It was clear that she had never resolved her feelings about this experience; she cried that she could never work it out now that her husband was dead. When I suggested that she visualize her husband sitting in the chair next to her, she began to cry. After a moment, I asked whether she could ask him for forgiveness. She hesitated; then, in the midst of her tears, she blurted out "I'm sorry, dear; I'm sorry!" After some wrenching sobs, she sat quietly for a few minutes. Her intense feelings were accepted and clarified, and she evidenced a restful sense of peace for the first time in my acquaintance with her.

A week later, in the fifth and final session, she recounted that she had returned to her friends at the Women's Club and at church. For the first time since her husband's death, she was once again admitting her friends into her life and accepting their emotional support. While she was still lonely, she felt that she was no longer entirely alone.

The five sessions with Thelma took place over a period of four weeks. She was a woman who had suffered the loss of a significant other person. Her bereavement had become a crisis in which she had been at least partially immobilized. In some respects, it was a crisis that could have been experienced by any person in similar circumstances; however, a complication in Thelma's case was that her grief work had been blocked by some unfinished business in her relationship with her husband. Once the issue of her guilt had been recognized and accepted, her grief work proceeded normally.

Thelma's grief work followed the usual pattern of the expression of loneliness, anger, and guilt. She had experienced sleeplessness and depression. She had talked about her husband and the kind of person he had been. She had secluded herself from her friends. Counselor responses had included recognition, acceptance, and clarification of her feelings, as well as emotional support and some problem solving. These interventions were similar to those used with other persons in bereavement crises, but they were specifically aimed at freeing Thelma to cope with her feelings and her grief in her own way.

The process of the generic level of crisis intervention in cases of bereavement is related to the target group of grief reactions in general. Although each person experiences his or her own situation idiosyncratically, there is a usual pattern of responses in grief work, and most persons follow this pattern in general. There is no need for a diagnosis of the psychodynamics of the individual's behavior. There is simply the need to understand the usual pattern of grief responses and to facilitate the expression of these feelings. My interventions in Thelma's crisis did not take into account any of her characterological problems but simply directed her back to the here-and-now of her predicament. Other types of crises activate their own patterns of responses. The chief consideration at this juncture is therefore to train counselors to identify these general patterns and to plan intervention strategies accordingly, without losing sight of the idiosyncratic features of each individual's experience.

There are some factors that limit the application of the generic approach. First of all, there are many types of crises that have not been sufficiently studied. It is impossible to outline the characteristic patterns of adaptive or maladaptive resolutions to these crises, because they have not yet been sufficiently identified.

A second limitation holds for any pattern involving human responses. As human beings, we have much in common and much that makes each of us unique. Our responses to crises will therefore be alike in many respects; yet each crisis will also be charged with highly idiosyncratic meanings. In addition, persons with various kinds of personality distortions may not respond in the ways we would ordinarily expect.

Since every human experience is filled with personal meaning, no two crises follow precisely the same course. When counselors' interventions do not seem to be successful, other experimentation needs to be done. In the event that interventions continue to be unsuccessful and an individual seems to continue in the same state of apathy or depression, it may be necessary to consult with a mental-health specialist or to refer the client for a more individualized type of intervention, perhaps involving more traditional treatment of chronic and characterological problems.

THE INDIVIDUAL LEVEL OF INTERVENTION

Mental-health specialists utilize both the generic level of intervention I have just described and an individual level of intervention. Essentially, the individual approach is distinguished by the use of psychodynamic diagnoses and assessments of particular persons. Ordinarily, an understanding of the intrapsychic and interpersonal processes of an individual is not necessary for interventions in the usual types of crises; however, occasionally a mental-health specialist may be needed to assess the dynamics of a specific individual's behavior in order to undertake treatment appropriate to that person.

This individual approach to crisis intervention differs from long-term or extended psychotherapy insofar as it is concerned with characterological patterns or established ways of responding only as they provide clues to an understanding of the person in a specific crisis. It is still crisis intervention, *not* long-term psychotherapy. It differs from the generic approach insofar as it aims at a different level of understanding of behavior and focuses upon the needs of a specific individual rather than upon those of a target group as a whole.

The experience of Phil, which was reported in my last work, illustrates some of the differences between the individual and generic approaches to crisis intervention (Whitlock, 1973). The fact that Phil was seen only twice over a period of two weeks also shows a difference between extended psychotherapy and crisis intervention.

> Phil was about twenty-eight years old, single, and had been working as a cook in a restaurant. He came to the counselor after having been almost completely immobilized for about two weeks. About two weeks before, he had walked off his job in the restaurant. He had not indicated a desire to terminate employment, but had simply not returned to work. . . . During the first few days he was sick in bed with physical symptoms. After a few days he felt able to get up, but he still stayed in his room most of the time and never left the house. He still felt he could not return to his job, even though he could no longer use his physical symptoms as an excuse.
>
> He had finally come in for counseling at the insistence of friends from whom he rented a room. He began by talking about his job and his feelings about not being able to return to his job. In his responsibility as cook he had several persons working under him. It was the first time he had been given such responsibility, and he did not feel capable of coping with it. To compound the problem, his anxiety was increased by a highly authoritarian chef under whose direction he worked. Exploring his reactions in previous positions, he indicated that in the past when he could not cope with such an authoritarian boss he had simply walked off the job and secured another. This reaction, then, was his way of coping with such a hazardous situation in the past.
>
> The first intervention involved questioning about what was different or new about this situation. Why did his previous means of coping not work in this situation? What was different here? It did not seem to be a different kind of situation, except that this chef had reminded him of his father. He was aware that he had resented his father, and that he had never worked out a basis for a relationship with him. He was aware that he simply could not

return to the job because of these feelings. However, he could not figure out why he was unable to seek out another job as he always had in the past, and why he found it difficult even to leave his room and the house in which he lived. As he talked about his situation in general, it became evident that he was renting his room from a couple who had befriended him years before and to whom he felt deeply indebted. In addition, this couple had gone to some trouble to assist him in securing this particular job, which involved greater responsibility and a higher salary than he had ever before earned.

It soon became clear that in leaving his job he felt guilty about leaving a position secured for him by his friends, who had become parent substitutes for him. The conflict between his inability to work under a "bad father" and his fear of rejection by the "good parents" was more tension than he could handle, and he became literally immobilized. Fearing that he would appear ungrateful to them, he was unable to indicate that he would either terminate his job and seek another or return to his position. His inner conflict made it impossible for him to move in either direction. He became immobilized.

The first intervention consisted of describing this data to him. The relationship between the authoritarian chef and his father and his usual means of coping with his tensions were described. The relationship between his images of the couple who had befriended him and the good parents that he needed was pointed out. This material was described in the context of his previous means of coping, and why this conflict made it impossible to work in this situation. In addition to describing this data to him, emotional support was given to the possibility of seeking another job. Additional interviews could have enabled him to explore different job opportunities. However, following the second interview he called to inform the counselor of the job he had secured just three days after the last session. He had gone out on two job interviews and had secured the second position.

It is clear that his characterological problems were not a part of the counseling with this individual. He had not worked out his problems with authority figures, but he was enabled to function adequately enough to move out of an immobilized state and secure a position. Although he obviously needed at least some psychotherapy, he demonstrated that he was not ready for any referral for additional psychotherapeutic work. Hence, even though he had not solved his characterological problem, he had returned to a level of functioning that was at least as capable as before the crisis. Since he had been able to talk over the matter with his parent substitutes, it may be inferred that his means of coping with this crisis was an adaptive one which increased his coping skills in general [pp.121–123].

The generic approach to crisis intervention is the one usually utilized by the mental-health worker; the individual approach is presented here to illustrate the differences between the two. This discussion may also serve to illustrate both the opportunities and the limitations of the generic approach for mental-health workers and to introduce the type of situation that may call for a referral to a mental-health specialist.

VARIED APPLICATIONS OF CRISIS INTERVENTION

Crisis intervention may be used in various contexts. First, it is commonly applied in different kinds of community mental-health and counseling centers in face-to-face situations. These agencies may be staffed by professionals in the mental-health field or by mental-health workers, clergy, community leaders, and others. The agency may be one that has a specific function, such as a suicide-prevention center, or it may be one that has a more general function of availability to persons in any kind of distress, such as a family-services facility.

Second, crisis intervention is increasingly utilized by persons in careers that regularly involve them in different kinds of human crises. Police are often called in instances of domestic crises involving some kind of violence or disturbance of the peace. Many police departments are now training their officers in crisis intervention so that they can work with persons in domestic and other crises, such as rape. Firefighters and emergency squads routinely encounter seriously injured persons, as well as bereaved persons in instances of accidental death. To work with persons in these stressful situations, they need training equal to the demands that confront them. Members of the clergy encounter persons in the midst of both the contractive experiences of dying and bereavement and the expanding experiences of marriage and childbirth.

Third, there are countless crisis telephone services throughout the country. Again, some services focus upon a specific crisis, such as suicide and its prevention, and others are "hot lines" serving a variety of needs, ranging from loneliness to the need for referral to other community resources. Hot lines are usually staffed by volunteers who have been trained by mental-health professionals, and the services are often available 24 hours a day. Telephone counselors meet important community needs, and volunteers who have only limited training may make effective interventions in crises simply because they are available at the moment of the most intense need. One resource that may be a helpful tool in this specialized service is *Crisis Intervention and Counseling by Telephone* (Lester & Brockopp, 1976).

Although the context of counseling and the type of action taken may differ considerably in these three types of application, the theory of crisis intervention remains the same. The basic methods will need to be adapted to specific situations and to the type of service involved, but the essential elements of the intervention approach are similar.

The Training of Crisis Counselors

The training of counselors is not limited to the teaching of counseling techniques. Anyone who is to be entrusted with the emotional conflicts of other people also needs some experiential preparation. Thus, professional counselors or therapists usually undergo some counseling or psychotherapy in the course of their training, to increase their self-awareness as well as their familiarity with the process of therapy. In all cases, an experienced therapist supervises the work of the apprentice. Social workers, clergy, probation officers, and others are trained for their work by professionals within their own disciplines. The preparation of all these individuals—mental-health professionals as well as others involved in community service—for counseling in crisis situations involves a specific kind of training. This chapter discusses some of the elements of counselor training in general and training for crisis intervention in particular.

An increasingly important group of counseling trainees is made up of the "new professionals," nonspecialists who are given limited training for counseling work. These mental-health workers are crucial to the concept of preventive mental-health care and to a psychology of the community. Since the fostering of mental health is the business of the entire community, the skills of various persons involved in service disciplines are needed to develop a community with sound mental health. A woman who is occupied with her family at home, a retired businessman, or a leader indigenous to the community are among those who might be trained as mental-health workers. The training of such persons does not eliminate the need for mental-health specialists, but it can develop valuable technical expertise without imposing the value structures inherent in more specialized forms of training. The length of time specialists must spend in training places an implicit value on the "authority" role and emphasizes the development and primacy of intellectual skills. Consequently, the same training that provides professional expertise can become a barrier that prevents some people from establishing rapport with, and trust in, the counselor. Moreover, the professional's own highly developed analytical skills can impede the experiencing of a personal relationship with the client.

Mental-health workers, in contrast, can make a significant contribution to the care and nurture of persons in virtue of the *experiential* wisdom they possess. Warm and loving persons who have not undergone the rigors of graduate education may possess the very human qualities that are needed to counsel effectively with persons in crises. There is no reason why training for counseling work must be an impersonal or analytical experience. Rather, it can be an enlivening experience that leads to greater awareness of self and others and to the development of the trainees' human potential.

THE NEW PROFESSIONALS: MENTAL-HEALTH WORKERS

The new professionals perform a unique function, even though their sense of identity is not always clearly developed. As an occupational group, they work on the boundaries of medicine, psychology, social work, and religion. They may function as a bridge between professionals in the mental-health disciplines and other citizens in the community. They differ from mental-health specialists in function and training, but their role is no less important. The only limitation of the new professionals is the extent of their training, supervision, and skill. Both the specialist and the new professional work with persons in crises, but there are some types of problems that belong specifically to the realm of the specialist and others that come within the province of the mental-health worker.

Professionals in the health disciplines deal most effectively with specialized needs. New professionals, on the other hand, serve a generalist function. They usually work within an integrative frame of reference and may provide a liaison among the various professions concerned with the mental health of persons.

THE SELF-UNDERSTANDING OF COUNSELORS

The response of counselors to the persons with whom they work is dependent upon many factors, the chief one being their own self-understanding. If counselors do not basically understand and accept themselves, all their other skills are useless.

Of course, self-understanding is relative and can only be proxi-mate. Nevertheless, a predominant sense of self-understanding and self-acceptance is crucial to the counseling role. I want to emphasize, however, that I am referring not merely to intellec-tual comprehension but to the experiential understanding of persons who have learned how to cope with the emotionally hazardous situations in their own lives. A basic point here is that mental-health workers can begin counseling effectively be-fore they have an intellectual grasp of the psychodynamics of their own behavior. Indeed, their more important assets may be the human qualities of love and concern for others.

There is a crucial dimension to self-understanding that is affective in nature rather than intellectual or conceptual. This affective dimension includes the differentiation between *iden-tification* and *empathy*. Although this distinction is made con-ceptually here, an understanding of the difference between these functions is the result of experiential self-knowledge.

Identification refers to the psychological mechanism by which one individual with unresolved feelings and conflicts identifies with the unresolved feelings of another person. Coun-selors who *identify* with people in crisis tend to become part of the problem rather than facilitators of a resolution. To the de-gree that counselors have not resolved their own conflicts, they will be unable to facilitate the growth and self-understanding of other people.

On the other hand, individuals who have encountered and identified emotional conflicts within their own lives may more readily be able to empathize with people in some kind of emo-tional trouble. *Empathy* refers to a "feeling with" another per-son. To the degree that counselors are able to relate the feelings of people in crises to their own experiences, they may be better able to facilitate resolutions. For example, persons with healthy self-understanding, who have themselves dealt successfully with bereavement experiences, may be able to counsel effectively with persons in the midst of grief work. People who have suf-fered in intense or even crisis situations are not necessarily any better than they would otherwise have been, but the nature of their being and understanding is certainly more complete. It seems reasonable to conjecture that one who has never suffered is incompletely human. Both my own personal experience and crisis theory suggest that the experience of suffering potentially leads to the enlargement of personality. This kind of experience broadens counselors' understanding of themselves and of the dynamics of crises.

THE CLINICAL ORIENTATION OF
MENTAL-HEALTH WORKERS

Mental-health workers who engage in crisis intervention will need to understand and utilize what may be called the clinical orientation. This frame of reference includes more than a logical approach to communication between persons. The language of poetry or of any intense communication includes considerable symbolism. Hence, counselors listen for symbolic or nonliteral meanings. They hear the actual words that are spoken, but they also attempt to understand what feelings or meanings underlie the statements of clients. Since words are symbols, counselors are simply trying to pay heed to the meaning of the symbolism at a specific time and place.

Clinically oriented counselors are therefore prepared to question anything that is said. Statements are not always taken at face value. In actuality, no verbal statement represents a purely objective analysis; it is always an interpretation. Although there are degrees of distortion, our needs and defenses provide psychological filters that influence our perception. We frequently see what we want or need to see rather than what is objectively there. Untrained counselors tend to take statements at their face value. They may be disconcerted by what they hear, but they tend to assume that persons literally mean what their *words* communicate, which is often not the case.

Clinically oriented counselors also try to discover the meaning of an experience to a particular person at a specific time and place rather than relying on a general understanding of types of events and behaviors. As I have written earlier:

> The clinical orientation reflects the philosophic influence of both pragmatism and relativism. The pragmatist is attempting to learn just what works. The relativist is preoccupied with the concrete situation. He is not interested in generalized rules of behavior which may be applied in any situation. He has seen the truth that all laws cannot be applied without ambiguity to both generalized and specific situations. In this way, the clinical orientation has influenced decision-making in every area of life precisely because it sees *persons* rather than rules. Of course, this frame of reference is not entirely new. The classic reply of Jesus to the criticism that he was breaking the commandment requiring rest on the Sabbath was that "the Sabbath was made for man, not man for the Sabbath" [Whitlock, 1973, p. 84].

The clinical orientation stresses the attitude of serious listening. Such listening provides the opportunity for individuals in crises to get in touch with their intense feelings, because they have the emotional support of counselors who are interested enough to listen. It also prepares the way for the consideration of alternative ways of coping with their crises.

Finally, a clinical orientation emphasizes the preparation of counselors to understand the nature of interpersonal communication. This is not so much a matter of learning the techniques of communication as it is a matter of learning experientially to respond to persons in ways that are relevant to the nature of the rapport that has been established. Communication in depth is not made possible simply through the application of any particular model; communication must be relevant to the nature and extent of each counseling relationship.

TRAINING IN COUNSELING SKILLS

Training in the helping process consists primarily of experiential learning. When counselors or helpers have learned about themselves in relation to others and to the inevitable stresses of life, they are ready to begin their work. Robert Carkhuff and others have developed a systematic skills-training system for counselors and helpers. The model of Carkhuff (1972, 1973) is based upon both research and practice. He delineates the skills needed by the effective helper at each stage of counseling. Ivey (1971) has developed a methodology called "microcounseling," which also includes systematic training procedures for the helping process.

Many others have contributed to the equipping of counselors to effectively fulfill their helping role. One of the most interesting and useful approaches to counseling is the recent developmental model of Egan (1975). Egan's work takes into account both social-influence and learning theory, while recognizing their limitations in the training of counselors and helpers.[1] His model is not a separate school of counseling but rather a systematically organized, eclectic scheme to be used in the

[1]There is no intention here of ignoring the contributions of the latter two theoretical positions. Years ago, Jerome Frank (1963) noted the elements of social influence present in various counseling approaches. Although such influence is clearly present in crisis intervention, any extensive utilization of this factor may increase the dependence of the person in crisis and, moreover, may be counterproductive when the counselor's cultural background is significantly different from that of the client. In regard to learning theory, any effective counseling procedure must reflect the basic principles underlying learning, unlearning, and relearning.

training of the "skilled helper." A brief overview of this position is presented here as a helpful model for the training of crisis counselors.

Egan's description of the counselor's role begins with the pre-helping phase of the counselor's activity. Essentially, this phase consists of verbal and nonverbal attending to the person in need. Stage One includes responding to the client with empathy, respect, and genuineness and grounding the helping process in concrete feelings and behavior. Effective helping at this stage also includes encouraging the client's self-exploration of feelings and behavior. Stage Two consists of the counselor's integrative understanding, including empathy with the client; the client's willing self-disclosure; a sense of immediacy in the present counseling relationship; the possibility of confrontation; and the exploration of alternative frames of reference for viewing behavior. In this stage, the counselor's function is to help clients develop, first, the skill of listening to themselves with some openness and, second, a dynamic self-understanding that eventuates in behavioral change. Stage Three includes all of the skills in the two previous stages and the elaboration of programs of action, such as assigned client "homework" or training in interpersonal skills. The counselor helps the client to learn cooperation and collaboration in setting and achieving goals, to acquire the ability to take interpersonal risks, and to develop the willingness to undertake some concrete action.

Such a model of counselor activity may be effectively used prior to specific training in crisis intervention. It is a general model that may be coordinated with the stages of actual crisis intervention identified in the following section.

THE STAGES IN CRISIS INTERVENTION

The methodology of crisis intervention is geared to helping individuals mobilize their inner resources. Hence, crisis-intervention counselors approach crises from the perspective of normality. Instead of allowing or encouraging regression, counselors encourage clients to see their problems as normal ones and to mobilize their own ego resources to cope with whatever problems have precipitated their crises.

Caplan (1964) groups the separate steps involved in the practice of crisis intervention into two basic stages. The first stage involves the exploration of the various aspects of the crisis situation. The second stage involves the work of problem-solving. It consists of exploring alternative ways of solving the problem posed by the crisis.

Stage 1

In the first stage, counselors are directed to explore the actual situations confronting individuals in crisis. In some situations, the exploration may be simple—for example, when a death in the family is the precipitating event. However, often the precipitating event is not readily accessible to the person in crisis. A man may be convinced that his divorce has precipitated the crisis. In reality it may be something else. Thus, the precipitating event is not necessarily identified by the story a client presents initially. Furthermore, individuals in crisis often cannot identify any event at all as the precipitating factor.

Since individuals tend to defend themselves against the pain occasioned by the precipitating event, the event itself may remain below the level of consciousness. Indeed, most interventions in any counseling or psychotherapy focus on the defense against recognizing and experiencing the particular experiences that have been painful. Thus, the counselor's first task in outlining the steps that may be taken as part of the intervention in a crisis is to try to identify the precipitating event. Directed questions are helpful tools in uncovering this event. What is threatening to the client? What is new in the ongoing situation, in *this* particular crisis? What is the *immediate* problem, as distinguished from the characterological problem?

Second, the counselor needs to identify the defensive maneuvers that are being used to avoid recognition of the painful event. These defensive maneuvers and some of their meanings must be understood before they can be interpreted for the person in crisis. Then the chief or most powerful of these defenses can be described to the client. Again, directed questions may help both counselor and counselee to discover these defense mechanisms. In what ways does this particular situation seem to be different from other similar situations? Who are the significant persons related to the crisis, and how are they involved?

Third, the counselor needs to listen for previous situations in the client's life that are similar to the present crisis experience. If the client has faced similar problems in the past, he or she may have developed means of coping, and the counselor needs to discover why these previous means of coping are not working. What new impasse has been brought about by this new situation? If the counselor is able to relate the uniqueness of this crisis event to the defenses being used against experiencing it, he or she will be able to interpret how the client is warding off his or her responses to the event. Formulating the dynamics of the situation will enable the counselor to understand more clearly the nature of the present impasse.

Fourth, a counselor needs to state the problem in clear, concise terms. Intervention at this point consists of describing the situation as clearly as possible, including the basis of the conflict as the counselor understands it. Such knowledge increases a client's sense of power over the situation. To the degree that a client understands the crisis event, he or she will begin to regain some hope of influencing its outcome.

Finally, the counselor needs to help the client to confront the crisis situation in manageable doses. People usually need some kind of relief from having to look at the whole of reality all at once. No one is so strong as to be able to look at a severely threatening reality without some relief. In addition, if these interventions have not been successful, the counselor needs to go back and explore the reasons why they have been unsuccessful.

Stage 2

This stage consists of problem-solving behavior. The counselor is directed to explore alternative ways of solving the problem posed by the crisis. Different ways of solving it may be worked out in collaboration with the client. In working out some means of coping, the counselor needs to review the various problem-solving methods that the individual has used in similar situations in the past. Some of these previous coping mechanisms may have been maladaptive in the sense that the individual emerged from the stressful situation less healthy than he or she was before. An analysis of such problem-solving behavior assists the counselor in working out a more adequate means of coping with the present crisis.

It is important to remember that learning how to cope with a crisis will not necessarily help solve long-standing characterological problems. For this reason, the counselor should be prepared to help the individual arrange a consultation with a mental-health specialist when the need is indicated by the following factors: (1) evidence of need for emotional understanding in terms of long-range goals, (2) a clear-cut motivation for additional therapy, and (3) the availability of mental-health resources and the financial ability to pay for the therapy.

EXPERIENTIAL METHODS OF TRAINING
FOR CRISIS SUPPORT AND INTERVENTION

The most effective training in crisis intervention is, of course, actual counseling with persons in crises. However, counselors need some training before actually engaging in counseling, and there are various experiential modes of training that can be helpful. In particular, simulated situations and role playing provide a rehearsal of crisis situations and hence may reduce the future counselor's anxiety and increase his or her skill. A counselor is not able to work effectively with a person in crisis until some point of contact has been established with that person's experience. Exposing the trainee to a variety of simulated crises can provide a heightened awareness of various experiences sufficient for the counseling task. Moreover, simulation of crises in familiar settings can provide the kind of training that will integrate theory with actual practice.

There are two crucial values of counselor training through simulation, role playing, and fantasy. First, an obvious value is that a simulation enables a student to be trained in a situation that is similar to an actual counseling situation with little risk to the persons involved. The second value is not as obvious, but it is equally important. Counselors in training for crisis intervention need to make contact with their own feelings and experiences, thereby claiming this knowledge as their own. When such knowledge is integrated within a person, it can facilitate the development of the personal authenticity needed for the task of crisis intervention. Although counselors will not have actual experience with all the human crises they will encounter, their awareness may be heightened through imaginative participation in crisis simulations. As an example, individuals who expect to counsel effectively with bereaved or dying persons need to make contact with feelings about their own dying. Hence, simulations of their own dying may be a crucial element in the training of counselors to work with dying and bereaved persons.

The emphasis in the training of mental-health workers is placed upon the dynamics of crises rather than upon the psychodynamics of individual behavior. Crisis-intervention counselors are not expected to be specialists in the dynamics of human behavior, but they are expected to understand the nature of crises and the ways change can be effected in crisis situations. Accordingly, the counseling situations presented in Part Two provide an exposure to various types of actual crisis situations. This exposure may help trainees achieve an understanding of a variety of crises and of a variety of ways in which to intervene.

This understanding can be further enhanced by the experiential exercises described in the following section. Although some experiential exercises are suggested at the conclusion of each chapter in Part Two, the following brief description of the theory underlying these exercises may enable both students and instructors to develop exercises that are more relevant to their own particular needs.

TYPES OF EXPERIENTIAL EXERCISES

1. Simulations and Role Playing

Since many kinds of crises come within the normal range of experience, simulations and role playing can be effective ways of training counselors for crisis intervention. A rehearsal of crisis situations can reduce the anxiety of counselors and increase their skills. Moreover, the simulation of a specific crisis in a setting related to the counselor's particular kind of work can provide the sort of training that integrates theory and practice. The simulation enables the trainee to make contact with the experiences and feelings that are likely to affect his or her work. Since counselors are not able to work effectively until they have established some point of contact between their own experience and that of their clients, trainees should be exposed to a variety of simulated experiences.

The simulations should position the prospective counselor in his or her present or future work setting, since the work setting will determine the type of counseling situations he or she will encounter. Although the counselor's self-understanding and the general techniques of crisis intervention are more basic than the specific function of a given role (such as that of a probation officer), simulating that particular role provides the most effective learning possibilities.

The use of role playing may enhance the potential of training simulations. A counselor's understanding of the psychodynamics of suicidal behavior, for example, may be enhanced if the counselor tries playing the role of a suicidal person. Since crises occur in the lives of normal persons, anyone may experience a crisis appropriate to his or her own circumstances. Hence, the playing of a role may enable a counselor to make contact with feelings akin to those of an individual in a real-life crisis and thus facilitate an understanding and appreciation of such a person's experience.

2. Psychodrama and Gestalt Therapy

The use of simulations and role playing may include the specific utilization of the methodologies of psychodrama and Gestalt therapy. Both psychodrama and Gestalt therapy focus upon the here-and-now. The techniques of role reversal, doubling, mirroring, and future projections enable counselors to make contact with their own feelings and may enhance their understanding of the psychodynamics of human behavior as well as the development of their counseling skills.

In one of my courses on crisis intervention, Lewis Yablonsky used psychodrama as a means of facilitating the understanding of the behavior of both parents and child in working out a resolution to a crisis in drug abuse. In other classes on crisis intervention, my students and I have often utilized psychodrama as one means of understanding crises and increasing counseling skills (Miller, 1967).

The "rules" and "games" of Gestalt therapy have also been utilized at various stages in the experiential teaching of crisis-intervention methodology. The "rules" may be utilized directly in the development of counseling skills, and the "games" in increasing psychodynamic understanding of behavior (Levitsky & Perls, 1970, pp. 140–149).

(1) Games of *dialogue* may vary from a dialogue between two opposite poles of one's personality to a dialogue that dramatizes any split experienced within a person. (2) *Making the rounds* refers to expressing feelings or thoughts to each person in the group individually instead of depending upon generalizations. (3) The concept of *unfinished business* refers to unresolved feelings about anything that the individual is directed to finish. (4) The *I-take-responsibility* game involves accepting responsibility for feelings, body behavior, or thoughts. (5) *Playing the projection* is similar to psychodrama and involves getting inside a feeling attributed to someone else by recognizing and accepting the feeling as one's own. (6) The game of *reversals* is also similar to a corresponding practice in psychodrama; it involves getting in touch with a wide range of behavior by acting out polar opposites of behavior. (7) The recognition of the rhythm of contact and withdrawal, as exemplified by the phenomena of figure and ground, emphasizes the bi-polar nature of the human organism's activity. Hence, the human need for withdrawal from activity is both recognized and accepted, and the acting out recognizes this need. An individual is directed to follow these feelings of withdrawal in his or her fantasy and then to return

to reality. The ongoing work is then resumed with the new things about the self that have been learned. (8) The *rehearsal game* involves a sharing of the rehearsal of social roles that an individual is expected to assume. The rehearsal develops increased familiarity with one's social role, such as that of husband or teacher or leader. (9) The *exaggeration game* includes the repetition of exaggerated gestures or body movements in order to facilitate understanding of the messages of body language. (10) The *"May-I-feed-you-a-sentence?"* game involves proposing particular sentences to be repeated by an individual. If the sentence is appropriate to the individual, the idea is developed and enhanced through the repetition.

The value of using these games of Gestalt therapy or the methodology of psychodrama as teaching tools depends, of course, on the knowledge and skill of the instructor. This outline simply suggests the possibilities of these two methodologies in teaching and learning the skills of crisis support and intervention and in developing a flexibility of personal responses to various life situations.

3. Guided Fantasies

The use of guided fantasies represents an elaboration of the methodologies already discussed. The purpose of guided-fantasy exercises is to heighten awareness of feelings potentially available to normal persons. The development of a guided fantasy is limited only by the imagination of the individual using it. A word of caution: this technique is a powerful tool that should be used with care. At least two common safety measures should be employed: First, persons should be *invited* to participate without any emotional pressure to do so; the choice of an individual not to participate should be respected. Second, participants should understand that, if their fantasies become too threatening, they may withdraw from the exercise at any point. Indeed, the most important safety measure in the use of fantasy is the ordinary mobilization of defenses that enables a person to withdraw from any serious threat to his or her psyche.

4. The Journal

Many beginners in the art of counseling and psychotherapy have already discovered the value of psychological journals or workbooks as learning tools. Use of journals in learning the techniques of crisis intervention is especially relevant for people who are already involved in some kind of counseling. Keeping a journal is not simply a matter of recording client or counselor responses. A journal will include a record of what is happening to the feelings, emotions, and intuition of the counselor. The journal methodology has been employed in training situations in which an internship constituted an integral part of the course. In such a context, journals provide running accounts of the inner experiences of the learners as well as the experiences of those with whom they are working.

Ira Progoff has contributed to the development of the journal methodology through his Dialogue House Workshops and use of the "Intensive Journal." Progoff's use of the journal is focused on personal growth, but I have found it helpful in integrating experiential and theoretical learning. Hence, I have adapted some of the features of the Intensive Journal methodology from my workshop experience,[2] using some of its principles to facilitate the learning of crisis-intervention methodology.

In keeping a journal, it is important to simply record feelings, thoughts, notions, images, and intuitions as they occur. One function of this recording is to enable the individual to "go with" the energy of his or her feelings, so that contact can be made with those powerful feelings that lie beneath the surface of everyday awareness. Recording these inner experiences as they occur and "going with" the momentum of thoughts and feelings enables a person to observe the experience as a whole instead of analyzing bits of it. There is a wholeness or gestalt to an experience that embodies its own characteristic meaning. The journal is concerned with the *now*, or present moment. While some recordings may refer to the past, they are included not for the sake of their own analysis but only to provide connections to present experience. A journal also reflects and utilizes the bi-polar or opposite parts of personal life and experience —for example, working on a single issue from two inner perspectives.

In teaching crisis support and intervention, I have first encouraged students to plan on keeping a daily log of their experiences throughout the course. Next, I have instructed them to select a recent period of time, involving a specific event or idea, and to record what happened during that period. Each person is then invited to share that period of his or her life with other members of the seminar or class, but no one is compelled or

[2]Dialogue House Workshop conducted by Ira Progoff at the Lloyd Center, San Anselmo, California, August 15–20, 1971.

pressured to do so. The next instruction is to select and record some past experience that constituted an intersection or cross-roads where a significant decision was made. Students are encouraged to recapture the feelings, thoughts, and emotions of the time and to record the totality of the experience. Again, time is provided so that those who elect to share their experience with other members of the seminar may do so.

The purpose of this instruction is to initiate the process of recording a log of experiences focused on both the experiential and theoretical dimensions of crisis support and intervention. Various types of entries can be made in the log, including fantasy dialogues, dreams, or imagery. Any way in which individuals can make contact with their own powerful feelings may facilitate growth and the development of professional skills.

PART 2

The Practice
of Crisis Intervention
in Real-Life Crises

The theoretical discussion of crisis intervention in Part 1 provides a framework for understanding the general nature of crises and the ways in which counselors can work with persons in the midst of their crises. All crisis experiences have much in common, but there are also significant differences between them. In Part 2, the dynamics of specific crises and types of counselor interventions are described in connection with accounts of actual crisis experiences and counselor interventions. Some of these situations have been included as examples of what crisis counselors may expect in actual practice. Different types of crises have been grouped in categories, but these categories, while helpful for facilitating understanding, should not be taken as indicating absolute or ironclad distinctions among the types of crises discussed. It is precisely what all crises have in common that makes a unified field of crisis intervention possible.

Maturational Crises

Personal development occurs through a series of maturational stages having both physical and psychological dimensions. Moving from one stage of development to another is more than an automatic process; it involves taking risks. While there is a developmental thrust from within the human organism to move from one stage to another, there is also a shrinking back from the implications of psychological growth. This ambivalence exists precisely because growth requires giving up some of the sense of security experienced in a present stage in order to move on to a different and unknown stage, with all the risks involved in such a transition. A 19-year-old girl expressed the poignancy of this dilemma when she said in one of her counseling sessions "Why can't we stay young always? It hurts so to grow up!"

Although all individuals move from one developmental stage to another with some degree of risk, the risk is increased significantly when environmental factors place additional stress upon an individual. In some instances, the combination of the stress of normal development with the stress imposed by environmental factors results in a crisis. As we have seen, when an emotionally hazardous situation is more intense than usual, and when there is insufficient time in which to develop some new means of coping with the loss of security, a crisis may occur. Crises related to the stress involved in developmental transitions may be called *maturational crises.*

A DEVELOPMENTAL MODEL

Erikson's developmental model of the "eight ages of man" provides a framework for understanding the psychodynamics of both human development and maturational crises (Erikson, 1963, pp. 247–274). For the purposes of this chapter, I have chosen to divide the stages according to the specific needs of crisis intervention. Hence, the first three of Erikson's developmental stages are grouped together as one stage, making a total of six.

1. Infancy, Preschool, and Early Childhood (Birth to Approximately Age 6)

Birth to Age 2. During the first period of life, the child acquires the basic building blocks for the establishment of healthy relationships with other human beings. This process begins in infancy with the development of *basic trust* in the first significant other person known to the infant—the mother. Although Erikson insists on the value of learning both *trust and mistrust* during this period, it is certainly a time in which the infant learns predominantly to trust that this person will be dependable in meeting the basic needs for food and comfort. The mouth is the infant's primary organ of gratification and exploration, and having oral needs met forms the basis for the beginning of a development of trust. If the feeding schedule is determined simply by the mother's schedule, the infant will have difficulty in identifying the feeding pattern and hence in establishing trust. If a previously established schedule is seriously disrupted, the infant will respond with restlessness and anxiety until the consistency with which needs are met is identified and a sense of trust in the maternal response is developed.

As the first stage of life progresses, the child begins to achieve a sense of self-control and autonomy. The *physical* or *psychosexual task* is learning to exercise control over bladder and bowels, since control over these functions belongs entirely to the child. Indeed, one exercise of power in relationships with parental figures is the demonstration of what the child chooses to do and what he or she chooses not to do. During this stage, the *psychosocial task* is to begin developing self-esteem through the exercise of freedom and self-expression. The young child has the opportunity to work out a balance between cooperation and willfulness. Failure to work through the psychosocial task of this stage may result in feelings of *shame* and *doubt* about the child's self-worth that will affect every facet of life in the remaining stages of development.

My daughter Carole was 2 years old when her mother died. Prior to her death, the usual schedule of caring for Carole had been seriously disrupted by the several periods of my wife's hospitalization. At the age of 1 year, Carole had been taken out of her home and cared for by a relative because her mother had been temporarily unable to physically care for her. Thus, during a period in her life in which she was developing her attitude of *trust versus mistrust,* Carole was deprived of the consistency of having her needs met by the significant other person in her life —her mother.

Following her mother's death, Carole was cared for during the day in a nursery-school and day-care facility. For more than six months, the teachers at the center noted that, whenever Carole got hurt, she never turned to an adult woman teacher for comfort. Her behavior appeared to be the result of the disruption of her development of basic trust in a maternal figure. She did not return to her developmental task of building trust until she had another maternal figure she could consistently count on.

Young children experience traumatic crises in their lives, even if they are unable to verbalize their feelings. Understanding the dynamics of an early-childhood crisis may enable a parent or parent surrogate to understand a particular child. Although interventions will not be the same for children as for adults, interventions that are informed by knowledge of the dynamics and anatomy of crises can facilitate the personal growth of the child.

Age 2 to Age 6. During the period from about age 2 to age 6, the child is involved in the process of including the other members of the family as significant other persons. The psychosocial task is the development of *initiative.* The child begins to develop a sense of direction and purpose, as well as a self-concept that permits undertaking something new and risky. To the degree that the child is unsuccessful in this stage, he or she will develop uncertainty and *guilt* about even dreaming of trying out new ideas. In addition, failure during this period will entail confusion of psychosexual roles and the loss of initiative in undertaking the learning of new skills.

When Carole was 5 years old, she was enrolled in kindergarten. She had been in a nursery school for over two years following her mother's death, so the context of a school was not strange to her. Indeed, she had looked forward to kindergarten with keen anticipation. She had talked about it and planned for it. However, some of her talking appeared to be an expression of anxiety about this new experience. On the morning of the first day of school, she vomited up her breakfast. A psychosomatic reaction to her anxiety seemed to account for the upset stomach. Despite her apparent ambivalence about this new experience, she still wanted to go to school. I had remarried since her mother's death, and Carole's new mother took her to the school. Upon entering the building, Carole blurted out "This is the end of me!" Yet her fear of initiating this new venture was coupled with an eagerness to risk it. Even though she was afraid, her psychosocial task of building basic trust was sufficiently well completed to enable her to take the necessary risks.

Counseling interventions with small children cannot be identified with the usual crisis-intervention theory and practice. During the first five or six years of life, a child is forming the building blocks of development that will provide the ego strength necessary for coping. Nevertheless, supportive interventions by someone who cares may enable a child to cope with a stressful situation and to utilize whatever emotional resources are available. In this instance, Carole's new mother provided loving support that helped her to cope with her stressful entry into school.

2. Later Childhood (Approximately Ages 6–12)

The period of later childhood extends from about the age of 6 to the time of puberty or adolescence. It has been called the "latency" period, but that description is accurate only in the psychosexual sense. The child is actively developing significant relationships outside the immediate family. Relationships with school and neighborhood take on new importance. The child is involved in gaining recognition by developing competence in producing something. The psychosocial tasks include developing a sense of *industry* with which to undertake projects with peers, and the development of self-esteem is dependent upon the competence the child is able to demonstrate. Failure during this period involves feelings of *inadequacy and inferiority.*

Joey was 8 years old and a behavior problem in his third-grade class. His teacher noted that, while he had always been a lively youngster, he had not been a "troublemaker" in class until about three months before Joey's mother came in for counseling.

Joey's mother had been upset about his behavior at home. He had tormented his 3-year-old sister and continually resisted his mother during most of the time they were together. Then Joey's teacher had called and arranged a parent conference. It had now been about five days since that conference, and Joey's mother was at her "wits' end." She didn't know what to do or where to turn. Realizing that she simply had to talk to someone, she arranged for a counseling session.

She began by relating that she and her husband had separated about two months before, after a few weeks of intense quarreling. She was presently involved in divorce proceedings, and she described how difficult this entire period had been for her. She knew that she had been impatient with the children, but now Joey's behavior problems were more than she could take. Since Joey and his problems were an integral part of his mother's crisis, I encouraged her to bring him to the next session.

Joey was a bright, alert youngster with an apparent interest in physically active games. He was not very verbal in the session, but his interaction with his mother revealed covert anger. It was obvious that Joey was deeply disturbed about his parents' separation. At the same time, his mother was preoccupied with her own problems of adjustment, and she expressed her feelings openly. Although Joey wasn't primarily involved in the session, he seemed to be listening. In the third and final session, he verbalized some of his resentment toward his mother. The resentment was focused on the interruption of the building of his entry for a soap-box derby with his father. Joey was not verbalizing the pain of his father's leaving, but I facilitated his experiencing of feelings about the interruption of his project. His angry feelings were directed primarily toward his mother as being somehow responsible for his father's moving out. He had turned his anger inward, however, with the result that he developed feelings of inferiority. His misbehavior secured the undivided attention of his mother, who otherwise seemed to be preoccupied. Being blamed for the misbehavior simply strengthened his feelings that something was wrong with him, which resulted in additional angry behavior.

Joey was helped out of his self-defeating behavior by counselor interventions focused on facing the fact of his parents' separation and achieving some understanding of the feelings of his mother and father. A restoration of good feelings about himself and emotional support from both his mother and father enabled him to reassert his feelings of adequacy and hence removed the primary dynamics of his problem behavior.

3. Puberty and Adolescence (Approximately Ages 12–18)

The period beginning with the onset of puberty and continuing through adolescence is a time of significant changes. Adolescents experience dramatic physiological changes, and they have the problem of developing the social and emotional skills to cope with these changes in body image and self-perception.

Their psychosexual tasks include the continuation of identification with their own sex while they begin to experience what it means to relate to the opposite sex. Significant other persons include their peer group, and at the same time they are beginning to learn the meaning of commitment to something or someone beyond their immediate world. Psychosocial tasks include emancipation from childish ties to their parents. Their work is one of self-definition and self-acceptance. They are actively engaged in working out a sense of *identity* in the face of psychological and cultural pressures toward *identity diffusion* and *role confusion*. Societal pressures militate against the development of any clearly defined self-image. Society's tendency is to blur the distinctions among persons and hence to undermine the youth's development of a distinct self-image. Failure at this stage results in a self-destructive rebelliousness or in the development of a frightened, dull, conforming human being.

Some unfinished psychosocial tasks from adolescence were evident in a case study I originally reported in a journal article (Whitlock, 1968, pp. 43–48). George was 19 when I first saw him. He was in his first semester of his sophomore year in college, and he had come in for counseling because of failing grades in his science courses at the mid-semester examination period. George had achieved outstanding recognition in high school as a builder of model spacecrafts. Since his academic record had been excellent in the past, he could not understand his present feelings of apathy or his academic failure. He had begun to feel anxious and fearful at the beginning of the school year in which he was now enrolled. In probing to discover whether or not something had happened within the past few weeks, I discovered that he had been classified 1-A by his draft board about five weeks previously. His student deferment had been set aside because of his grades during the prior semester. Although his lack of motivation to study had begun about six months prior to the draft notice, he had begun to experience panic at the time of the draft reclassification.

During his first and second years in college, George had been attempting to discover the direction of his career. He had not been able to make any final decision about his occupational role, and the threat of the draft had exerted additional pressure upon him to decide immediately. When this pressure would start to become intolerable, he would drive up into the mountains and hike the trails by himself. He knew that if he was drafted his freedom of choice and movement would be curtailed. Since the draft meant that he could no longer participate meaningfully in decisions involving his own goals, he began to experience apathy in his studies. Actually being reclassified climaxed the deprivation of freedom and resulted in panic, and by the time of his second counseling session he had developed an ulcer. Unable to cope adaptively with his role confusion, he had developed a maladaptive means of coping. The development of an ulcer successfully eliminated the problem posed by the draft, but it was a maladaptive resolution of his personal crisis. This resolution was achieved in a period beginning about five weeks prior to his decision to consult a counselor.

This case is more typical of late adolescence than of young adulthood. First of all, the age of this young man illustrates the problem of "role confusion." During the critical years of late adolescence and early adulthood, individuals are confronted with the problem of choosing their values and discovering who they are in terms of the roles they are to fulfill in life. During these years a person is in danger of role confusion. Up to this point, George had been able to successfully evade his psychosocial tasks of developing his identity and defining his role clearly because of the control he had been able to exercise over his environment. The pressure of the draft, which he could not control, involved him in a panic reaction of flight from the necessity of making choices and from the recognition of his own inability to do so at the specific time dictated by the arbitrary deadline of the draft classification.

The need to reach some resolution of the crisis within a limited span of time is evidenced by the rather dramatic somatic effort that culminated in the development of an ulcer in the fifth and sixth week. The body reacted to the psychic threat by offering a resolution to the crisis. It is significant that the ulcer appeared shortly after the first counseling session and during the sixth week following the receipt of the draft reclassification. Although not every person of this age and in this circumstance will react with the same panic, any young person may be confronted with a similar crisis or role confusion. Young people need time to explore their choice of values and goals with some degree of freedom. These values and goals may be expressed through various commitments, including the choices of career, education, and marriage. In ordinary circumstances, counselor interventions include the exploration of these life choices in such a way that an individual experiences some sense of power and influence over his or her destiny. When arbitrary circumstances, such as the draft, block the usual way of developing coping skills, a maladaptive resolution may be used as the way out of the situation.

4. Young Adulthood (Approximately Ages 18–35)

The years of what might be called young adulthood overlap the later years of adolescence, but this stage includes its own developmental particularities. As the case of George shows, the tasks of this period may be compounded by unfinished developmental work from the previous stage. Since the tasks of the adolescent period are so complex, and since the transition to adulthood is so decisive, the amount of unfinished psychosexual and psychosocial tasks may be considerable. Indeed, the degree to which individuals have not completed some of their developmental tasks will become dramatically evident in young adulthood.

These are the years in which individuals usually begin to accept full responsibility for themselves, as well as for others in the establishment of a family. Young adults come to their full psychosexual maturity in both its physiological and psychological expressions. Hopefully, their psychosocial maturity is sufficient to enable them to risk giving to another person in the development of a mutually rewarding experience. The personal potency of adults is expressed through the ability to develop *intimacy* with at least one other human being. Young adulthood is also a time for heightening one's self-esteem and for relating to others in cooperative ventures that involve both risks and opportunities. Failure to complete these psychosexual and psychosocial tasks successfully results in the experience of *isolation*, of hostile dependency, or of overcompensatory aggressiveness.

Like George, whose crisis was discussed in the section on adolescence, Henry showed both unresolved psychosocial tasks from adolescence and an unwillingness to be responsible for himself in adulthood. I saw him for several sessions while he was in prison. Henry was 29 years old and unmarried. He had been convicted of writing checks with insufficient funds and was serving time in a minimum-security state prison. A transcription of the taped counseling sessions provides a record of Henry's perplexity as he expressed it to me: "I want to know why. That's right, I mean, they say . . . I mean . . . I know myself, and my friends tell me, people here tell me, I'm not criminally intended, which I'm not. I mean, I've never stole nothing.

I never stole in my life. It's just that when I get a heat on, I think I'm John D. Rockerfeller. I'd like to know why. What happens?" Early counselor interventions included questions about how he had responded to other situations in his life.

Henry had been a star high school and college football player, and a hero of the campus. During the Korean war he had flown as a Navy pilot and hence was again in an elite position. After his discharge, he experienced a brief letdown. Shortly after, he went into the real-estate business and made a number of important sales that netted him several thousand dollars in two months. In his own words, "I think the first month I was in there I made about twenty-five hundred bucks, and Jesus—it was all big money, and boom, I was living like a king! I had a big new car, I had all tailor-made suits, I moved away from the home with my mother and moved downtown and got an apartment. Moved one woman in, three days later moved another one in—threw her out and got another one."

He was a "big shot" again. When sales fell off, he continued spending money. In a bar with his buddies, he would play the "big shot" and buy drinks for everyone; then he would simply write a check, regardless of whether he had the money in his account to cover it. Although he had always been drinking when he wrote these checks, his basic problem seemed to be related to his need to feel important and cared for. He sought the recognition of other persons by buying their presence through the drinks he set up for them. Similarly, he confused his need for intimacy with a woman with his being able to buy any woman he wanted. Indeed, he was so preoccupied with his dependency needs that he was unable to accept responsibility for himself and unwilling to risk the development of an intimate relationship with one other person. He sought support for a precarious sense of self-esteem by buying recognition instead of risking failure in his interpersonal relationships.

Counselor responses consisted of listening to his story and intervening at some points. Although Henry's situation was initially a stressful one, it only became a crisis when he experienced the panic of finally facing the fact that he was in prison. He was so scared of what had finally happened to him that he was afraid of repeating his behavior after completing his four months of confinement. He requested a counselor immediately upon arriving at the prison, and it was clear that he was concerned about himself.

The support I was able to provide facilitated Henry's examination of himself and of his feelings about his sense of self-esteem. Interventions included confronting him with responsibility for himself and exploring ways in which he could feel good about himself without playing the big-shot role. While continuing to defend himself against recognizing the painful reality of his actual situation in life, Henry gradually tried out some of the alternative roles available to him. Playing these roles gave him an increased sense of power to effect some changes in his behavior.

5. Middle Adulthood (Approximately Ages 35–55)

The precise age span indicated for any of the adult periods is largely arbitrary, but there are identifiable tasks that characterize each period. Middle adulthood gives individuals the opportunity to include the larger community within the sphere of their significant relationships. Some of the psychosocial tasks include establishment in a job or career and pursuit of some concern that may take a person beyond himself. It is a period characterized by Erikson as concerned with *generativity,* or the establishment of self in relation to the next generation. The concerns of middle adulthood include productivity and creativity in culture, education, and the development of one's tradition.

Failure to complete the previous life stages successfully results in an inability to exercise the power of persons in this stage of life to contribute to the enhancement of human meaningfulness and enjoyment. Failure at the middle-adulthood stage results in *stagnation* of the individual and the loss of that person's contribution to the advancement of both self and society.

In one of the predictable crises of middle adulthood, John experienced a loss of meaning in life and was temporarily immobilized by his internal conflict. John was 39 years old, married, and the father of two children. He had taken a leave of absence from a business firm about two weeks earlier because of his inability to concentrate on his work, and he was searching for something that seemed to be missing in his life.

John had been very active in a conservative Protestant church and, at the time he took his leave of absence, was considering preparing for the ministry. He came in for career evaluation and took a battery of personality and occupational-interest tests to determine his interests and fitness for the ministry. The Strong Vocational Interest Inventory showed a high degree of interest in several phases of accounting and office work with which John was already acquainted, but only a fair degree of interest in the ministry and related occupations. The Gilford-Zimmerman Temperament Survey suggested a friendly, thoughtful, cooperative, and somewhat restrained person. It also noted tendencies toward submissiveness, depression, and hypersensitivity. The Minnesota Multiphasic Personality Inventory showed a freedom from any serious pathology but noted a tendency toward worry, useless thinking, and some forms of compulsive behavior. The results of these exploratory tests suggested the need for further projective testing before he could be encouraged to consider the ministry as a career.

About a week later, John came in to discuss the results of the tests and to seek further clarification of his personal and career possibilities. He was depressed at the outset of the session, and my responses included empathic listening to his distress. In answer to my questions, he revealed that he had been having difficulty getting to sleep. As I supported his exploration of his feelings, he began to talk about himself and to reveal a conflict in which he was involved. He had become very interested in a woman other than his wife. This interest had begun about ten weeks before. At first he had only seen her for lunch, but during the past five weeks he had been seeing her more often, and during this time he had come to realize how seriously he was becoming involved. He had become aware that he was thinking about her whenever he was at home and that he was comparing his wife with her. Despite some ambivalent feelings about his behavior, he had been denying any infidelity by referring to the relationship as a "spiritual" one. My interventions included encouraging John to explore these feelings and confronting him with his responsibility for himself and his feelings.

John's restlessness and dissatisfaction with his occupation were focused on his relationship with the young woman. His feeling that he was missing something in his religious life was combined with a consideration of the ministry as a career that would satisfy his longing for personal meaning. It appeared that his psychosexual needs had awakened the man who had become stagnant and unproductive. This awakening had involved him in a stressful reexamination of his personal life and its meaning. Further counselor interventions included a realistic look at his interests and abilities in relation to his restlessness and his relationship with the young woman. The challenge to his value structure increased the stress, but he involved himself in problem solving and eliminated the consideration of a career change.

Focus upon the conflict between the valuing of his marriage and his interest in the young woman forced him to face the issue squarely and to resolve it.

6. Late Adulthood (Approximately Ages 55–75)

The exact age span represented by the phrase "the later years" is impossible to determine. Moreover, a person may manifest some of the characteristic marks of both middle and late adulthood in the same experience. Nevertheless, Erikson's designation of this general period as "maturity," or late adulthood, is a helpful one. Late adulthood includes the dynamics of all the previous life stages. It is marked by the culmination of all the psychosocial tasks that have been completed successfully. It is a time that includes a greater possibility of wisdom, precisely because the primary tasks are not those of establishing or producing. The potential psychosocial crisis concerns the dimension of *integrity*. Individuals who have successfully completed the previous stages of development can experience a sense of integrity as a climax of life. Failure to complete the previous stages with at least a relative degree of success, on the other hand, creates an existential anxiety. To the degree that mature men and women experience failure in relation to their families or careers, their anxiety may result in *despair*. Despair may be expressed behaviorally through psychosomatic symptoms, depression, or excessive use of alcohol or other drugs.

Both the dangers and possibilities of this period are manifold. A woman experiencing menopause at the age of 45 may show some of the physiological characteristics of late adulthood, including a significant loss of function. At the same time, she may, for example, develop a lively interest in teaching children and in introducing them to the values of a tradition that she has come to appreciate. The possibilities of this period are just now being explored. The renowned organizational consultant, Peter Drucker, gave expression to these possibilities when he remarked "Here I am 58 years old, and I still don't know what I'm going to do when I grow up."

James H. Barrett, author of *Gerontological Psychiatry*, has maintained that the aging individual has certain developmental tasks that must be mastered. These tasks are both *regressive* and *compensatory* (Barrett, 1972). The regressive developmental tasks noted by Barrett are:

1. Accepting the physical decline of the body.

2. Accepting sexual change in self and in the spouse. Though sexual interest and activity may continue, physical decline and individual physiological differences . . . may reduce sexuality in old age.
3. Accepting and adjusting to changes in dependency and independency status.
4. Accepting the role of receiver, instead of giver . . . without loss of self-respect.
5. Acceptance of a reduction in social contacts due to physical impairment, loss of status, and death of friends [p. 4].

These tasks may require the intervention of a counselor or simply the concern of a caring person in exploring with individuals the reality of their situation. If the developmental transition, perhaps in combination with external events, results in a crisis, the first stage of intervention includes examining the actual situation confronting the individual who has experienced a significant and emotionally hazardous change in his or her relationships with self or with others.

The compensatory developmental tasks listed by Barrett include:

1. Developing new leisure-time interests.
2. Education towards new skills which may be used for part-time employment.
3. Adjustment to a healthy, prescribed diet, even though it may be bland.
4. Adjustment to a new environment.
5. Reconciliation to a younger generation with new and different ideas.
6. The maintenance of acquiring status.
7. . . . alteration of self-concept to include loss of friends, family, and abilities without feeling a loss of intrinsic worth [p. 4].

The compensatory-developmental tasks involve the counselor in a second stage of intervention—the encouragement of problem-solving behavior. In this stage, interventions are directed toward the exploration of alternative ways of resolving the individual's actual situation.

POSTSCRIPT

Persons who experience crises in connection with maturational changes may experience some degree of failure in completing their developmental tasks successfully. Although there may be characterological problems that are involved in any such failure, maturational crises are related to both developmental and situational factors.

Since everyone is subject to the intense and ongoing processes of maturational development, we are all vulnerable to their associated, normal pressures. These processes run their course over an extended period of time as transitions are made from one stage of development to another. Increased awareness of physiological and psychological changes alters people's perceptions of their environment. They experience a loss of the secure position enjoyed in one stage of development, and they are compelled to work out a new relationship with a changed environment. An increased sense of disequilibrium results. If the changes are too radical, or if sufficient time is not available in which to develop coping skills, a crisis may develop.

In addition to the potentially hazardous transitions that normally occur in human life, there are accidental changes that radically alter an individual's relationship to the environment. When normal maturational changes are combined with accidental changes, the intensity of the changes is often so severe that a crisis develops. An understanding of maturational development may therefore facilitate an understanding both of maturational crises and of those combinations of circumstances in which crises tend to develop. In view of the fact that every stage of development has its own psychosocial tasks, any crisis may be related both to the accidental situation and to the developmental tasks of the individual in his or her particular stage of life.

EXPERIENTIAL TRAINING

I. Suggestions for the Instructor

The suggested exercises may be either directed by the instructor or initiated by students themselves as assignments out of class. It will be helpful to direct at least one of these exercises in class, since fantasies have greater strength if they are directed by a leader. Each student should be allowed the freedom to choose whether or not to participate in a fantasy exercise.

II. Experiential Exercises

A. Select a particular childhood age, and identify something of significance that happened to you at that time.

1. Be your child in your imagination.
   a. Take the time and silence to fantasize yourself as a child. It will be helpful to find a comfortable position, either lying down or sitting up, and to close your eyes.
   b. Become aware of your breathing. Give attention to your inhaling and exhaling, but do not change the rhythm of your breathing.
   c. Relax your body as a whole, and experience that relaxation.
   d. Become aware of each part of your body. Begin by relaxing your feet, then your legs, your thighs, and so on.
   e. When you are totally relaxed, enter into your fantasy of being a child again. What kind of situation are you in? What is happening to you? What are you feeling? Who is with you in this experience? What is the outcome of your experience?
   f. When you are ready to leave this experience, become your actual age again, open your eyes, and rejoin the class.
2. Select another member of the class, and tell that person about your fantasy.
   a. Relate how old you were and what the circumstances of your situation were.
   b. Talk about your feelings as a child.
   c. Explore your present feelings in your dyad.
   d. Ask for feedback.
   e. Reverse roles. Listen to the other person's fantasy, exploring the same questions as before.
B. Select a period from your adolescence or adulthood when you were confronted with some crossroads experience in which you chose to go in one direction rather than another.
   1. Imagine yourself at this particular age.
   2. Write out this experience of choosing in the manner of a journal entry. Include the description of the situation, what happens, what you are feeling, who is with you, and the final outcome.
   3. Share your journal account with the class. The instructor coordinates this telling of individual stories as follows:

a. The accounts are accepted as recorded—that is, without analysis but with questions and comments from the members of the class and from the instructor.
b. The instructor accepts, clarifies, questions, and in general facilitates the telling of each story and the exploration of the dangers and opportunities posed by the events related in each of the stories.

Crises within Families

Any crisis involving an individual who is living in a family is in some sense a family crisis. However, some crises are ones in which something happens primarily *within* an individual, whereas others are primarily interpersonal. Since crises involve both dimensions of experience, no clear line of demarcation can be made between individual and family crises; it is rather a matter of emphasis. Stressful situations that are primarily interpersonal in relation to the family constellation are included in this chapter. Those that may typically result in a decisive break such as divorce are discussed in the chapter on contractive crises. Of course, any marital conflict may eventually result in divorce; such conflict is included here if the couple is working on the conflict within the marriage.

THE THREAT OF LOSS IN MARITAL CONFLICT

Marital conflict always involves stress and often results in a crisis. The *danger* of the conflict is that it may increase the distance between the spouses and result in a permanent disruption of the relationship in divorce. The *opportunity* is that through the conflict some issues may be defined and resolved in a way that strengthens the relationship. Coping successfully with one crisis or conflict provides the basis for resolving future ones.

In *The Intimate Enemy*, George Bach (1964) emphasizes the *value* of marital conflict. Since marital conflict can be constructive as well as destructive, the goal of the counselor or therapist is to assist the couple to utilize the constructive dimension of conflict to facilitate the growth of their relationship. Counselors and psychotherapists who have worked with couples in conjoint and family therapy have understood these dynamics. Bach stresses the techniques of "fighting fair" rather than "unfair."

Eric Berne (1961) and the transactional therapists have emphasized the identification and the breaking up of "games people play" that are destructive to the relationship. Regardless of differences in approach, the dynamics of a marital encounter usually include considerable similarities. My own training with Walter Kempler in psychotherapy with couples and families emphasized Kempler's identification of two basic rules of experiential family therapy: "(1) attention to the current interaction as the pivotal point for all awareness and intervention, and (2) involvement of the total therapist-person who brings overtly and richly his full personal impact on the families with whom he works—not merely a bag of tricks called therapeutic skills" (Kempler, 1970, p. 150).

In my experience, learning to cope with marital conflict is a process rather than an end product, but it is a process in which skills are learned and powers are rediscovered. Although marital conflict does not always constitute a crisis, it is always more or less stressful, and its resolution often requires the assistance of a counselor or therapist. My approach is to make interventions in relation to *current* interactions between the individuals involved and to participate actively in the therapeutic process. Interventions are directed toward the *what* and *how* of behavior instead of toward an attempt to explain why it occurs.

As an example, we may consider the marital situation of Harold and Mary. I had originally seen each of them separately. They were 23 and 22 years of age, respectively, and they had two small children. Harold had made his original contact because of feelings of depression resulting from a loss of personal and vocational meaning. He was working in a social-work agency while completing college and had been planning to go on to a graduate school of theology to prepare for the ministry. As the result of his studies and his personal struggles, he had rejected his conservative religious beliefs, and his faith had collapsed. At the same time he was experiencing the meaninglessness of his marriage. He indicated that he had lost sexual interest in his wife, complaining that she was so passive that she was not interesting.

In the midst of this inner turmoil, Harold had become involved in an affair with a woman in his office who was several years older than he. She had made the first overture; Harold indicated that, while not literally seducing him, she had "said what I didn't dare to say." In any event, he would often leave his home after dinner, go to her apartment, and return home around three o'clock in the morning. In this way, he had made it obvious to his wife that he was having an affair, and indeed had told her about it. It was almost as if he would do anything to get some aggressive response from her. I saw them both sep-arately until it was clear that they both wanted to keep their marriage intact. When Harold indicated that he wanted his wife and his marriage more than he wanted the other woman, he ter-minated the affair. At this juncture, conjoint therapy sessions were arranged. Only interventions relevant to the couple's in-teraction in the here-and-now were planned. Although the type of counseling involved was essentially experiential family ther-apy, it included anxiety-provoking interventions.

The conjoint sessions began with each of them talking to me. My response was "Say that to her" or "Tell him—he's right here." Their early responses were that these things had already been said and that saying them hadn't made any difference. I responded that they needed to talk to each other about these very feelings that whatever each one had said hadn't seemed to make any difference to either of them. Thus, my initial inter-ventions consisted largely of directing them to interact with each other and of refusing to be placed in the position of the "answer man" or "middleman." They both tended to withdraw from each other and from their feelings of both anger and ten-derness. Mary began the sessions with the attitude "Now that the affair is over, I can relax." She refused to acknowledge that Harold's affair was a symptom of something radically wrong with their marriage and that the same symptomatology was still evident in their relationship.

In the early sessions, neither of them could make any hos-tile statement to the other without smiling. The incongruity between the words expressed and the nonverbal message of smiling was obvious, and I pointed it out whenever it occurred. When Harold criticized Mary, she agreed with him. Whenever he would get the courage actually to express feelings of anger, she would retreat into tears, and he would try to comfort her. The series of interventions at this juncture consisted simply of describing how they behaved in interactions with each other and of pointing out to both of them how Harold was controlled by the passive behavior of the "underdog." As Fritz Perls observed, the underdog always wins! The only trouble was that, when Mary "won," in actuality she lost Harold again. When Harold did muster up the courage to express angry feelings, I supported his outburst, which facilitated the rediscovery of his own power as a person in the relationship.

In the early sessions, Mary controlled Harold by alternately protecting him and utilizing her tears to make him sorry for her. In this mothering role, she criticized me for "dissecting" Harold by describing his behavior. She made it clear that she did not want to be a participant in this kind of endeavor. However, when her controlling behavior was described as destructive to their relationship, she began to understand how her control resulted in self-defeating behavior. Her avowed purpose was to keep the marriage and to reestablish a healthy relationship with Harold, but her controlling behavior frustrated this development. She said she wanted a relationship with Harold, but in actuality she cut herself off from him. She showed this same behavior with the therapist. One of my interventions at this point pointed out her ambivalence: "You say you want help, but you act as if you want me to leave you alone." As she was confronted with her self-defeating coping mechanisms, she began to see her contradictory behavior for what it was. At one point she became aware of her own body language. She pointed out how she held her head to one side in the way that her 4-year-old daughter did when she said she wanted to be left alone yet still wanted to get attention.

In a series of ten sessions, the direction of their encounter changed. Although no permanent solution to all their problems was achieved, the crisis in their relationship had passed, and they had begun to rediscover something about themselves. In referring to what had been happening in their therapy, Harold said "I discovered that things were different. I don't try to be different—it just happens." Mary began to recover some of her overt aggressiveness, while Harold recovered some of his loving, sexual feelings for Mary—even though he remarked "I don't know how it happened." They both said that they now experienced some recovery of power over what was happening in their relationship. It was no longer a situation in which the therapist was the one with the power of observation and understanding. They had regained some control over their own relationship, despite the fact that it was scary business.

Although this situation was not a "crisis" in the precise sense of the word used in this book, it can legitimately be described as a marital crisis. Strictly speaking, the interventions I have described consisted of experiential family therapy rather than crisis intervention, but they do represent therapeutic interventions in a specific kind of critical situation. Furthermore, the first series of consultations were focused upon the immediate, precipitating circumstances. The consultations that followed were focused upon the characteristic pattern of the couple's present interactions and included an examination of the basis of their continuing transactions.

THE THREAT OF LOSS IN PARENT-CHILD CONFLICT

Wise parents know that there is bound to be a certain amount of conflict between themselves and their children. Nevertheless, such conflict is usually threatening; in fact, it has been so threatening to some middle-class Americans that the term *filiarchy* has been coined to define the domination of parents by their children. The source of a child's power is the parents' fear that conflict will result in their children being cut off from them. The threat parents feel is the expression of both a basic insecurity about their role and identity as parents and a fear of intense feelings, especially those of anger. The threat of parent-child conflict is experienced more typically at the time the child reaches adolescence. Conflict is usually intensified as the result of blocked communication over a period of time prior to the actual event that precipitates the family crisis.

The dynamics of the conflict between Susan and her parents include various dimensions of interest to any counselor. Susan was 17 years old and in her first semester at the university. She was the only child of a couple who had been very successful in a business together. They lived in a beautiful home in a suburban community in Southern California. They were members of a prestigious church in their community, and, although they were not very active, they valued their membership in that particular church.

Susan had been referred to me by the university chaplain because of the intensity of the conflict between herself and her parents over her intention to marry David, who was Jewish. David was 21 years old and was about to graduate from the university. Although David was a Reformed rather than an Orthodox or Conservative Jew, his religious tradition was important to him. Susan had grown up in the Protestant tradition, but she was probably closer to the Reformed-Jewish theological position than to her home church at this time in her development. At any rate, the religious issue did not represent any problem to her, and she and David had decided to rear their children in Judaism. In addition, both of them were involved in what were termed the radical movements of the early 1960s. They were active in C.O.R.E. and participated in civil-rights demonstrations.

Susan's parents were very upset by both the religious and political differences between their daughter and themselves, and they felt threatened. The threat they experienced was due more to the fear that they would be cut off from their daughter's life than to their religious or political differences as such. The possibility of being cut off from certain religious rituals and experiences represented the threat of a significant loss.

Shortly after I saw Susan for the first time, she called frantically for a special appointment. At that time I suggested seeing her together with her parents, since the focus of her distress was the conflict and lack of communication with her parents. Her father was unable to come to this session, so her mother began by talking to me about not being able to talk to Susan anymore. My first intervention was to direct her to talk this over with her daughter. When she again tried to talk to me about Susan, I firmly directed her to say whatever she had to say to her daughter. When she started to talk to Susan, she began to cry, and in a moment they were both crying. Interventions during this first family-therapy session consisted of facilitating their interactions and helping them to listen to each other.

During the second session, the religious question surfaced. Both parents expressed their feelings to Susan in the form "You will be damned if you reject Christ." When they were confronted with the limited degree of their participation in the actual work of their church, their fear of being cut off from Susan's life with David became evident. They were fearful that, if Susan's children were trained in Judaism, they, as grandparents, would be cut off both from the Christian holidays and rituals they valued and from the Jewish holidays that would now represent their daughter's tradition. The threat of this loss precipitated feelings of fear and anger. Interventions consisted of identifying and describing these fears. When Susan could see their fears as personal rather than ideological, she was able to respond to her parents with some understanding.

Between the second and third sessions, Susan was arrested during a civil-rights demonstration. Her father called and wanted advice about whether or not to put up bail to get her out of jail. When I refused to make any decision for him, he decided to let her work out her own problem, even if it meant that she would remain in jail for a day or so. Despite some uneasiness about his decision, he remained firm. Although Susan did not like being left in jail, she respected her father's feelings about her participation in the demonstration. In the third session, they expressed warm feelings for each other, and some genuine acceptance occurred.

Prior to the fourth session, a letter to Susan from a Mid-western university was delivered to her home address. Her parents were upset that, without telling them, she had applied to the same university at which David had been accepted for graduate work. Tension about this incident and a discussion of her plans to go to the Midwest with David occurred during the fourth session. They were listening to each other and were able to communicate, despite differences in their attitudes and opinions.

Susan celebrated her 18th birthday a few days before the fifth session. Her parents had made a special point of inviting David to a birthday dinner at their home, but he had not been able to come. They expressed disappointment that he was not at the party, but they showed some new attitudes toward Susan. They began to understand how they could be domineering without really being aware of it. In a problem-solving session, they showed a new willingness to let Susan make her own decisions. They still wanted her to remain at the university, at least until the completion of her first semester, but they were willing to leave the decision up to her.

In a session with Susan and David before David's departure for graduate school, we clarified some of the issues that had been relevant to their relationship. Susan was able to raise some of her own questions about her readiness to be independent of both her parents and David. Since she recognized some of her unresolved dependency needs in relation to her parents, she began to question her readiness to establish a durable relationship with David. Although she decided to drive to the Midwest with David, she also decided to return to Southern California and to complete her unfinished business with her parents before marrying him. This occasion was one of the few instances in which I have observed a young couple postponing a wedding in order to work through some unresolved needs in relation to parents. This sixth session concluded the crisis portion of this counseling relationship.

During the next five sessions, most of them with Susan and her mother, Susan explored her dependence on her parents. Indeed, she and her mother were very dependent upon each other. Susan had suffered from rheumatic fever at about 12 years of age and had had to stay in bed for about six months. This time had been a fearful one for both of them. Susan told her mother that she had been afraid that she would never walk again but that she had never told her mother of her fear because she hadn't wanted to worry her. Her mother had likewise been worried, but she hadn't let her daughter know just how worried she was. Each had tried to protect the other from unpleasant feelings and thoughts, thereby placing a severe strain on open communication between them. They gradually became able to discuss everything—including plans for Susan's wedding, which had been set for January, following completion of her first semester at the university.

Not all of the problems between Susan and her parents had been resolved. Nevertheless, the crisis in their relationship had been faced, communication had been reestablished, and she and her mother were now able to plan the wedding together. In addition, Susan was able to clarify some of her unresolved dependency needs, and this clarification provided a more sound basis for her marriage. Some months following these consultations, I received notes on separate occasions from Susan and her mother. Her mother expressed her gratitude for the kind of communication she had experienced with Susan throughout the planning of the wedding. Although the relationship with her daughter had changed, she had gained a new kind of friendship with her. Susan wrote several months after the wedding, expressing her appreciation for the help in resolving some crucial questions and reiterating her belief that the decision to postpone the wedding had been a wise one.

THE SENSE OF FAILURE ASSOCIATED WITH PREMATURE BIRTHS

A unique kind of family crisis can occur in connection with the premature birth of a child. Irrational but real feelings related to a sense of failure are common, and they must be acknowledged and understood in the context of the family. In addition, some women actually contribute to the occurrence of prematurity through such factors as inadequate diet or heavy smoking. Whatever the cause of a premature birth may be, feelings of guilt and failure need to be acknowledged and clarified. The birth of a premature baby is a stressful situation in any family, regardless of whether or not it is anticipated. There is always fear for the well-being of the infant, and measures need to be taken to prevent any serious psychological consequences to the mother or father.

A crisis-intervention text written by nurses reported on the four phases the mother of a premature child must work through if she is to come out of the experience in a healthy way: (1) The mother must realize that she may lose the baby. This anticipatory grief involves a gradual withdrawal from the relationship already established with the child during the pregnancy. (2) She must acknowledge failure in her maternal function to deliver a full-term baby. (3) After separation from the infant during its prolonged hospital stay, she must resume her relationship with the baby in preparation for the homecoming. (4) She must prepare herself for the job of caring for the baby through an understanding of its special needs and growth patterns (Aguilera, Messick, and Farrell, 1970, p. 58).

While the immediate crisis of prematurity comes within the purview of the nurse or physician, the mother and father of the premature baby will cope with their own emotional hazards one way or another. A minimal understanding of the dynamics of the stress associated with prematurity should help them to cope more effectively.

First of all, the infant will be taken to the nursery for premature infants immediately after delivery; hence, neither the mother nor the father will get more than a glance at the new son or daughter. They will have little opportunity to reassure themselves about the condition of the child directly, and, since the infant is subsequently isolated from all but the medical personnel, they will have little opportunity to allay their anxieties. Furthermore, since there is a realistic possibility that the child may either die or be abnormal in some way, the hospital personnel are often guarded in their responses to the parents.

In my own counseling experience, I have not encountered a crisis associated with prematurity, but in my reading and in contacts with nurses in my crisis-intervention classes, I have noted the importance of the stressful dynamics of prematurity. The following case history illustrates these dynamics.[1]

Assessment of the individual and his problem. Laura and Peter G. were a young couple who had been married for three years. Peter, five years older than Laura, was the oldest of four children. Laura, a petite young woman, was an only child. They had a daughter 2 years old and a son 2 months of age who was born prematurely.

Peter's company had transferred him to another city when Laura was seven and one-half months pregnant; she went into labor the day after moving into their new home 100 miles from their home town, where both their families lived. She delivered

[1]From *Crisis Intervention* (2nd ed.), by Donna C. Aguilera and Janice M. Messick, pp. 69–72. Copyright 1974 The C. V. Mosby Co., St. Louis, Missouri. Reprinted by permission.

their son in a private hospital with excellent facilities but under the care of an obstetrician previously unknown to her due to their recent move. She was upset by the strangeness of the hospital, by the new doctor, and by the precarious physical condition of the son she and Peter had been hoping for. Laura did not want to discuss her fears with Peter, because she knew he was also concerned about the baby, and she did not want to add to his worries. Laura did not feel free to discuss her fears with her doctor, because she did not know him, or with the nurses, because they "always seemed so busy." She also thought that since she had had a baby before, she should know the answers to all the questions she had in mind.

After she and Peter brought their son home from the hospital, Laura had episodes of crying and was experiencing symptoms of anxiety, including insomnia. She felt physically exhausted and increasingly fearful concerning her ability to care for her son. No matter what she did, the baby slept only for short periods and was more fretful when awake than their daughter had been. Because of the baby's small size, Peter was afraid to help with his care, so Laura was responsible for all his physical care.

Peter's mother arrived for a visit "to see how the new baby was doing." She had been critical of Laura's intention to move at the time of Peter's transfer, advising that Laura should wait until after the baby's birth. Laura had now begun to think that she should have followed that advice. Her mother-in-law and she often had talks about the rearing of children. Laura had begun to have confidence in her own mothering abilities as a result of her daughter's good health and average development, but now she was doubtful again because of her apparent inability to care for her new son.

Planning of therapeutic intervention. The event that precipitated the crisis was the visit of a mother-in-law who was critical of Laura's ability to care for her new baby. "I can't understand why the baby cries so much. You must be doing something wrong. My children always slept through the night by 2 months of age and took long naps during the day," were typical of her constant comments. Peter seemed reluctant to take sides against his mother, so Laura received little support from him in dealing with these criticisms. She was finally unable to cope with her feelings of inadequacy, which were intensified by her mother-in-law's visit, and as a result became extremely upset, cried uncontrollably, and was unable to care for the baby at all. Peter's employer commented to him that he seemed upset and asked if there was anything wrong at work. Peter told him that the problem was not his job but Laura's behavior since the birth of the baby. His employer recommended that they seek help at a nearby crisis intervention center.

The goal of intervention determined by the therapist at the crisis center was to assist both Laura and Peter in exploring their feelings regarding the premature birth of their son, their changed communication pattern, and the lack of support Peter was giving Laura.

Intervention. During the first few weeks, Laura was able to discuss her feelings of inadequacy in the mothering role and to tell Peter of her anxieties regarding their son, of her fears that he would be abnormal, and of her belief that the premature birth was her fault because she had insisted upon moving with Peter at the time of his transfer. Peter, in turn, could tell Laura of his feelings of guilt at not being able to help more during the move, and also of the blame he placed upon himself because the labor was premature. The therapist assisted them in seeing the reality of the situation. Although the move may have been a factor in the premature onset of labor, there could have been other causes.

Peter discussed his insecurities regarding the handling of such a small baby; Laura was then able to tell him that she felt the same way and she feared she might be doing something wrong with this baby. The therapist gave them information about the differences in the behavior of a normal child and the care required for a premature infant. She reassured Laura that she was doing well and that in time the baby would adjust to more regular hours. She also encouraged Peter to help his wife so that she could get more rest; in turn Laura helped Peter to gain confidence in holding and caring for their new son.

Anticipatory planning. As Peter became comfortable in caring for the baby, he was encouraged to share the responsibility of caring for him in the evenings. This enabled Laura to get more physical rest. Peter's emotional support helped her to relax, and she began to sleep better.

The therapist discussed their need to continue to improve communications between them. It was stressed that they must reestablish a pattern of social activities with each other. They were assured that their new son could survive for a few hours with a competent baby-sitter while they went out to dinner or to play cards with other couples.

Most of their energies and concern during the past two months had been concentrated on their son. It was recommended that they also devote some additional time to their two-year-old daughter. This was a stressful time for her, too! Since her mother and father could not give her their sole attention, she would be competing for time with her new brother, and the feelings of sibling rivalry would emerge. She would need to feel that her position in the family was also unique and important—that is, a daughter and their first born. Time should be planned for her to have some activities with her parents. This would emphasize that she was "old" enough to be included in their activities.

They were warned to expect some acting-out behavior and possibly some regressive behavior in her bids for "equal" attention.

During their last visit Laura and Peter were assured they could return to the Center if they felt the need for help with a problem.

This case history provides an introductory understanding of the dynamics of one couple's response to the premature birth of their child. Peter and Laura brought their problem to a crisis-intervention center after the child had come into the home. Laura's equilibrium had been further upset by her mother-in-law's criticism. Laura saw herself as a failure in the mother's role, and her inability to communicate her concerns to her husband and doctor, coupled with her inexperience in caring for a premature infant, resulted in increased anxiety and depression. After determining the precipitating factor in this crisis, the counselor encouraged Laura's expression of her feelings and gave her some realistic understanding of the problems of prematurity. Helping Laura to mobilize the support of her husband and to improve her communication with him enabled her to cope with her crisis in a healthy and adaptive manner.

THE LOSS ASSOCIATED WITH BIRTH DEFECTS

Every couple expecting a child hopes simply that the baby will be all right. Sometimes a couple has a preference for a child of a particular sex, but their principal hope is always that the baby will be normal, both physically and mentally. It is a tragedy whenever an infant is born with a physical or mental impairment. Such an event always results in considerable stress in the family and often results in a crisis. I described in an earlier publication how one family's crisis was occasioned by the birth of a mongoloid child:

> Betty was twenty-five, a college graduate, married, and lived in a small town near the city. She had delivered her first child about eight weeks prior to her coming in for counseling. She explained that about three weeks before her counseling appointment, her family physician had informed her and her husband that their baby was a mongoloid child, even though it was a borderline case. She was now staying with her parents in the city where she had taken the baby for some medical checkups with specialists at the suggestion of her physician. She had received

a definitive diagnosis about ten days prior to her counseling session.

She was depressed and somewhat apathetic. She began talking about her reason for coming to the city. The session with the doctors ten days previously had destroyed any hope she had for good news. The first intervention was simply an encouragement to talk about her feelings. She revealed that after the birth of the baby she had shown him off proudly to her friends. When the family physician finally told her the truth, he confessed that he had been aware of the situation from the first but simply could not bring himself to tell her the truth. She was encouraged to express her feelings, and she talked about the trauma of hearing the first word of it from her physician. However, she had not let herself think much about it until the specialists had examined the baby. Now she lived with her grief for her child. Her feelings of grief were accepted, and she began to express hostile feelings, especially toward her family doctor who had not had the courage to inform her of his original diagnosis. She expressed bitter feelings against God who allowed such a thing to happen. These feelings were accepted and supported by interpreting that God was concerned with her honest feelings.

She indicated that her parents and friends had urged her to put the child in an institution for the mentally retarded. She expressed some guilt feelings for desiring this solution, and she seemed most apathetic when she talked of it. She seemed to assume that since her family physician, parents and friends had all urged her to place her child in an institution, there was no other solution. However, she began talking of taking care of her child, and another intervention was to encourage her to talk about this and to explore the possibility of such a plan, contrary to what seemed to be everyone's advice. Almost immediately she began to express some aliveness. As she was encouraged to explore other possibilities, she began to appear brighter, increasingly alert and more interested in her future. Another intervention consisted of encouraging her to learn more about the occurrence of mongoloid birth, and pointing out the fact that there was no reason to believe that the remainder of her children would not be normal. Being reassured that such births occur erratically seemed to give her increased hope of influencing the outcome of her crisis experience [Whitlock, 1973, pp. 138–140].

The course of this crisis was marked by depression and apathy. Betty's depression was evidently related both to grief and to hostile feelings that had not yet been expressed. Her apathy seemed to be related to feelings of hopelessness. By supporting her expression of grief and hostility and by increasing her knowledge about the situation, the counselor enabled her to experience a growing hope of influencing the outcome of the crisis.

Crises seem to follow a similar course in the case of other kinds of birth defects. The problems facing the parents will, of course, be different if the defects are physical rather than mental, but their initial reactions seem to be quite similar.

THE LOSS EXPERIENCED IN RELINQUISHING A CHILD FOR ADOPTION

A trauma that may involve an experience of a significant loss is the relinquishing of a child for adoption. In the past, counseling in such cases has usually been the exclusive domain of social workers employed by adoption agencies and homes for unwed mothers, and a considerable proportion of this type of counseling will continue to be handled by public and private adoption agencies in the future. However, an increasing number of unwed girls are having their babies while continuing to live within their families, homes, and communities. In addition, some couples with several children are beginning to relinquish babies for adoption. Increasingly, counselors in various settings are being sought out for this type of counseling. Hence, mental-health workers need training to prepare for the possibility of such counseling.

An additional facet of this problem is the recent increase in the number of unwed teenage girls who decide to keep their offspring. Although this option is always available to a woman, considerable maturity has often been shown by very young girls in deciding to put their babies up for adoption. Through counseling made available to them by adoption agencies, these girls have been exposed to anxiety-provoking methods of intervention and have been confronted with the realities of rearing a child without the physical and psychological support of a husband and family. Other girls, reflecting the romantic illusion encouraged by counterculture influences, have decided to keep their infants—a decision that has often been followed by a period of painful reality testing. During the first year, and often extending into the next, an infant is entirely dependent and thus in some ways meets a young woman's need to be needed without placing many demands upon her maturity. However, when the child begins the inevitable struggle for autonomy, beginning with the negativistic stage at about age 2, the young mother is confronted with the demands of mature adulthood. The prospect of such future reality testing should be one concern of counselors who work with young, pregnant women.

Women who decide to give up their children for adoption

represent a broad spectrum of society in terms of both age and social position. Some are married women who have no other children; others have children either they or someone else is caring for; some are divorced or widowed. Their reasons for relinquishing their children are correspondingly varied. One woman may want to avoid the stigma of unwed parenthood, although this response is occurring less and less frequently, especially among teenage girls. Another will give up a child because her circumstances are such that it is too difficult to care for the child properly. Married couples have occasionally decided to put a child up for adoption simply because they could not care for the fifth or sixth child adequately. A married woman who is carrying a child fathered by a man other than her husband will often decide to place the child up for adoption, since keeping the child might be detrimental to her marriage.

A mother who relinquishes her child, and in some instances the child's father, usually experiences considerable emotional stress. Even the consideration of placing her child in someone else's family can lead to a crisis. Even though the decision may be a voluntary choice, it is usually made in relationship to other issues and personal concerns. The conflict of ambivalent feelings may be sufficiently powerful to immobilize a person, and a counselor may be needed to help sort out priorities and to facilitate the necessary decision making. The *danger* of such a period is that a person may simply seek to relinquish her child as an easy solution to a personal dilemma rather than struggling with its consequences. The *opportunity* is that the intensity of feelings engendered will enable the person to explore alternatives and to demonstrate considerable maturity in whatever decision is made. The degree of maturity achieved by a woman in this circumstance will be expressed in the way she adapts to the reality of the relinquishment or in the way she responds as a mother in accepting responsibility to rear her child.

In counseling these women, social workers have preferred contact early in a pregnancy. Early contact provides as much opportunity as possible for the exploration of the feelings involved and for the clarification of priorities and goals. The beginning stage of contact is usually when a woman states that she has an unwanted pregnancy. Initially, she may be seeking a way out of a difficult situation, perhaps inquiring about getting an abortion or about adoption procedures. Hence, the strategy of the counseling is simply to listen carefully to what she is saying. If she is not emotionally aware of the reality of her pregnancy and what it means, the counselor can facilitate that discovery. A woman may, in extreme instances, deny her pregnancy or her feelings about it. In the first sessions, it is necessary to help her to emotionally accept the reality of her pregnancy and to come to terms with her feelings about it.

The second intervention may involve confronting the woman with what it will really be like to relinquish her baby for adoption. This intervention will usually involve an exploration of her feelings about giving up her child and the acceptance of the difficulty of doing so.

A third intervention may involve a continuation of the second, including some anticipatory grief work. A woman who either is considering relinquishing her child or has already done so will experience feelings akin to grieving or bereavement. Since the relinquishment is voluntarily chosen, the feelings of guilt associated with bereavement may be particularly strong. Although the expectant mother has not had the opportunity to establish a long-term relationship with her child, she often has developed a bond between herself and the unborn fetus growing within her. As the time draws closer to the permanent separation, the separation anxiety of the expectant mother usually increases, and it may involve actual grief work. The grief work involved in relinquishing a child for adoption is significantly different from that involved in the loss of a child in death, not only because the loss is voluntarily chosen but also because it lacks the finality of death. In spite of counseling, the mother may continue to wonder whatever happened to her child. A part of her grief work may include the exploration of her feelings about this part of her experience. Guilt feelings, which are a part of any grief work, are usually a crucial dimension of the work of relinquishing one's child. The expectant mother may feel that she is giving up responsibility for her child, when in reality she may be expressing the most mature kind of responsibility. A part of the problem is the uncertainty of not knowing whether her child will have more of a chance in life with an adoptive parent than she could have provided. Consequently, the mother naturally has doubts about whether she is really making the best decision for the child. The existential guilt experienced in other contexts is also relevant here. The relinquishing parent may experience the guilt of unfulfilled promise and commitments. The expectant mother especially may have had fantasies about what her child will look like, what the child will be like when he or she first walks or talks. She may wonder about the first day in school and about how her child will develop as an adult. All these feelings may become a part of the grief that is experienced in the loss of a loved child.

An additional dimension of anticipatory grief work is that of hope. A fourth counselor intervention may consist of facilitating the expression of hope the relinquishing parent has for the future of her unborn child. The expectant mother who has fears about how she can provide for the development of her child's potential can be encouraged to hope that her child will have a suitable opportunity in an adoptive home.

The fifth set of interventions may be a continuation of the fourth in supporting the expectant mother in whatever plans she is making and in the hopeful feelings she has for her child's future. These interventions may consist of specifically facilitating her decision making and the actual planning of her future. It may consist of exploring with her just what kind of adoptive parents she would want for her child. It usually involves a description of the process by which adoptive parents are selected and expressions of both adoptive parents and their children about their experiences of family life. She can be assured that adoptive parents will tell the child that he or she is adopted, that they were happy to adopt him or her, and that they will provide any answers they can about the natural parents. She can be told that, when adopted children are old enough to ask, they are given the opportunity to read the statements of the adoption-agency social worker about the natural parents. She can be assured that these children are told that they were loved and were relinquished for adoption precisely because that was the way they could have a home and family that could provide for their care and development as persons.

Feelings of sadness and deprivation may be a part of both anticipatory grief work and the completion of the unfinished business or bereavement reactions after the separation has actually taken place. Hence, a sixth set of interventions may focus on any unfinished grief work. In spite of anticipatory work, there may be some unfinished grief work that does not become apparent until the actual separation has occurred. At this time sadness may also be mingled with feelings of relief that the whole thing is over. Ambivalence is normal. If a woman is distressed by her pregnancy and the intrusion it has made into her life, she may be relieved when the baby is finally born and the relinquishment accomplished. Counselor intervention consists simply of accepting these feelings of relief as normal reactions without increasing any feelings of guilt.

Although I have outlined a pattern of client responses and corresponding counselor interventions, each person experiences such a trauma in her own way. The counselor's role is to be available when a person cries for help, to be genuinely concerned about that person, and to understand just how interventions are affecting the person in the midst of this kind of crisis.

Counseling with a relinquishing parent has been largely limited to adoption agencies, but it is likely that these problems will increasingly be brought to health-services workers in various contexts. A typical counseling problem from my own experience was presented by Anna's situation. Anna was 18 years old and had recently graduated from high school. She became pregnant by her boyfriend in high school. She was in love with him, and they had talked about getting married. However, after graduation he had decided to enlist in the Marines, and he was in training for service in Vietnam at the time she came in to see me. She was living at home in a typically middle-class family and community. Her father was a professional man, and her mother was active in various community organizations. She was about three months pregnant when I first saw her. She was obviously ambivalent about seeking an abortion, even though her initial reason for seeking counseling was to secure an abortion.

My first response was simply to listen to her and to reflect back the ambivalence she had related to me. Beginning with her expressions of love for her boyfriend, my first intervention confronted her with her ambivalence about terminating her pregnancy. We moved to the second intervention, that of exploring the alternatives open to her. The alternatives available to her included going through with an abortion or else having the child and either keeping the baby or relinquishing him or her for adoption. The third intervention involved assisting Anna in the clarification of the alternative that she had chosen—namely, to have the baby—and supporting her in following through. A fourth intervention included some problem solving in working out the practical arrangements for her referral and care. Although the decision of whether or not to relinquish her child was yet to be worked out, Anna had faced her present reality and had already made one important decision.

POSTSCRIPT

Potential crisis situations occur in every family. Although not all of the hazards discussed in this chapter will be experienced in every family, they are potential crises for any family. Individuals may understand the crises in their own family life as they increase their understanding of the nature of such crises. Mental-health workers may increase their understanding of family crises and of ways to cope with them by studying some of the kinds of crises that have already occurred. These crises may be resolved in such a way that personal growth occurs and family relationships are strengthened. Failure to resolve family crises adaptively usually results in some form of disintegration of the family and often results in personal disorganization.

EXPERIENTIAL TRAINING

I. Suggestions for the Instructor

The entire exercise may be included in the class period, but the sociogram may be worked out either in the class period or as an assignment out of class. The family simulation may be worked out most effectively during the class period itself.

II. Experiential Exercise

A. Construct a simple family sociogram showing the relationships the members of your family have with one another.
  1. Family members include parents or parental substitutes and siblings, with the ages of each one indicated.
  2. A simple sociogram is constructed by identifying all the members of the family, using triangles for males and circles for females, as shown in Figure 7-1.

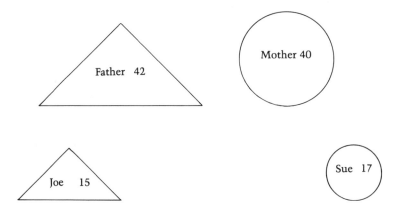

Figure 7-1.

  3. The relationship of family members to one another is diagrammed, with a solid line indicating a positive relationship, a dotted line indicating a negative relationship, and a broken line indicating an ambivalent or mixed relationship, as shown in Figure 7-2.

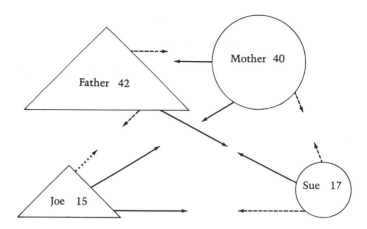

Figure 7-2.

In this family, Father has an ambivalent relationship with his wife and with his son, Joe, and a positive one with his daughter, Sue. Mother feels positive toward her husband and son but ambivalent about her daughter. Joe has a positive feeling about both his mother and sister but feels negative about his father. Sue feels positive about her father but ambivalent about both her mother and brother. Of course, if this sociogram has been constructed by Joe, the diagrammed relationships represent only his feelings at a particular time in the life of this family.

B. Using your sociogram as the basic design of your family's relationships, identify a crisis or an area of tension or conflict and describe it.

C. Select people from the class to play the other members of your family, and prepare them for their respective roles.

D. Conduct the role play, playing your own part, and correct the behavior of other members of the family when necessary by reversing roles and taking their parts until they better understand their roles.

E. Some member of the class should be selected as the counselor who intervenes in the family crisis or conflict. The person whose family is being portrayed plays his or her own part and makes any necessary corrections in the simulation.

F. Other members of the class act as observers of the counselor's role, noting down their observations and questions and discussing their evaluations of the counselor's effectiveness when the simulation has been completed.

Expanding Crises

Some crises are basically contractive experiences, in the sense that they primarily reduce or limit options. Other crises primarily represent expanding possibilities: there is some loss that must be risked, and hence some crisis to endure, but the loss is not the predominant factor. There are, of course, numerous kinds of expanding experiences. The ones included here are representative of the kinds of emotionally hazardous experiences that include some potential for expanding options in life.

Although all crises come appropriately within the scope of preventive psychology, the expanding crises are especially relevant to the concerns of preventive psychology and education. For example, education in preparation for the expanding experience of marriage is an expression of the primary level of prevention. This first level includes the development of an environment conducive to healthy growth. In the event of marital conflict, early intervention in the interpersonal crisis, which may prevent the development of a more serious problem, is an excellent example of the secondary level of prevention. In the event of a marital disruption, the introduction of family therapy or individual psychotherapy as an expression of the tertiary level of prevention may be needed to prevent the development of a serious psychopathology within the individual or the family.

The type of intervention appropriate in the expanding crises is essentially anxiety provoking. Interventions are designed to realistically confront individuals with the possibilities inherent in experiences with predominantly expanding potentialities.

INTIMACY AND MARRIAGE

The development of the ability to maintain an intimate personal relationship with another person is a psychosocial task of young adulthood. The expression of this intimacy in marriage is, of course, voluntarily chosen. Although it is not usually considered a crisis, it is evident that any experience that is surrounded with the kinds of rituals and practices associated with marriage represents a significant event that may bode either good or ill. It is certainly no neutral happening, and anything that is thus fraught with meaning is bound to include both *danger* and *opportunity*.

While I was studying with Gordon Allport over 20 years ago, he mentioned a series of lectures he had given on marriage. The title and the main emphasis of the first lecture was "Marriage Is for Adults." Allport's main thrust was that a stable marriage was possible only to persons who had achieved a fair degree of maturity, because marriage failure is largely a personality failure. Although my memory may have oversimplified his comments, there is a basic truth to the insight that a healthy marriage requires the development of mature skills of coping with the complexities of commitment and intimacy.

There are countless books on the subject of marriage, and I have discussed the specific crises of marital conflict and divorce elsewhere in this book. At this point, I want to discuss one aspect of marriage that is related to the hazards involved in the establishment of commitment and intimacy. In the contemporary scene, the problem of *self-alienation* seems to be one of the important dimensions of marriage crises. I believe that, to realize our nature as persons, we must each take the risk of being fully ourselves in an intimate relationship with another human being. The refusal to risk exposure in relationship is described in the myth of the Garden of Eden and is expressed by a person's desire to *control* rather than to *be with* the other.

This denial of humanity is related to the psychodynamics of self-alienation. In self-alienation, a person is preoccupied with a partial quality of himself or herself and expends considerable emotional energy on zealously protecting this partial quality. An alienated person does not respond to another as a whole person taking risks but only with a defense of this partial self, which is thereby protected and enhanced. The result is an estrangement from both self and others. Alienation from the total self is experienced precisely because neither commitment nor intimacy is risked. Defenses are preserved intact, but the experience of oneself as the center from which come living acts of love and reason is lost. The self-alienated person becomes an object, and any other person becomes a mere object as well, precisely because the wholeness of the person is denied. The potency of passion is available only to the person who is involved in the giving and receiving of the whole person as it can be experienced in intimacy.

Although the institution of marriage as such is not necessary for intimacy, some dimension of commitment as expressed by marriage is crucial to any development of intimacy. One cannot achieve intimacy just by "doing what comes naturally." Nor is intimacy the necessary product of something like a marriage contract; it is an ongoing process of being and doing. If the notion of a contract is appropriate in any sense here, perhaps it is not the noun *contract* we should think of so much as the verb *contracting*, which characterizes a lively and wholesome intimacy. This activity of *contracting* involves the commitment of two persons in dynamic interaction with each other, with the inevitable risks and opportunities of intimacy. It is a *happening*, and it involves a *willing* for something to happen. It is *not* the expression only of the conscious processes of decision-making; it *is* the expression of the whole person.

Helen and Joe were looking forward to getting married, but they were also experiencing considerable ambivalence. Joe had been a bachelor for his 35 years, and he was unsure of himself as he considered marriage. Helen had been married once; she was now divorced and had a young daughter. Since her first marriage had been a disaster, she too was uncertain about herself and her impending marriage. They called for a consultation about three weeks after their decision to marry. They were both tense as they began talking. The wedding had been planned for the following month, and Joe had started talking about his fears of accepting responsibility for Helen and her daughter. On her part, Helen began to question her responses to Joe. Both had tended to withdraw from the early intensity of their relationship. They felt conflicting thrusts toward intimacy and toward separation. An initial counseling intervention was simply supportive of this ambivalence. A second intervention consisted of confronting them about sharing their fears instead of avoiding them. Because they had not shared their fears, they had not fully acknowledged them even within themselves, and as a result they had become alienated from themselves. In the midst of the sharing encouraged in the counseling session, they considered together some of the problems involved in parenthood. Although they did not resolve all of their anxieties, they moved through the critical stage of their relationship in two sessions, and they began to feel more comfortable with the questions that remained.

The *danger* involved in establishing a marriage commitment is that a dimension of selfhood that makes true intimacy possible may be denied. The self-alienation that results from a denial of genuine feelings is disastrous to the development of healthy individuals and a human society. The *opportunity* of such a commitment is that a person's full human potential may be actualized through intimacy with another human being.

Most of the critical hazards of intimacy are encountered early in the relationship. In lecturing about marriage and the family, I have always specifically included a discussion of the first year of marriage as a crucial point in time. Nearly every kind of stress is experienced during the first year, and preventive education should therefore be directed to that span of time. In marital counseling and family therapy, most of the stresses and conflicts can be traced to interpersonal transactions that originated in the first year of marriage.

PREGNANCY

Pregnancy usually involves some elements of crisis. To a woman, the most powerful "three little words" may be "You are pregnant." When the pregnancy is planned, this announcement is a source of celebration; when it is entirely unexpected, it may cause considerable stress; when it is unwanted, it may precipitate a crisis. Even a desired pregnancy is an emotional hazard, however, in the sense that it presents both a *danger* and an *opportunity*. One meaning of the word *pregnant* is "filled with promise," and the potential of expanding meaning is represented by the introduction of an entirely new and unique human being into the world. Pregnancy is filled with promise precisely because the new possibilities are limitless. No one can anticipate the potential inherent in this new life.

Inasmuch as pregnancy is one of the natural events in life, a crisis of pregnancy is, in one sense, a maturational or developmental crisis. The stresses of pregnancy might be discussed in the context of the psychosocial tasks of young adulthood. Pregnancy is an expression of the development of intimacy with another human being—an expression of a joint venture involving expanding self-awareness and a developing sense of responsibility for each other. However, it is not simply a developmental task. In its normal occurrence, it is a venture that is voluntarily chosen and that involves its own risks and opportunities.

During a time of significant progress in the medical treatment of pregnancy, the psychological considerations have largely been ignored. Only recently has the medical profession begun to look at pregnancy from a holistic perspective. Dr. Somers H. Sturges has urged that the definition of gynecology be broadened to include the *total* care of the pregnant woman. The eminent psychiatrist Helene Deutsch has pointed out that the interdependence of psychological and physiological processes in human beings is nowhere so clearly evident as in the female reproductive activity (Tanzer, 1972).

As an extension of this perspective, Dr. Grete Bibring developed a comprehensive, theoretical view of pregnancy as a whole. In her prenatal clinic she noted a disproportionate number of women who were referred for psychotherapy. They presented serious emotional problems, and yet they improved significantly after brief periods of treatment. She concluded that pregnancy was a crisis involving profound psychological as well as physical changes (Tanzer, 1972).

As I write these words, Emalee is about seven months pregnant. Although we are somewhat older than most couples having babies, we are expectantly looking forward to this event. Nevertheless, Emalee is working out a new relationship with herself and with the lively fetus growing and developing within her. And in some ways a new relationship with me is being evolved. The physiological changes occurring within her body and the psychological effects of her perception of herself and her change in body image have their effect upon her mood swings.

A crisis may occur if Emalee's feelings about the changes in her body image result in negative feelings about herself. If she is in serious conflict between wanting the baby and, at the same time, resenting this distention of her body, she may experience a crisis. She may experience both hostile feelings directed toward the unborn fetus and guilt for having such feelings. She may experience conflict between her desire to be pregnant and hostility directed toward me for her impregnation. If any of these conflicts are too intense, and if she does not have the skills with which to cope with such conflicts, she may experience a crisis in which she needs someone to intervene.

The *danger* in such a crisis would include the denial of any of these feelings or of fear about the well-being of the fetus, about our relationship, or about her adequacy in the actual delivery. The *opportunity* would include the expansion of self-awareness and of understanding and appreciation for both her unborn fetus and me. If her feelings were not acknowledged and resolved effectively, her feelings for the newborn infant would be affected negatively. If she were able to utilize her feelings in effecting increased self-awareness and interpersonal understanding, the meaning in her life could be significantly expanded and enriched.

CHILDBIRTH

Like pregnancy, childbirth is one of the natural events in life. In one sense, therefore, a crisis of childbirth is a maturational or developmental crisis. In most instances, however, childbirth is voluntarily chosen, and it is characterized by its own risks and opportunities. Unfortunately, more has been written about the risks or dangers of childbirth than about the potential meaning of the process itself. Childbirth has usually been endured only because of the end result. Until the recent development of natural childbirth, it was usually perceived as the cross that women had to bear as their lot in life. Indeed, a little child who had heard his mother talk about "the cross I bear" concluded that he had come from "a cross-eyed bear." Attending a class with my wife on natural childbirth, I have found it interesting to discover how many women have heard "horror stories" about the birth process from their mothers.

My purpose here is not to argue for natural childbirth but simply to develop the notion of the birth process as a crisis experience. The *danger* of childbirth includes the actual physical dangers to both the mother and the baby. I do not want to downplay these real threats; indeed, everyone is grateful for the splendid developments in the practice of obstetrics and gynecology that have significantly reduced the physical dangers to both mother and child. However, there is the danger of losing some of the potentially expanding *opportunities* in this natural process of life. By the beginning of the 20th century, childbirth had acquired the status of an *illness*. It had lost the sense of being an experience of personal meaning and had become a medical problem. Progress in medical science had taken the experience of childbirth out of the home and familiar environment and had placed it effectively in the hands of the physicians and the hospitals. The irony is that the welcome progress in medical science is the very factor that has dehumanized the birth process. Only recently have physicians and hospitals joined such early pioneers as Grantly Dick-Read (1944) in humanizing the medical involvement in the process of childbirth. Classes are now being conducted to acquaint prospective mothers and fathers with the medical procedures involved in childbirth and with the new and sometimes strange environment of the hospital.

Childbirth can be one of the experiences that expand the consciousness of both men and women. The recognition that childbirth is not an illness handled by the physician but a co-operative process of a woman's labor restores the sense of power to the woman, where it belongs. Indeed, the cooperative process of labor may involve the woman, her husband, and the doctors and nurses. Restoring the sense of power to the woman gives her an expanding experience of her own competence and worth. In a day in which women have lost some of the traditional modes of developing a sense of self-worth, it is important to re-capture the potential meaning of a significant hallmark of the mother's being and existence.

There are several important ways in which the process of childbirth is related to the dynamics of a crisis event. One way in which childbirth is a crisis is that, once the fear has been realistically faced, the ease of the process is significantly in-creased. Although all pain and discomfort are not eliminated, the process is facilitated by freedom from fear and anxiety. With-out the *fear* of pain, the natural functioning of the musculature, with its own coordination of contraction and dilation, proceeds with increased ease.

Another way in which childbirth is a crisis event concerns the biological nature of the process itself. Normal childbirth is inextricably related to the *labor*—that is, the *work*—of the mother. The physician and nurse may assist her in the process, but it is the woman's labor—her pushing of the fetus—that re-sults in the birth of her child. Although medication may be ad-ministered to ease the pain and discomfort of the cervix and vagina, the abdominal muscles need to be operative in order to enable the mother to do her necessary work. She is inevitably involved in doing everything that she can do by herself, and the doctor and nurses should not do anything for her that she can do for herself.

Childbirth is also a crisis in the sense that the here-and-now of the process is the reality with which a woman must cope. It is obvious that the delivery, like any crisis, will be re-solved one way or another within a certain specified period of time. But there is more to this observation than the obvious. Without the necessary coping skills, a woman can temporarily block the resolution or at least make its achievement more dif-ficult. Her fear can interrupt and disrupt the natural processes of muscular coordination. On the other hand, a woman can de-velop mechanisms with which to cope with the normal stresses of childbirth. First, she can learn to listen to her own body throughout the pregnancy and the delivery. Amazing things are happening within her as a unique human being is formed with his or her own developing neurological and physiological processes. Physiological changes occur within the woman's body to accommodate this happening, and she can become sensitive to these changes without becoming hypochondriacal. Second, she can learn to exercise her muscles to provide the maximum options in the process of delivery. Proper exercise not only increases the effectiveness of her musculature but also maximizes the expansion of her consciousness and heightened awareness of her body. This heightened awareness enhances the meaning of the experience. Freedom from fear provides the base on which all the other coping mechanisms are built and frees the woman to experience the expansive nature of the birth process. Third, the husband and wife can together develop the skills that increase the woman's control over her own body, as in the practice of husband-coached childbirth (Bradley, 1965). Exercise, breathing, and panting techniques can permit the maximum utilization of the woman's musculature in effecting a more comfortable delivery, as suggested by the Lamaze method (Bing, 1969).

Bodily and breathing exercises facilitate a woman's labor in several ways. They can first of all assist a woman to work with her own muscles rather than against them. Second, they can enable her to relax when it is appropriate and to utilize her strength most effectively when it is needed. Third, they can be utilized to maintain a woman's contact with the here-and-now of her labor. Her feeling of compulsion to push and expel her fetus represents an important physiological function and is often the most effective body signal heralding the *kairos,* or the time for delivery. Although the woman needs to be sensitive to these feelings, there are moments when pushing would involve an undue hardship to the fetus. At these moments, with the cooperative efforts of her husband and doctor, a woman can effectively utilize the technique of panting, for example, which will enable her to resist the compulsion to push. Her use of this kind of technique mobilizes the resources both of herself and of those who are assisting her in a way that effects a more comfortable delivery and hence provides her with an expansion of her own understanding and a heightening of her awareness of the meaning of this self-fulfilling experience.

The development of these coping mechanisms enables the woman to regain her sense of power over what happens to her body and to her consciousness in childbirth. The only point I wish to make here is the importance of the woman's sense of power over her own destiny. I am not espousing a particular form of "natural childbirth"; male chauvinism has already said too much about what a woman should and should not do in childbirth. Childbirth is the woman's crisis, and she can learn how to cope with it in a way that can make it an expanding experience for her. A counselor, friend, or husband may be the one who facilitates the development of her coping skills. The woman may also be helped to open channels of communication between herself and those who assist her in the process of giving birth to her child. These helpers usually include the doctors and nurses, of course, but her husband may also be involved as the significant other person in an expanding experience of self-fulfillment.

Barbara and Stan had experienced some severe conflicts in their marriage, but they had reached a point in their relationship at which they felt ready to begin their family. They had planned together for the pregnancy and had attended a class in husband-coached childbirth. Barbara had asked Stan to attend the class and had wanted him to be involved with her in the various stages of childbirth. However, as the date of her delivery approached, she became anxious and depressed. After talking briefly with the instructor of her class, she was referred for some psychological consultations.

Barbara showed considerable stress, and it was evident that she needed to talk with someone, despite her reluctance to seek out a counselor. She showed some initial confusion as she related how she had wanted to get pregnant and had planned for the delivery with anticipation. She was grateful that Stan had attended the class despite an initial reluctance to do so. It appeared that everything was working out well, but she had begun to feel panic about the approaching date, and she had become confused and depressed.

As her expression of her fears and confusion was supported, Barbara began to relate some of her feelings about Stan. She revealed that, even though she wanted Stan to be with her, she lacked confidence in his being available to her as she needed him. She recounted that her father had been an alcoholic and had been drunk the night she was born. Her mother's description of this experience had become a painful memory, and she had tried to forget it. As a result, she had not thought about it for several years, but now it was a vivid and depressing memory.

Accepting the expression of her depression, I asked Barbara whether any unusual experiences had occurred during the past few weeks. She recalled having been upset with Stan when he had come home somewhat drunk about three weeks earlier. While she hadn't thought much about it, she did recall having experienced some anxious feelings that night. Interventions included directing her to explore those feelings, relating them to the memory of her father's problems and to her present situation. Although she was reluctant to think of Stan in relation to her father, she explored some of her feelings in her first and second sessions, and she decided to talk things out with Stan. In the third and final session, she told me that she had talked with Stan and experienced a significant sense of relief. She discovered that the episode with Stan had triggered the memory of her father's irresponsibility and had increased her anxiety about his support in her impending experience with childbirth.

Interventions in Barbara's case clarified the nature of her crisis. Her crisis was engendered by the conflict between her anticipation of the delivery of her child and her fears that her husband would not give her the necessary support. She had sought Stan's participation in the childbirth class partly because of her desire for a fulfilling experience and partly because of her fears concerning his adequacy in the parental role. In addition, she experienced fears about her own adequacy in regard to both the delivery and the subsequent care of the child, and she needed Stan to be supportive in this fearful situation.

In summary, the psychological *danger* in childbirth is that the woman will not resolve her crisis adaptively and hence will react negatively both to herself and to the newborn baby. Dr. Grete Bibring has said "These disturbances in the earliest attitudes of the mother to the newborn baby may lead to the establishment of a vicious cycle in the form of mutually induced negative reactions of frustration and rejection between the mother and child, and finally result in the well-known chronic malformation in this relationship" (Tanzer, 1972, pp. 69–70). The *opportunity* is the possibility that the woman will achieve an expanding and heightened awareness of herself and of her relationship with both her husband and her newborn child.

PARENTHOOD

The actual undertaking of parenthood creates its own unique set of emotional hazards and potential crises. It begins with the decision of a couple to give and receive the love they have for one another and to share that love with the child created out of their experience of loving. To "make love" is a poetic way of beginning the process, and the birth of a child is a demonstration of the potency of such a creative encounter. The problem is that men and women begin the work of parenthood unprepared for its responsibilities and stresses. Potentially critical situations will normally arise simply because of the personal interactions among the unique individuals within a family. Although some potential crises may normally be expected, many parental crises could be avoided by preventive measures.

First of all, it should be realized that the prospect of parenthood involves significant changes in the lives of both husband and wife. The English anthropologist Sheila Kitzinger has been quoted as saying that the woman experiences "such enormous changes in identity that sometimes, almost for the first time, a girl comes face to face with what she is and what she wants to be. It is, in fact, a tremendous opportunity for growing up emotionally" (Tanzer, 1972, p.71). It is therefore crucial to care for the psychological needs of the woman who is preparing for parenthood. In a profound sense, prospective parents are busily realigning themselves and their world to make room for new and shifting relationships with each other and with a new person in the family constellation.

Sheila and Stuart had a conventional beginning. They were both young when they married shortly after their graduation from high school. Stuart had been accepted in a training program in an insurance company, and, while his income was minimal at first, he worked hard at his job. Sheila got a job as a secretary and initially was making more than Stuart. Since he worked long hours, they didn't have much time to be together. After about six months they decided to start their family, and almost immediately Sheila became pregnant.

Stuart continued to work long hours even after their son was born. Although they experienced many of the usual conflicts, they seemed to work through most of their difficulties until the baby was about a year and a half old. At this time Sheila began to complain about her isolation and to talk about going back to work, despite their earlier agreement to wait until the baby was 3 years old and able to attend a nursery school. Sheila began to resent her son and at the same time to feel guilty for doing so. She directed some of her hostility against Stuart, who didn't understand what he perceived as a change in Sheila.

When the baby was about 2, and probably expressing some of his developing autonomy, Sheila slapped him very hard on one occasion, and her action frightened her. As she tried to talk it over with Stuart, they decided to come for a counseling session together.

Sheila related her feelings of being isolated from her usual contacts with other adults. Her job had had its drawbacks, but it had been exciting to interact and to work with others in the office, and she missed having that excitement in her life. She was happy with their baby, and she loved him. However, although she understood something about the developing child, his increasing tendency to resist her was threatening to her.

Sheila's conflict was accepted and clarified. She was relieved to learn that others have experienced many of the same conflicts. She was also able to express resentment of Stuart and of his long hours of work that left her with the sole care of their son. Interventions of support for her feelings enabled her to express herself more openly.

Sheila's most threatening experience was her striking of her son in intense anger. It was difficult for her even to talk about it. Since she had not been able to express many of her feelings about this incident with Stuart, she was now verbalizing some of her feelings for the first time, and they were simply accepted. The first two sessions consisted of the telling of her tale and the exploration of her feelings. There was little evidence of the usual dynamics of child abuse, and I perceived the stress as primarily situational.

As she talked about her anger in the third session, we explored the nature of the actual problem she faced. She identified her problem as a conflict between what she wanted with Stuart and with their son and what she wanted for herself. Once the problem had been somewhat defined, interventions included exploration of alternative ways of meeting her needs and of coping with her anger. Stuart became more open to talking with her and understanding her needs for personal fulfillment, and Sheila recognized her fears of talking about her own needs. As she came to recognize the problem and to choose some ways in which to cope with her needs for fulfillment, they both saw some hope of working through this threat to their parenting and to their life together. The opening of lines of communication between the two of them was a significant change in what had been happening and provided a basis for future development in effective parenting.

The continuing stresses of parenthood include all the significant interactions and events that occur in the intimacy of a family. The "games people play" are played most effectively in the family. Furthermore, each developmental stage of the child involves its own stresses and interpersonal tensions. The *danger* of these hazardous moments is the tendency to withdraw from the responsibility of parenthood, to avoid the intensity of parental struggles by withdrawing from the parental role. The *opportunity* is the enlarging of each person's perspective on life and on his or her relationship to it through the stresses and interactions occurring between parents and children.

CAREER CHOICES

Career choices are usually the result of a variety of factors in dynamic interaction. Motivating factors include the conscious and unconscious needs that may be met by a specific occupation. The actual occupational decision making is the result of family influences, socio-economic and educational background, occupational interests, and capabilities. In addition, in my experience in occupational psychology, I have noted the importance of certain *critical incidents* in the exploration of career possibilities. These incidents have some distinct similarities with the characteristics of crisis events. They may be decisive moments, or at least turning points beyond which something decisive occurs.

The *danger* of these critical incidents or crisis events is that unresolved emotional needs will become the determining factors in the decision making, rather than a realistic appraisal of abilities and sustained interest. The *opportunity* of the critical incidents is that deep motivational forces within the personality may be tapped. Hence, an occupational choice may result in the maximum development of an individual's potential, rather than simply the exercise of some aptitudes in a career chosen according to the possibility for financial advancement.

In an earlier book on the career psychology of ministers and ministerial candidates, I included a portion of a sermon preached to his congregation by a 39-year-old clergyman who had decided to leave the ministry for another occupation. In reference to the critical incident related to his original career choice, he said the following:

> But what if, in a tumultuous thirty-ninth year of life in which there has been more growth than in any other period of one's life,

there comes a question, what was the nature of the choice I made to become a minister? In answer, it is clear to me now that it was based upon immature reasons not then realized or pointed out. The choice was then immediately acted upon and reacted to by people in such a way that continued liberty in the choice was taken away. It is not that the choice would have been reversed, but the choice would have been strengthened properly had it remained an open decision with the possibility of reversal while the life was still so immature in relationship to such a decision [Whitlock, 1968, p. 53].[1]

In this case, the critical incident or crisis event in the process of occupational decision making was resolved maladaptively. A realistic appraisal of his abilities and interests was not made; as a result, his premature decision robbed him of the actualization of his potential. Nevertheless, career choices are basically expanding crises, because the choice of a career is "full of promise." A given choice may cause disappointment and failure yet fulfill the purpose of what has been labeled in career psychology as "meaningful failure." When individuals learn something about themselves through some kind of failure, their failures are significant learning events.

In the general field of career psychology, including career assessment and development, there is an increased emphasis upon a continued analysis of careers in terms of changes within both the individual and the economic order. In view of the technological revolution and radical changes in production and consumer demands, more and more people will need to consider the possibility of making several occupational changes during a lifetime. Indeed, Peter Drucker, a well-known consultant in organizational development, has estimated that in the next 10 or 20 years the average person will have several different careers during his or her working years. Thus, occupational changes will in all likelihood be made with increasing frequency in the future. Such career changes will inevitably cause considerable stress, and they may result in crises. Yet they need not be contractive experiences; they can provide expanding possibilities for the individuals undergoing these changes.

To quote again from the sermon of the clergyman who had decided to leave the ministry for a new career, he had concluded

---

[1]From *From Call to Service*, by Glenn E. Whitlock. Copyright © MCMLXVIII, The Westminster Press. This and all other quotations from this source are reprinted by permission.

that he needed to make a career change in response to the changes that had occurred in this "period of growing selfhood." He went on:

> I am a different person today than I was up to a year or two ago. The reasons for being in the ministry that were valid for that more immature person are no longer valid for the person I am now. . . . These [developments] have had serious inner repercussions as the years have gone by. They have finally forced this total re-evaluation of life. They brought the necessity of realizing my selfhood as a maturing person through the responsible remaking of some of life's choices where this possibility still exists [Whitlock, 1968, p. 54].

Although there are many reasons for making occupational changes, these transitions can often be expanding experiences. I have observed the frightening deadness of persons who have chosen to settle for a merely secure position. Others, who have chosen to move out beyond security to meaningfulness, have expressed potency and aliveness. They have resolved their crises of uncertainty by choosing to be open to the actualization of their aliveness and potentialities.

THE POTENTIALITIES OF EXPANDING CRISES

There are situations and events in life whose predominant tendency is to expand the options available to developing persons. Nevertheless, these transitions include both the dangers and the opportunities present in any time of significant change. Although all the experiences discussed in this chapter are marked by expanding possibilities, in each instance a maladaptive resolution will usually result in some degree of personal disaster. The potential for expansion simply emphasizes the opportunity inherent in any crisis event for personal growth and development. *Maturational crises* are also predominantly expanding experiences in this sense.

EXPERIENTIAL TRAINING

I. Suggestions for the Instructor

The experiential exercises for the expanding crises consist of imagery and fantasy. Their purpose is to enable a person to enter the inner world of expanding experiences that may become crises. These exercises are usually most effective if the instructor directs them, but they may be used as assignments for triads or dyads outside of the class period.

II. Experiential Exercises: The class members form triads.

   A. Guided fantasy of a marriage decision.

      1. In your imagination, become the age you were when you proposed marriage to a desired person, or received a proposal of marriage from a desired person.

         a. Take a comfortable position, close your eyes, and relax your entire body.

         b. Become aware of your breathing, but do not change the rhythm of your inhaling and exhaling.

         c. Relax your body, and become receptive to your imagination.

         d. Imagine the marriage proposal and take time to think about your proposal or your answer. What questions are aroused by this decision? How do you feel about this decisive step? What changes will your marriage make in your life-style? How do you feel about these changes?

         e. Choose a "counselor" in your triad to consult about your questions and your feelings.

         f. Open your eyes, and rejoin your triad.

      2. One person in the triad talks about the questions and feelings aroused in relation to the marriage decision, another is asked to act as the counselor, and the third person is an observer of the process. Each person takes about five to ten minutes for his or her questions; then the roles are changed so that each person will play all three roles. After each session of exploring questions and feelings, the observer takes five to ten minutes to make observations about the counseling process.

   B. Role-play of pregnancy and preparation for childbirth in a dyad.

      1. One person takes the role of the pregnant wife; the other takes the role of the husband in a husband-coached childbirth. (Ideally, each dyad should consist of a man and a woman, but the sex of the participants in the role play is not crucial; besides, the roles should be switched so that each person has the opportunity of playing both roles.)

         a. The woman lies down on the floor on her side, as a pregnant woman lies to lighten the weight of the baby upon her body. As the pregnant woman, you are asked to close your eyes and imagine that you are eight months pregnant. How do you feel about your pregnancy? How do you feel physically in your

eighth month? What changes have occurred in your
life as the result of your pregnancy?
  b. As the husband, you are asked to kneel beside your
     wife and to coach her. After giving her a minute or
     more to imagine her pregnancy, help her to relax.
     Give her directions to relax, beginning with her
     feet and including various parts of her body.
  c. In this relaxed state, the wife practices the onset
     of contractions while her husband coaches her.
     Practice the contractions in this way: Your con-
     tractions have begun, and you are to gulp a mouth-
     ful of air and let it out in spurts through your open
     mouth, as in panting. Let all your air out in seven
     parts. Repeat this exercise several times for the
     duration of the contractions (about 30 seconds).
  2. After one role-play is completed, the persons are asked
     to continue in their roles and to direct questions to
     each other, listening to the expression of feelings or
     conflicts about the pregnancy and about the childbirth
     exercises. Switch roles so that each person will have
     the opportunity to play both roles.
C. Guided fantasy of a career decision. The class members
   form triads.
  1. Select a period in your life in which you have a career
     decision to make. It may be your initial career choice
     or a change of careers as the result of developing inter-
     ests or of a termination of your present career.
    a. Take a comfortable position, close your eyes, and
       relax your entire body.
    b. Become aware of your breathing, but do not change
       the rhythm of your inhaling and exhaling.
    c. Relax your body, and become receptive to your
       imagination.
    d. Imagine that you are confronted with this decision
       of choosing a career. What questions are aroused
       by this decision? How do you feel about this deci-
       sive step? How do you feel about yourself in this
       new career? What changes will occur in your life
       as the result of this choice? How do you feel about
       these changes?
    e. When you are ready to leave your fantasy, open
       your eyes and rejoin your triad.

2. Select one person in your triad as a counselor; the other is an observer.
   a. Tell your story to the counselor, and share your feelings, questions, and conflicts.
   b. After about five to ten minutes, terminate your counseling session.
   c. Switch roles and repeat the process until each person in the triad has had the opportunity to play all three roles.
   d. Each observer should take notes of the counseling dyad he or she observes and should then share this feedback with the two persons involved.

9

Contractive Crises

Although expanding and maturational crises include the *danger* of becoming contractive or limiting experiences, they also represent the *opportunity* of expanding awareness and new possibilities. Some crises, however, primarily represent contractive experiences that reduce a person's options in life. Although such crises include the *opportunity* of developing some alternative and compensatory behavior, they always involve some significant loss. The *danger* of a contractive crisis is that the loss that is experienced may result in a permanent loss of self-esteem.

Loss of self-esteem can take many forms. The nature and extent of the loss depends upon both the maturity of personal development and the individual's sociocultural milieu. Self-esteem is the basis of competence in both personal and occupational life. A temporary diminishing of self-esteem in a crisis is a significant loss that affects a person at a level of depth, and it must be recognized and accepted. If the mechanism of denial is utilized, the result may be the development of physical or emotional disorders. Recognizing, accepting, and learning to cope with a temporary loss of self-esteem will enable a person to mobilize his or her inner resources.

Developing a sense of self-worth involves both becoming a unique individual and experiencing one's unique self as being *significant*. The achievement of identity, or individuation, is a part of the developmental or maturational process discussed in Chapter 6. A sense of significance may be based on both a religious valuing of persons in the scheme of things and the fulfillment of a particular mission in life. The valuing of the *being* or existence of a person, independently of achievements, is a philosophical or religious decision that provides the individual with a sense of unconditional worth or significance. The sense of significance attached to the *doing* of an individual is related both to the concept of fulfilling one's mission in life and to the concrete role in which that mission is fulfilled. A man who perceives his role largely as that of a wage earner and provider for his family will suffer a contractive crisis if the opportunity to fulfill that role is denied to him. A woman who perceives her role predominantly as a mother will experience stress and possibly suffer a crisis if she experiences failure in that role.

THE EXPERIENCE OF LOSS THROUGH FAILURE

There are two dimensions to the problem of failure. The possibility of failing at something in particular is a realistic expectation of everyone, but it is also potentially traumatic. Even more serious is the experience of oneself as *being* a failure. This feeling undermines and distorts everything a person undertakes, and it always involves a traumatic loss of self-esteem.

The Experience of Being a Failure

Some people see themselves as "losers." Everything they undertake is contaminated with their sense of failure. Expecting not to succeed, they provide evidence for their self-fulfilling prophecy by their behavior. It sometimes seems as if they make certain that they will fail, but this may be an unconscious phenomenon. Detention facilities for youth and prisons are filled with persons who are victims of their own sins of failure. Indeed, although they are often unaware of it, they have frequently ensured their own capture. While I was working in an internship in counseling at Chino State Prison in California, the favorite program of the inmates was "Crime Doesn't Pay." The unrealistic scripts aside, the theme that crime doesn't pay represented the gross incongruity of their lives. Crime *does* pay for those who succeed! Some inmates even understood how they had set themselves up to get caught. The dynamics of failure are not the same as those of neurotic guilt, which sometimes causes people to call attention to themselves so that they will get the punishment they feel they deserve. People who perceive themselves as failures simply fulfill their own prophecies that they will fail.

William Glasser's extensive work with delinquent girls led him to conclude that the one thing all the girls had in common was an attitude of "resignation" (Glasser, 1965). They all resigned themselves to failing, as they saw it, at making it in the world. They failed in their relationships with their parents.

They failed in school. They failed to form warm relationships with either adults or their own peers. I have worked extensively with adolescents and young adults who see themselves as failures. This problem is one of character disorder, and it calls for extensive psychotherapeutic work. No profound characterological problem is going to be resolved by crisis intervention. Nevertheless, individuals who characteristically respond in this way to the stressful situations in their lives may be assisted to develop better means of coping when they are in the midst of a crisis.

Glasser's approach to this type of problem has been labeled *reality therapy* (1965). He has utilized his treatment primarily in work with adolescent delinquents, but he contends that his approach is applicable to a broad spectrum of society. It is clear that the concepts of reality therapy and anxiety-provoking crisis intervention are interrelated. Confronted with the here-and-now of a crisis, persons are particularly vulnerable to change in the direction of either constructive or destructive resolutions. A man who sees himself as a failure, and who is in the midst of a stressful or crisis situation, will experience the *danger* of a maladaptive resolution, such as committing a crime as the "easy way out." On the other hand, he may experience the *opportunity* of facing his reality head-on, accepting it as reality, and accepting the possibility of working out alternative ways of coping with his situation.

The psychodynamics of failure have both psychological and ethical dimensions. Some preachers, such as Billy Graham, and a few psychologists, such as O. Hobart Mowrer, have overemphasized the ethical basis of this psychological state of mind and hence oversimplified the problem of failure. The recognition of a moral dimension in decision making cannot be identified with a simplistic, Pelagian view of free will. Nevertheless, my clinical experience confirms that this problem does have an ethical dimension.

Paul Tillich's analysis of anxiety is helpful here. Tillich (1952) identifies the concept of non-being as a source of anxiety: "Anxiety is the existential awareness of non-being" (p. 35). Anxiety is present when a person is aware of the possibility of non-being. Non-being is that which prevents the self from affirming itself. The greatest threat to the self is death, but threat is also present when the self is prevented in other ways from affirming itself. A sense of being a failure is, in reality, an awareness of the ways in which the self is prevented from affirming itself. In some instances, economic and cultural deprivation is responsible for this hindering of the self. The injustice of such deprivation is a political issue and requires political action to be corrected, but that dimension of concern cannot be developed here. The psychological dimension of the problem of failure is that the self prevents itself from affirming itself. Ordinarily, this dimension of the problem will not be resolved by crisis intervention, because the sense of being a failure is a characterological problem that can usually be resolved only by long-term psychotherapy.

Although the problem of failure cannot be resolved by brief intervention in a crisis, individuals can be confronted with the reality of their stressful situations. They may respond to anxiety-provoking interventions by engaging in reality testing in a way that involves accepting responsibility for themselves. Through the experience of a supportive relationship, and with a sense of self-acceptance, they may develop the courage to affirm themselves in response to their particular stressful situations, in spite of some block to such self-affirmation in the past. A person who has suffered personal or sociocultural deprivation and yet experiences support and acceptance may be enabled to take a small step forward in a particular situation of stress, in spite of the handicaps.

Individuals who have felt themselves to be failures may thus be able to utilize specific failures as learning experiences. Encountering one segment of reality with the unusual intensity of a crisis may provide the basis for considerable progress in a short period of time. The *danger* is that the stress of a specific failure may result in additional decompensation. The *opportunity* is that, by facing up realistically to a failure in the company of a person who is supportive and caring, an individual may be able to come out of the situation with increased integration. A person can be enabled to respond to the reality of a failure in such a way that it becomes a meaningful failure. It will become a meaningful failure to the degree that the person has utilized the reality of the situation to learn something about the causes of the failure and about alternative ways of coping with it.

Charles was 32 years of age and an accountant. He had been divorced after only two years of marriage. He was referred to the counseling service by a minister who had seen him just a few days previously. He had talked with his minister because he had been arrested and was being prosecuted on the charge of writing a check with insufficient funds. He was in the process of pleading not guilty, since he claimed he had no intent to defraud. However, he was frightened, and the minister sensed that there was more to this situation than a simple mistake or a careless violation of the law. Charles was in a serious conflict, since he had never experienced himself as a criminal.

In talking with me, Charles told of repeated failures in his life, including his marriage. He revealed some unrealistic expectations of himself and a lack of ability to plan for the future. Although there seemed to be some sociopathic tendencies, including a low degree of affect, he had successfully completed his B. S. degree with a major in accounting, and he was now experiencing feelings of genuine threat. At any rate, he appeared to be open to some counselor interventions. The event that precipitated his conflict was, of course, his arrest on the charge of writing a check with insufficient funds. Although he insisted that he had thought he would be able to cover the amount of the check before it cleared the bank, it was evident that his projection had been unrealistic. I questioned him about any previous situations in which his expectations might have been similarly unrealistic. He recalled that he had contracted some debts in the past that he had not been able to pay and that his mother had paid them. Asked why he had not asked his mother or anyone else for money this time, he indicated that he felt guilty about doing so and, moreover, that his mother had remarried two years earlier and had moved to the East Coast. Despite some initial resistance, when he was confronted with the similarity of the situations and his unwillingness to accept responsibility for himself in them, he began the process of accepting his failure and his responsibility for it.

By the conclusion of the fourth and final session, Charles appeared to be more relaxed, and his plans to repay his debt were realistic. Although his characteristic ways of responding to such problems would probably continue to give him trouble, his resolution of this crisis was an adaptive one, and he was now better equipped to cope with future problems. Extended psychotherapy was not a viable alternative for him at this particular time, but he did appear to be open to exploring the possibility after resolving his financial situation.

In summary, Charles had experienced a series of failures, but he used a traumatic failure to begin focusing upon his lack of responsibility for himself. He discovered, or rediscovered, some courage to affirm himself—to be *responsible.* He affirmed his ability to give a positive direction to his life, and he did so in spite of the ways in which he had been defeating himself in the past.

The Loss of Self-Esteem in the Experience
of Particular Failures

An individual may, of course, experience a particular set-back without suffering a serious loss of self-esteem. A young man may experience considerable stress if he loses a job in which he has invested something of himself, but ordinarily he will pick himself up and go out on other job interviews. However, when the loss of a job entails a significant change in a person's relation to himself or herself and to others, what is normally a stressful situation may trigger an actual crisis. To the degree that such a change involves a loss of self-esteem, the individual will experience increasing stress on his or her capacity to function. For example, a man may lose his job and, because of his age or the condition of the economy, experience a significant diminishing of his sense of self-esteem. Such a feeling of failure and loss of self-esteem may well result in a crisis.

Jonas experienced such a loss a year before I first met him. He was 50 years old when he lost his position with an air-conditioning firm. He had worked for the firm for over 19 years, the last 12 as a salesman. He had worked his way up to a top sales position within the firm. His work had consisted of contacting builders and contractors, and he had thoroughly enjoyed the nature of this work outside the office. He lost his job partly because of a disagreement with a new sales manager, a younger man who had been with the firm for only ten years.

Jonas was a college graduate, married, and the father of three children. He had a son in college and daughters in high school and junior high. He had become accustomed to a comfortable standard of living, with a beautiful home in the suburbs on which he was still making payments. He was a member of a church in the community, and he had participated in community projects as a concerned citizen.

Jonas' first response to the loss of his job was one of shock, and at first he was unable to determine just what he wanted to do. He floundered for several weeks, and during that time he experienced feelings of anxiety and depression. It is my impression that he experienced a crisis at this time and within a few weeks resolved it by himself, but with some maladaptive coping mechanisms. He had not explored his loss of self-esteem and hence had denied some of his deepest feelings of panic and anger. At any rate, the resolution of his crisis involved a decision to buy a small shop. I first saw him about a year after this change. He appeared somewhat dependent and passive, and he was bewildered by the things that were now happening to him.

Jonas' wife had encouraged him to arrange for some counseling. He began by complaining of tiredness. He related that he always went to bed very tired but that he awakened about 3:00 A. M. and could not get back to sleep. He worried about himself and his feelings of adequacy, and about his children's future. His son was enrolled in a community college and was living at home, and Jonas knew that with his present income he would not be able to provide adequate assistance to his son or to his daughters, who were planning on college in a few years. In addition to talking about the loss of his job the year before, he related that his shop would never be able to provide an adequate income and that he had become bored with it. He had recently taken a part-time sales position, and his wife worked in the shop while he was out. In the past two weeks, however, he had been worrying increasingly about his inability to make a sufficient number of sales. His physician had prescribed some medication to help relax his tension and enable him to sleep.

During the first session he primarily related these circumstances surrounding his life, and I listened to him and accepted his "cry for help." He had never before talked with a professional counselor, and he took some time to feel relaxed about it. He began to explore some of his feelings about himself and about his loss of self-esteem. These feelings had begun a year before with the loss of his job, in which he had invested considerable emotional energy. He continued his exploration of these feelings during the second session a week later. He also began to discover a relationship between feelings of low self-esteem in his present part-time sales position and his original feelings following the loss of his job. When he revealed a conflict between his failure in selling and his feelings about the inferiority of the product he was asked to sell, he began to clarify just what he felt about this job. Since I was involved in field-testing an instrument with Charlotte Bühler at the time, I gave him her Questionnaire on Goals and Fulfillments and an Occupational Interest Inventory.

Bringing in the two instruments at the third session, Jonas related that his company had terminated its part-time sales positions until it could add additional lines that were more competitive in both quality and price. His qualifications about the quality of the product had been recognized, and he felt supported by these objective reasons for his inability to make competitive sales. The fact that he had explored these feelings about the product at our prior session enabled him to cope with the stress of his present termination. Indeed, he was considerably less anxious than he had been the week before, and he revealed that he was sleeping better and had not taken any medication for several days. When he had awakened early in the morning, he had been able to get back to sleep without a sleeping pill.

In the fourth and fifth sessions, Jonas continued exploring his feelings about himself, as well as the information that he learned from the inventories on values and occupational interests. These instruments were utilized simply to provide him with additional information about himself that he could use in determining alternative ways of coping with his values and interests. He reported that he continued to be more relaxed and better able to sleep. He was increasingly active in exploring some of the data revealed in the inventories. He realized that many of the goals that he had deemed important had not been attained. He had not been able to "compete successfully" or to "accomplish things in life" or to "develop himself as a person" and "take advantage of his opportunities." At this time, he made the concrete decision to sell his shop, because it provided neither the necessary income nor the meaning he sought for his life.

At the time of the sixth session, Jonas was negotiating the sale of his shop. He had not yet made a final decision about his occupational future, but he had examined his occupational interests and had discarded the possibility of teaching. His occupational interests were integrated around the fields of personal/social and business interests. The type of interest was verbal. Hence, he experienced an integration of his interests and values around the area of sales work, which increased his sense of self-esteem and personal competence. All in all, he now felt competent to take control of his own life.

Jonas was both a product and a victim of a competitive society in which some people are successes and others are failures. His self-esteem had been developed on the basis of his ability to compete successfully and hence to provide for himself and his family. He was a victim of these values insofar as he was branded a failure if he stumbled along the way, unable to compete successfully and to support his family. The kind of crisis he experienced could have been experienced by anyone in our society. Although changing the social order to eliminate this kind of pressure may represent a *higher* order of preventive endeavor, a *prior* concern is to provide particular individuals with the counseling assistance that will enable them to mobilize their own inner resources to cope with their present situations.

In the case of Jonas, although his characteristic way of responding to pressure may continue to constitute a problem, crisis
therapy had the limited goal of facilitating his development of
psychological mechanisms with which to cope adaptively with
stressful situations.

THE LOSS EXPERIENCED IN DIVORCE
AND IN OTHER BROKEN RELATIONSHIPS

The loss experienced in any broken relationship may give
rise to a crisis. To the degree that a relationship is bound up
with an individual's sense of personal significance, he or she will
suffer a contractive crisis if the relationship ends. This kind of
crisis may include both the loss of a sense of communion with
another person and a loss of self-esteem.

A loss of self-esteem is often experienced by the one who
is left alone. The following example of the loss experienced by
a woman in her divorce was reported in my last book. I include
this account here because of the kind of crisis that occurred and
because of the ways in which she coped with it.

Grace was a woman of 38 who had been married for about
15 years. She had three children, ages 7 to 11. Her husband had,
in her words, come home one night about two weeks before and
entirely unexpectedly stated that he wanted a divorce. Since then
he had actually consulted an attorney, and she had to secure legal
advice for herself. According to her, the announcement came as
a complete surprise. However, as she talked she realized there
had been times when she wondered about what was happening
to her marriage. In the first interview she became increasingly
aware of the distance that had developed during the previous few
years, especially during the previous two years.

In the second and third interviews, she began to express negative and hostile feelings. Her husband's business had demanded
extended periods of time away from home, and she became aware
that he paid very little attention to either her or the children even
when he was home. She was able to verbalize her feelings about
his neglect of the children. Two of their children had asthmatic
conditions, and one was serious enough to necessitate hospitalization. She was able both to accept these feelings which she had
buried and to express them towards her husband. She also became
aware that she had really given up on any hope to establish a
really open and growing relationship with her husband.

During the next few interviews she began to express an increasing amount of hostility toward her husband. She began to
blame him for everything that happened. She recalled that when
she had accused him of neglecting her and the children while he

was home from a business trip, he quarreled angrily with her. She withdrew from the quarrel, and he ended up spending even more time away from them. An intervention at this time consisted simply of interjecting that a relationship always involves two persons, and that she would need to examine what kind of "pay-off" or "reward" she got from withdrawing from the quarrels. While reflecting on the fact that they had not had any real quarrels for about two years, she became aware of the kind of compromise she had made simply to keep some kind of peace and stability in the marriage. She began to see how much his anger threatened her, and that she had accepted his withdrawal as an easier solution to her own anxiety about the relationship.

Although she continued to express anger toward her husband in the next few interviews, she began to examine what problems she had brought to the marriage. When she began to blame her husband and feel sorry for herself, the counselor intervened to confront her with her own responsibility to be fully herself in the relationship.

During the sixth session the counselor's intervention consisted of exploring with her some constructive steps which she would need to take. These steps involved the need to secure a job and sell her house, which she could no longer afford to keep. As she began to cope with these very concrete tasks, she began to express some hope for herself and her children.

The increased ego strength which she gained through the discovery that she could take care of herself enabled her to begin to examine some of her long-buried guilt feelings in relation to her children. She began to see that she had chosen to stay with her children instead of spending time with her husband in his hobbies and sports interests. She discovered she had not been a companion to her husband in some ways because of her overprotection of her children. At the same time, she experienced some feelings of rejection of her children. Interventions by the counselor involved acceptance of her guilt feelings and support for her increased awareness of her own responsibility for the break in the relationship with her husband.

Interventions in the seventh through the ninth sessions consisted of additional support as she applied for a part-time job to supplement her income and as she worked to get her house ready for sale. Other interventions included the suggestion that she re-examine her relationship with a women's group at the church, which she had discontinued at the time of the divorce, and to look into the possibility of the organization "Parents Without Partners." By the time of the ninth and final session she was experiencing some support from this new group and had developed a friendship with a man who had the care of two children from his divorce.

In the first two interviews Grace seemed to be seeking some

understanding for the cause of the divorce, but in reality she was gradually working toward the acceptance of the fact of the divorce. One intervention at this juncture was to assist her in accepting the reality of the separation and in coming to this awareness gradually and in manageable stages. Another intervention was the acceptance of and encouragement to express her negative feelings.

Interventions during the second and third interviews consisted of support for the expression of her hostile feelings toward her husband which she had successfully suppressed, and in some instances repressed to the extent that she had actually forgotten she ever had such feelings.

During the next few sessions the counselor interventions consisted of breaking up her "game" of blame and self-pity. She was confronted with her own responsibility for the relationship and the way she had evaded quarrels in order to keep "peace." His anger had been more threatening than his withdrawal, and hence, she compromised her responsibility for the relationship.

Her coping with the very constructive steps of securing a job and selling the home increased her ego strength to the point where she could begin to examine some of her buried guilt feelings. They involved a pattern of over-protection of her children in order to compensate for her guilt at resenting them for interfering with the time she could have spent with her husband. Hence, this pattern involved her in choosing to stay with them rather than going off with her husband at times when he could have been with her.

Her increased acceptance of her own responsibility for what had happened to the relationship and the support she experienced from both the counselor and her new friends in "Parents Without Partners" enabled her to take full responsibility for herself and her children in their new life together. There was no attempt to work with the characteristic ways she dealt with her dependency problem, but her behavior was adaptive in this instance and her acceptance of her responsibility for herself showed considerable growth in her ways of coping with such a situation [Whitlock, 1973, pp. 132–136].

The dynamics of the loss in divorce are often similar to those of losses experienced in other broken relationships. These dynamics may be present in varying degrees in a broken engagement or in the termination of an affair. As a contractive experience, the end of a relationship may involve some elements present in bereavement, including, at certain points, something akin to grief work. It may involve both a conflict of values and a grieving for a significant loss. Although each individual experiences a divorce in his or her own way, there are patterns of responses that occur in instances similar to the one just described; a similar pattern of responses may occur at least in situations in which the break is initiated by one of the individuals over the objection of the other. This pattern would not necessarily be duplicated in every situation, but the similarities in such experiences enable counselors to understand the usual course of contractive crises of this kind.

LOSS OF FUNCTION

Any significant change in individuals' expectations of themselves or of their relationships with others involves a loss. A loss of some personal function represents such a change. The loss of function in aging has been included in the discussion of the maturational crises of the later years. Some specific losses are related to maturational changes, others to situational changes, and still others to a combination of both.

Loss of Physical Health

A loss of normal physical health in either illness or old age is, of course, a significant loss. A man's loss of health may lead to a loss of his function as the wage earner. His inability to fulfill the role of provider for his family can represent a serious loss that must be accepted as a reality that cannot be changed. If a woman is the sole support of her family, her loss of health may impair her ability both to earn a living and to care for her home and children. Such a change in her role represents a significant loss of function that may result in a crisis. Moreover, this type of loss may result in the additional experience of a loss of self-esteem. When persons' role expectations can no longer be fulfilled, they may suffer the loss of their sense of self-worth.

Loss through Surgery

The loss experienced through a surgical procedure can seriously affect a person's self-image. The removal of a breast in a radical mastectomy, for instance, involves a radical change in a woman's body image, and she must look at herself in a new way. She will usually be fearful that her husband will no longer find her attractive or that people will see her and treat her differently. Since the body image contains considerable personal meaning, a change in body image can lead to significant loss of function and of self-esteem. In the case of a hysterectomy, the loss will not be physically evident, but it represents the loss of the possibility of bearing any more children, and hence a loss of function. Women ordinarily relate their early awareness of their feminine attraction to the time of the development of their curves and breasts and to the beginning of menstruation. Since a woman usually associates the meaning of these experiences with her attractiveness as a woman, it is normal for her to experience anxiety about the loss of function resulting from either a mastectomy or a hysterectomy. The significance of such loss is discussed in more detail in the chapter on changes in body image.

Menopause and Impotence

Menopause, which occurs in women around the ages of 40 to 50, is a potential time of stress in maturational development. Medically, menopause represents physiological changes in decreasing glandular activity, but the menopausal syndrome includes psychological components as well. A person consists of both physical and psychological influences interacting dynamically with each other. While the physiological changes in menopause are real and involve some physical changes, ordinarily the physical components of the menopausal syndrome will not greatly affect this period of life. However, the interaction between the physical and the psychological influences may cause considerable stress and precipitate a crisis. Although there is no reason why sexual activity should cease with menopause, often there is a lessening of interest due to diminished glandular activity. There is no organic reason why sexual activity should cease or even decrease, but the diminished interest has psychological implications. Just as in the case of surgical procedures, this loss of function poses a threat. A woman usually associates the beginning of her sexual interest with the time in life when she began to be noticed and to be sought after by the boys. Hence, the diminished interest in sexual activity may be associated with the feeling that she is no longer desirable as a woman. Erich Fromm (1963) suggested in his essay "Sex and Character" that the woman's psychological problem in relation to sex is that of feeling attractive to men. A loss of feeling attractive to men may therefore represent a significant loss in a woman's estimate of her self-worth.

The problem of diminished sexual interest and ability is most evident in men in connection with their potency—that is, their ability to maintain an erection sufficient for the sexual encounter. Fromm (1963) suggests that if the woman's question is "Does he want to have me sexually?" the man's question is

"Can I make it?" Since the man's ability to demonstrate his sexual capability is more obvious, he undergoes a kind of trial. His anxiety is centered on the question of failing. Failure in potency represents a loss of function or of role expectation and therefore may involve a significant loss of feelings of self-worth.

There are other losses of function, but some of the same principles included in this discussion may be applied to other experiences as well. In addition, there are countless ways in which a sense of self-esteem can be lost. All these experiences are to be taken seriously, and any of them may precipitate a crisis. The *danger* in such a crisis is that an individual may succumb to a passive resignation to the loss, resulting in apathy or some other maladaptive response. The *opportunity* is that, while the individual recognizes the reality of the loss, he or she may be enabled to adopt an active stance toward it and hence to develop compensatory bases upon which self-esteem may be reestablished.

COPING WITH A LOSS OF SELF-ESTEEM

A loss of self-esteem is similar to any significant loss. When people experience changes in the expectations they have of themselves or of their relationships with others, they may sustain a significant loss. The *first* intervention in crises of this kind consists of listening to the pain of the loss and assisting individuals to make contact with their intense feelings. These feelings may include anxiety, anger, guilt, and despair. There may be a grieving for the loss and a feeling of aloneness or alienation from others. Helping individuals make contact with these feelings, and with those mechanisms that defend them from the pain associated with their feelings, will facilitate their acceptance of a loss as a reality that cannot be changed.

A *second* intervention may involve the exploration of previous means of coping with a serious loss. Exploring the coping mechanisms that have been used in the past and the reasons why they are not working in this instance may help individuals develop ways of coping with their present experience of loss. Questions such as the following can be used to explore previous coping skills: "Have you ever been faced with a similar situation? What happened then? What seems to be different about this situation?" In addition, a counselor may be able to discover who the significant other persons are, and whether or not they played a part in helping an individual cope in the previous situation.

A *third* intervention may involve exploring alternative ways

of experiencing a sense of success or self-fulfillment and reestablishing a feeling of self-esteem. A *fourth* intervention may
include opening up some channels of communication with significant other persons. This step may include establishing
support systems that will provide the emotional support individuals need to maintain self-esteem while adjusting to a significant loss.

Some of these interventions may be effectively used with
some clients and some with others; they simply need to be available to the counselor to use as needed in specific instances. Directions for the use of any interventions are merely guidelines
suggesting possible ways to facilitate the development of a person's own coping skills.

EXPERIENTIAL TRAINING

I. Suggestions to the Instructor

These exercises can be conducted either inside or outside of
class. Directions for the formation of the triads may be given
in the class sessions and the exercises themselves conducted
outside of class if students are able to meet on their own. If
the triads meet in class, you may circulate around them and
observe how they are proceeding. You may wish to plan time
at the conclusion of each class period for process observations shared with the entire class.

II. Experiential Exercises

A. The class forms triads. Within each triad, decide who will
take the initial roles of counselor, counselee, and observer.

B. The role-play involves a man who is the sole support of
three children. He is 58 years of age and has spent the last
20 years in the employment of a company that has just
fired him in a reorganization move. He has been informed
that, since he cannot fulfill the requirements of the position under the reorganization, he has been given one
month's severance pay. He is bitter because he knows he
made significant contributions to the company as the
business was being established. He knows that the business is a profitable one but that a new president wants
to make a record for himself and for the company. At 58,
he knows that he cannot find a position that will pay an
adequate salary, and he has two children in college and

a third in high school. He is depressed, and he finds that he can't get his affairs organized to seek new job interviews. In fact, he hasn't left his home for two weeks following the termination notice. Someone has suggested consulting a counselor at the family-services center.

C. Tell the counselor in your triad about your difficulties for about five to ten minutes.

D. Switch roles and repeat the process so each one will have the opportunity of playing each role.

E. Feedback should be preceded by some information from both the counselor and the counselee.
   1. Questions to the counselee: Did you feel heard? How could the counselor have helped you more effectively? How do you feel about the counselor now? Other questions?
   2. Questions to the counselor: Do you feel that you heard the counselee? What was left unfinished in the counseling? How do you feel about the counselee now? Other questions?
   3. Each observer should have taken notes and should then share his or her own feedback on the processes of the various counseling situations.

F. Additional role-playing of contractive experiences may be designed to meet special counseling needs.

10

Crises Related to Changes in Body Image

A change in body image is usually a contractive experience. The crisis of a loss experienced through a *radical* change in body image is always a contractive one. As in any experience of loss, there is a remarkable similarity between the process of coping with a change in body image and that of grief work in bereavement. However, a change in body image is a unique case of loss, and its unique meaning needs to be understood if it is to be coped with adaptively. The rationale for a separate treatment of this kind of loss is based upon the unique dynamics of the concept of body image.

First of all, it is important to understand what is meant by *body image*. The body is not simply flesh and bones arranged in a unique way. If in one sense a person is more than a body, there is a real sense in which a person's body *is* that person. The only way we recognize people is through their bodies. What we perceive, however, is not merely particular arrangements of physical characteristics. When I look at someone's body, what I see—unless I'm directing my attention specifically to merely physical characteristics—are both the physical dimensions of that person and something of his or her selfhood. My perception of a human being—of a human *body*—involves a recognition of the whole person.

It is equally true that we perceive *ourselves* as particular bodies. For example, a woman relates to her body not merely as a physical organism but also as the carrier of her total selfhood. The "gestalt" of that physical perception or image is integral to her sense of selfhood. Since she perceives herself as a psychosomatic whole, her body carries the weight of both psychomotor development and personal meaning. In the event that her body is sufficiently well coordinated for her to develop a particular skill to a high degree, she relates personal meaning to that skill. Her selfhood becomes related to the skill she has developed as a baseball pitcher or as a surgeon. Her possession of this skill represents more than just a physical accomplishment or the fulfillment of a role; it is the development of a *person* that significantly affects her self-perception.

Any change in body image, therefore, involves an altered perception of self. It follows that the more radical the change, the greater the possibility of a radically altered self-perception, and significant changes in self-perception are usually difficult to work out. People seek out psychotherapy with the avowed purpose of undergoing some change, but they often display ambivalence as they seek to settle instead for a release from those symptoms that are causing them pain or discomfort. Working out a change in self-perception is a painful process. It includes letting go of the past, facing the fact that the past cannot be changed or recovered, and accepting the losses this reality may entail.

RADICAL CHANGES IN BODY IMAGE

A change in body image inevitably entails a change in perception of self. Such a change can be avoided only if the psychological defense of denial is used. In this case, the degree of denial determines the extent to which self-perception becomes distorted. The athletic male whose physical competence is impaired may deny the reality of that change. Another man may deny the seriousness of a heart condition; his refusal to change his perception of himself may result in either death or invalidism. A woman may deny the effects of a disease or injury that impairs her coordination, and others then perceive her as fooling herself. The alternative to denial is to learn to look at oneself in a new way. And this change in perception of self can be a painful unfolding of self-understanding, with all the shock such an awareness of self can entail.

When a change in body image is so obvious that it cannot be ignored or denied, a crisis may occur. Such a crisis includes the *opportunity* that the need for a change in self-perception will be obvious. A man who suffers the paralysis of his limbs, for example, cannot deny the necessity of a change in his perception of himself. The *danger* of such a crisis is that the experience of deprivation may be so great that apathy or despair results. Thus, the paralytic may lose his motivation to struggle to retain even those functions that are left to him.

A crisis occurred in the life of one young man whose normal development was disrupted by a serious illness that caused a radical change in body image. The illness struck at the very time in which he was involved in working out his own identity in relation to himself and his peer group. Paul was a 17-year-old high school student and a first-string halfback on the football team. He had shown considerable promise in the first few games of his final football season. In the midst of that season, he contracted polio. I saw him initially in the hospital at the request of his mother and the medical staff, who were concerned about his depressive and suicidal reactions.

Paul was a tall, muscular young man with considerable personal involvement in the athletic ethos. Developmentally, he had been in the process of forming his identity around the athletic image. His significant relationships were with his peers and with his coach as an adult model. Paul's coach was important to him especially because his parents were divorced, and Paul was living with his mother.

His suicidal responses began immediately following the culmination of the medical crisis. Following the initial physical struggle for survival, he began to feel better. During that period he had the energy to reflect and to be self-conscious about his physical condition, especially in the presence of his peers. Since his hospitalization extended over a year's time, interest on the part of his peers and his coach diminished, and their visits became increasingly infrequent. Paul was thus deprived of peer support at the very time he needed it most.

Paul's physical impairment included a general weakness throughout his body. His arms and hands were most severely affected, his legs less so. After a few months of bed care, the application of hot Kenny packs, and some hydrotherapy, he learned to walk again. He regained almost normal usage of his left leg, and he was able to walk without a brace as he learned to lock his right knee. Although his instability meant that he could be easily knocked over, he did regain the ability to walk short distances, and later he was able to walk several blocks with the assistance of a cane. However, his arms were seriously impaired. He regained sufficient use of them to be able to feed himself, but he could not raise his arms to comb his hair or to reach for objects on a shelf. This inability to care for himself in crucial ways continued to be a critical problem for him.

Counseling sessions during a period of several months included listening to Paul and, at times, simply sitting with him. The most critical period occurred during the first four months. Interventions during this time included establishing rapport and listening to his feelings of panic and his talk about his lost dreams. He was depressed and lonely. He experienced a period of emptiness in which he was searching for his identity in the midst of an identity diffusion and role confusion. Being robbed of his developing sense of identity, which had been built around the athletic image, he was now frantically searching for the answer to the question "Who am I?"

Interventions included not only listening to his feelings of loneliness and panic but also accepting them as feelings that would be expected of any young man in such a situation. His encountering of the reality of his physical condition was supported, but always with the reminder that exercise and training could enable him to regain some of his strength. He was also referred to a vocational-rehabilitation counselor, who helped him plan college courses and the choice of a career. When I happened to see Paul several years later, I learned that he had married and completed college and was now earning his teaching credential while teaching in a high school. The development of an identity based on a new body image, and the discovery of a role that he could fulfill, had enabled him to cope with a very difficult physical handicap and hence to reassert his control over his own destiny.

A young university chaplain also had an intense experience with a radical change of body image. At the age of 29, Philip contracted polio. He spent over a year in the hospital, after which time he was confined to a wheelchair. Philip's thoughts about this period in his life provide a useful illustration of some of the problems raised by such a change in body image in an adult. His total experience extended over about three years and included two crisis periods about two years apart.

Beginning with about the fifth month of hospitalization, Philip felt well enough to begin dealing with more than his immediate symptoms. During this period, the emotional support he received from other polio patients in the ward and from the hospital staff was of primary importance. The nature of his condition involved hope for recovery, and the hospital community became a buffer between himself and the world outside the hospital. The community became both physically and psychologically therapeutic for Philip, enabling him to develop a gradual awareness of a new body image. The physical treatment was directed toward limbs that no longer functioned and hence demanded conscious attention. The process of muscle reeducation involved concentrating on a single muscle of a foot or toe as the physical therapist lightly touched it and listening carefully for the body's faint response. These treatments facilitated Philip's learning of how to live with a different body image and constituted the first intervention in his crisis. The intervention consisted of the reality testing of actual physical capabilities within a supportive community. Experiencing a new body image, so decisively different from the one he had known before, required a gradual movement toward acceptance of the reality of his situation.

The first time Philip went outside the hospital grounds in his wheelchair, however, he felt like a strange being in a new world. He was no longer surrounded by other patients and by those who provided care and treatment. He felt the stares of strangers and encountered a hostile world of stairs and curbs, a world unfriendly to him and to the wheels on which he depended. He experienced a crisis of shock and denial. He was angry at the world and bitter toward God for allowing this awful thing to happen. Supportive interventions at this point included the efforts of an understanding counselor, who listened to him and accepted his angry and alienated feelings. Confronting interventions included his physical treatments, which were reality oriented and which provided some evidence of potential physical capabilities.

Another dimension of the threat triggered by this change in body image consisted of existential guilt and anxiety. Philip's disability led him to experience a feeling of powerlessness over his own destiny. With such a drastic change in his ability to be physically responsible for himself, he experienced the guilt of unfulfilled commitments and the anxiety of unfulfilled dreams. At the same time, these feelings were coupled with a fierce determination to regain what physical strength he could, and he began an examination of some alternative career options. The exploration of these alternatives comprised the next intervention. This intervention included learning about some of the ways in which he could once again take some responsibility for his career. Vocational rehabilitation provided some intellectual tools and financial support that enabled him to take a step in coping with the reality of his new body image. He discovered new ways in which he could recover some power over his life. Polio had robbed him of power over some body movement and, to some extent, over his own destiny. Learning some facts about career possibilities provided some tools with which he could once again hope to take charge of his own life.

As he began studies in graduate school, Philip experienced another crisis. It was extremely difficult for him to ask someone to help him up a curb or, worse still, to carry him up stairs. He even experienced emotional pain whenever anyone came up from behind to voluntarily push his wheelchair. There were both feelings of anger at these people for having normal bodies and a resistance against his dependency. Philip's struggle with his own dependency needs occasionally resulted in overcompensatory behavior, indicating an inability to cope satisfactorily with his changed body image. His responses were those of embarrassment and self-consciousness. It was as if he was still unable to perceive himself in a changed way, unable to accept this changed image of a body that was no longer normal, physically active, or attractive. Although he rightfully resented others' pity, the mere fact that he was the object of pity was a painful reminder of a body that was now crippled.

Although Philip gradually developed an acceptance of himself and of his new body image, he experienced a continuing struggle and resistance to the change in his perception. He cried over his loss and cried out because of it. His weeping was, in part, the painful weeping of a grief experience as he grieved for the lost functions of his body, but it was also an expression of the anger he directed against God or Fate and against the limbs that refused to follow his command. He sought to retain his perception of a normal body image and, at the same time, struggled to say "goodbye" to those body functions that no longer served him. He struggled to accept his real losses without, at the same time, losing what he still had. His counselor's support and confrontations were crucial interventions at this point in his development.

At this juncture, Philip was a participant in group psychotherapy. Over a period of about two months, he experienced a sequence of intriguing dreams, which he related to the group. He had noted previously that he had never dreamed of himself in a wheelchair. Now he began to admit new dimensions of experience into awareness. At the outset, he began to dream of the trails he had once hiked extensively in the high Sierras. In these dreams, he first experienced an increasing difficulty in managing the difficult trails. Next, he admitted into his awareness the image of limping. Finally, he was able to see himself in his dreams sitting in a wheelchair.

Philip was consciously aware at this time not of capitulation or defeat but simply of acceptance. The result of this sequence of dreams, occurring concurrently with a psychotherapeutic effort, seemed to be an acceptance of a reality that could not be changed. The change in self-perception occurred as the result of both considerable personal struggle beforehand and the current psychotherapeutic support and interventions. The ultimate acceptance of his body image grew out of his struggle with the conflict between resistance to dependency and honest mourning for an irrevocable loss. His grieving was painful, but it enabled him to say "goodbye" to his normal body image and to finish that particular segment of his life. The resolution involved letting go of the past so that there would be room for the present.

SUDDEN CHANGES IN BODY IMAGE

A radical change in body image may occur gradually in the event of a disease such as multiple sclerosis. In the case of such conditions as polio or a stroke, the change in body image may be sudden, but there is generally hope for partial or complete recovery. In addition, there is usually sufficient time for the afflicted individuals to learn how to face their new reality gradually and in manageable doses. People who have the necessary time can be helped to accept a changed body image gradually, without suffering panic. Time allows them the chance to work out mechanisms or skills with which to cope with a changed condition.

People involved in accidents, however, often suffer sudden, radical, and even permanent changes in body image, without having the time necessary to develop coping mechanisms. As a result, they may be immobilized by a serious crisis. In my most recent book, I related the case history of a man who had suffered such a trauma in a railroad accident. His story is worth repeating here, because it well illustrates how sudden and unexpected a serious loss of this kind can be.

> Joe was about 26 years old, unmarried, but engaged to be married in a few months. He was a high school graduate and was working for the railroad when he lost both legs in an accident in the railroad yards. He was seen in the hospital less than a week after the accident at the request of both his doctor and his family. He was very depressed and apathetic. He had a religious background. Although his immediate family had not said anything about it, some relatives and friends were implying that the accident was the way God tested a man.
>
> In an initial intervention he was encouraged to talk about how he felt about himself. It was difficult for him to get in touch with his feelings, but as his negative feelings were accepted he began to express some hostility. He slowly began to express feel-

ings of hostility toward the railroad, God, and his relatives and friends who had suggested that somehow God was involved in his predicament. As he became increasingly free to cope with his hostile reactions, he was reminded of his responsibility for himself.

As he became more able to talk about his physical condition, he seemed to be adapting to his new situation gradually but painfully. He began to talk about his missing legs in a way akin to grieving. He expressed feelings that can only be interpreted as grief for his lost limbs. He was encouraged to express his hostile and grieving feelings, but the focus of the intervention was upon the constructive steps he might take in order to cope with life with such a handicap.

In conjunction with the physical therapist in the hospital, new information was imparted to him regarding the possibilities of artificial limbs and just what steps would be necessary to train him to walk again. Interventions also included consideration of some occupational therapy in the hospital and vocational rehabilitation which would enable him to retrain for a new kind of job.

The focus of these interventions was upon his gradual awareness of the reality of his new situation, his hostile and grieving feelings, and the constructive steps that he could take in order to cope with life under the new and difficult circumstances of a serious physical handicap. The gradual awareness of the extent of his physical handicap was a part of the crisis process and was completed in six sessions. After his release from the hospital, however, he was seen for about 20 additional weeks, during which time he worked with the gradual acceptance of his new body image. Such therapeutic work on the acceptance of body image could be a part of any therapy with a person who has a physical handicap, but it would usually involve crisis intervention only in situations where some significant loss had been recently experienced [Whitlock, 1973, pp. 140–141].

Joe's accident was an experience of greater intensity than he had ever before experienced, and its suddenness deprived him of sufficient time in which to work out a resolution to his new situation. A crisis occurred. The *opportunity* in this crisis was that Joe might be able to come to an acceptance of his loss and of his new body image in a relatively short period of time. The *danger* was that his depressive and apathetic reactions might result in maladaptive resolutions to his predicament. The danger of his depressive responses was that he might take measures to end his own life. The danger of his apathetic responses was that he would give up what he still had and capitulate to his dependency needs, thus becoming a helpless invalid.

As Joe experienced the freedom to express his feelings and to grieve for his lost limbs, he learned to accept the unchangeable reality of his loss. To learn adaptive means of coping, he had to first accept the loss of his legs. With this acceptance, he was no longer in a panic over his helplessness and could accept responsibility once again for his own destiny.

During Joe's recovery at home, he was also learning to cope with his feelings about his fiancée. Although she endured considerable emotional pain while working through her own feelings, she was even more accepting of him than he was of himself. She was free of any feelings of pity but was painfully aware of the changes the accident would make in their lives. At the time of termination of his counseling interviews, Joe was learning to accept his continuing feelings of existential anxiety. He was learning to cope with his feelings of unfulfilled dreams in a way that involved adapting to his real losses rather than denying them.

VOLUNTARY CHANGES IN BODY IMAGE

Changes in body image also occur voluntarily, through the choice of various forms of plastic surgery. Even though these changes are usually not radical, and moreover are voluntarily chosen, they may be experienced as traumatic losses. In any event, such changes require emotional as well as intellectual understanding of their consequences. An individual may understand the nature and extent of the change that the surgery will effect, and may even be happy with the results, yet still experience a trauma and need to work through an emotional acceptance of a new body image and its implications.

Any body image a person has developed, or is in the process of developing, is bound to have significant meaning, whether positive or negative. An individual who has an ugly birthmark may have highly negative reactions to it. Nevertheless, the birthmark may have considerable meaning for the person, and the loss of that meaning is a significant loss. In one of my previously published case studies, I described the experience of a young woman who had used her body image as a mechanism of defense against admitting into her awareness something unpleasant about herself. I refer to this case study again because of the interesting psychodynamics of her behavior.

Beth was twenty years old and unmarried. She was not in school at the time, but had graduated from high school a few years before. She had previously held a job as a clerk in a store but had now withdrawn from any activity whatsoever and simply stayed at home. When she was seen for the first time, she was a very withdrawn and frightened person. Her mother brought her to the counselor because she was concerned about the radical change in her daughter, her withdrawal into herself, as well as her hostile responses. Although Beth was an attractive young woman, she began by complaining that she was ugly and that she would never attract a man because of her ugliness. She complained especially about the structure of her face, saying that her eyes were too small and close together, and that it was altogether an ugly face. She kept insisting that no one could help her because the structure of her face and the position of her eyes could not be changed. As a result of her feelings of hopelessness, she was apathetic about life. She was not motivated to leave her room or to go out and get a job, and she had very little interest in life. The first intervention consisted simply of permitting the verbalization of her negative feelings about herself and accepting these feelings as hers. As she talked, she revealed that she had had plastic surgery on her nose about three years before. She had felt good about the results. She had not had any counseling at that time. An intervention at this point consisted simply of encouraging her to talk about this change in her body image, and how she felt about herself. Since she had not had sufficient opportunity to explore her feelings about this change in her facial appearance, she had not learned an adaptive means of coping with her original feelings of ugliness about her nose.

When the counselor intervened with questions about her experiences during the past two or three weeks, she revealed that her boyfriend had broken off with her about two weeks prior to this appointment, and that she had begun to withdraw after that. Although she had been dating several times a week, she had not had any possibilities of a date for more than two weeks. She felt she was not sought out for any dates because of her ugliness and that she would never have a chance for another such relationship. In the course of the questioning, she related that her mother and father were divorced and that she had visited her father about three weeks previously. It was just before her boyfriend broke off their relationship.

She talked about how she resented her mother and how close she had felt to her father. When the counselor questioned her about the visit, she told about her father's new family. She related that she had felt somewhat out of place, and that her father's attention was directed primarily toward the children in his new marriage. She felt largely ignored, and then her boyfriend had told her he didn't want to see her again.

Intervention at this juncture consisted of encouraging her

to verbalize her feelings about being hurt in both situations, and these feelings were both accepted and interpreted. It was interpreted to her that she had suffered rejection in both situations. Her need for acceptance by her father had been accentuated by her boyfriend's rejection. When she had experienced rejection in the past, she had used the excuse that her nose was ugly. She had not developed any means of coping with the rejection, but had evaded it by turning to her feelings of ugliness. Surgery on her nose had robbed her of the use of this means of coping with her feelings. Now she "discovered" that her eyes were so small and close together that her face was ugly, but in a way that could not be changed. Hence, no one could help her, because no one could change the structure of her face. She was now confronted with the problem of rejection, but not in an examination of her characterological problem of her relationship with her father, which was broken at a crucial point in her psychosexual development by the divorce. She was confronted with the possibility of discovering other ways to cope with her feelings of rejection and lack of popularity with young men. Additional intervention involved experimentation with job interviews and additional social contact as well as examining her limited patterns of interest and involvement with others which made her a less interesting person [Whitlock, 1973, pp. 119–121].

By using her perception of her original body image as a psychological defense against the reality of rejection, Beth had endowed it with considerable meaning. This use of her supposed ugliness had been a maladaptive means of coping, but it had served her immediate need to evade a painful reality. Since she had not mourned for the significant loss involved in her surgery, she had not fully accepted her change in body image. The psychodynamics of her behavior following the surgery were the same as before; only her objective looks had changed. In her mirror she objectively perceived a change in the looks of her nose, but her self-image remained the same precisely because she would not emotionally accept the meaning of a changed body image.

There are other voluntarily chosen changes in body image that may affect persons in different ways. The changes in the bodies of women in pregnancy have often been cited as a source of threat. Even if a pregnancy has been planned, the woman may experience the threat of no longer feeling physically attractive to her lover. An unwanted pregnancy simply compounds that threat. Acceptance of the change in looks is possible to the degree that the new body image is endowed with meaning. Active involvement of both husband and wife in the meaning of the birth process and of the baby itself constitutes a mechanism for coping with this change. Since the woman's body will return to its former shape, this kind of change in the body is, of course, unique. Interventions supplying information about the birth process, reassurance of the woman that she will indeed regain her former figure, and active involvement of the husband in the preparation for the delivery and in the delivery itself will increase the possibility of acceptance of this temporary change in body image.

POSTSCRIPT

Changes in body image inevitably alter individuals' self-perception as a result of the change they experience in relation to their environment. Regardless of whether a change in body image occurs accidentally or is voluntarily chosen, the affected individual needs to accept the reality of some loss and the meaning of the change in relation to his or her environment. Almost anyone who experiences such a change will need some kind of personal or psychotherapeutic experience through which its significance can be understood. Failure to cope with both the reality of the loss and the change in relationship with the environment may result in existential anxiety about meaning and guilt about unfulfilled promises.

EXPERIENTIAL TRAINING

I. Suggestions to the Instructor

Since the crises resulting from changes in body image are usually contractive experiences, the following exercises are similar to those suggested in the previous chapter.

II. Experiential Exercises

A. The class forms triads. Within each triad, decide who will take the initial roles of counselor, counselee, and observer.
B. This role-play concerns a person who has been seriously crippled by an accident. At present, he is in a wheelchair, but with adequate physical therapy he has hopes of being able to walk with crutches. He is 35 years of age and has been a skilled plumber. He can no longer function in his job, and his employment has been terminated. He is married and has three children, ages 3, 5, and 9. He is living

on his disability-insurance checks, but the income is minimal, and the family will need to reduce their standard of living. He has been depressed for about two weeks following his last visit to his doctor. His wife has been concerned about his depression and has asked him to consult a counselor at the family-services agency.

C. The counselee tells his story to the counselor for about five to ten minutes.

D. Switch roles and repeat the process so that each member of the triad has the opportunity to play each role.

E. The observer should remember to secure information from both the counselor and the counselee.

    1. Questions to the counselee: Did you feel heard? How could the counselor have helped you more effectively? How do you feel about the counselor now? Other questions?

    2. Questions to the counselor: Do you feel that you heard the counselee? What was left unfinished in the counseling? How do you feel about the counselee now? Other questions?

    3. Each observer should then provide feedback on the process of the counseling.

F. Additional role-playing of changes in body image may be designed to meet special counseling needs.

Crises Related to Miscarriage, Abortion, and Rape

Among the many traumatic losses that people may suffer, the losses associated with miscarriage, abortion, and rape deserve special attention. Although these experiences are, in varying degrees, common in our society, their dynamics are often poorly understood. I will discuss each of them in turn, but it is worth noting that all three tend to engender patterns of responses that have obvious similarities to those engendered by other serious losses discussed in this book, including the deaths of loved ones and radical changes in body image.

MISCARRIAGE AS A TRAUMATIC LOSS

As I write about the trauma of miscarriage, I am aware of some feelings of threat, because my own wife is pregnant. Knowing intellectually that a miscarriage is unlikely does not eliminate these feelings of threat, but it does help to lessen them. I also know that miscarriage fulfills a function not unlike that of pain, which is the body's way of signaling that something is wrong; miscarriage, like pain, can prevent more serious damage. I experience a continuing diminution of my threat as I reflect on the profound meaning of this biological fact.

Although miscarriage is a relatively common phenomenon that can occur in any pregnancy, an actual miscarriage is often traumatic, regardless of whether or not the pregnancy has been planned. Even if a pregnancy is unplanned, some emotional attachment to the fetus usually develops, although sometimes unconsciously. When a woman has chosen her pregnancy and has shared her plans and hopes with her lover, the possibility of a crisis in the event of a miscarriage becomes greater.

I first reported on one such crisis and on my counseling with the woman involved in the interdisciplinary journal *Pas-*

toral Psychology (Whitlock, 1970, pp. 45–46). Here I will amplify my comments about this counseling experience in order to further clarify the nature of the woman's loss.

Jane was 24 years of age and had been married for about a year. Her husband was about five years her senior and was a very stable person who offered her both love and security. I talked with her about three weeks after her miscarriage. She had reacted at first with deep disappointment, and for the past two weeks she had become increasingly upset, apathetic, and depressed. Her husband became concerned about her increasing apathy, and she finally realized her need to seek help when she kept feeling worse. Her friends had encouraged her not to talk about her miscarriage and kept reassuring her that she would get over her disappointment and feel better very soon. She had felt free to consult the counselor at a church counseling service because of her religious convictions.

She began by talking about the deep sense of disappointment she had experienced. She and her husband had both been very happy upon learning that she was pregnant. They had planned for the pregnancy together; her husband had been especially happy and had talked about elaborate plans for their first child. Now she felt that she had failed her husband.

Early in the first interview, Jane began to talk about an abortion she had obtained several years prior to her marriage. The first intervention involved accepting the feelings of guilt she expressed about her abortion and encouraging her to talk about these feelings. Her guilt feelings represented some unfinished business from her past that had now surfaced to become a disruptive factor in her relationship with her husband.

At this point it seemed to be important to Jane that she was talking to a counselor related to some religious tradition. There were some elements of confession in this session, and forgiveness was expressed both in the counselor's acceptance and in a descriptive intervention pointing out the nature of God's forgiveness. Although it did not seem to be a predominant theme, her feelings of guilt were related to a gnawing fear that the miscarriage was God's way of punishing her for the abortion and to a neurotic fear that she would never be able to have another baby. Since her guilt feelings were related to her fears in this way, the interpretation of forgiveness was intended to help her accept that the occurrence of this miscarriage did not in any way indicate that future pregnancies would also result in miscarriage. She was advised to talk with her physician about this question as well, but she was relieved to have this emotional support and interpretation.

In the second and final session, she expressed grief for her unborn fetus. Although she was not aware of having had fantasies during her earlier pregnancy, she had had numerous fantasies during this one, especially in relationship to the plans and hopes that she had shared with her husband. She was now grieving for the loss of the fetus that had been the result of their love. Acceptance of her grieving feelings, both in the sense of accepting them as normal and in the sense of understanding her pain, was important to her. Her grief work seemed to relieve her, and she did not feel the need for any additional appointments.

In a miscarriage, a woman suffers a significant loss. The course of the crisis usually includes some physical complaint, feelings of apathy and depression, and feelings of guilt and grief. Hostile and angry feelings may also be experienced. Jane's hostile responses were primarily related to her guilt feelings, which were apparently hostile feelings directed against herself.

The feelings that occur following a miscarriage reflect the experience of some loss. In the event of an immobilizing crisis, these feelings tend to follow the course or pattern of any experience of a significant loss. A woman who has been carrying a fetus has, to some degree, developed a relationship with it. Often the fetus begins to be personalized, and its loss may be experienced as a personal loss. In addition, although the loss experienced in a miscarriage tends to give rise to a characteristic pattern of responses, for each woman the experience will have a unique personal meaning.

ABORTION AS AN EXPERIENCE OF LOSS

Any consideration of abortion must be extremely complex. The problem includes social, medical, ethical, and psychological dimensions, all of which are inextricably related. The usual tendency is to oversimplify, and hence to distort, the entire question of abortion. One extreme position, for example, is the so-called "tissue" school of opinion, according to which a fetus is nothing more than a nonhuman piece of tissue, no different from any bit of barely formed protoplasm. One psychiatrist has argued, for example, that an abortion should be considered morally neutral surgery, not unlike an operation for the beautification of a nose (which can itself be a serious matter, as the chapter on changes in body image shows). At the opposite extreme is the position that utilizes the concept of natural law in asserting an absolute obligation to respect the life of the fetal "human being," thus giving rise to all the casuistry practiced to determine the moment at which human life begins.

It is beyond the purpose of this discussion to present all the dimensions of the issue of abortion adequately, but I do want to clarify the complexity of the problem and to suggest ways in which an individual can cope with feelings about an abortion, as well as ways in which a counselor can work therapeutically with cases of unwanted pregnancies.

First of all, my position is that the question of whether to have an abortion is a matter that should be left between a woman and her physician. Those of us who have counseled extensively with women seeking to terminate their pregnancies, and who have worked for legislative changes in abortion laws, welcomed the recent Supreme Court decision overturning restrictive state abortion laws. By this decision, the Court appears to have brought some resolution of the severe injustices inflicted upon women

Nevertheless, the solution of making abortion simply a matter between a woman and her physician may create as many problems as it resolves. I believe the solution is correct, but at the same time I insist that physicians must be prepared either to counsel with women seeking to obtain abortions or to refer them to mental-health workers or other professionals who are specifically trained to prepare women for abortions. Preventive education in this area includes at least the disciplines of social work, psychology or psychiatry, and ethics or theology. Specific medical decisions are of course reserved to the physician, but the ethical and psychological issues are inextricably related and are not simply a matter of medical or psychological expertise. Preventive education and crisis intervention may together provide a methodology sufficient to the complexity of this issue.

Counseling women with unwanted pregnancies involves a combination of preventive education and crisis intervention. Since the woman is encountering a critical incident in her life, she may need some counselor interventions. The nature and timing of these interventions depend upon the counselor's understanding of the range of psychodynamics possible in an issue as complex as that of abortion.

Some comments about my own development as a counselor with respect to the question of abortion may illustrate the complexity involved. In the early stages of my experience in counseling with women facing the predicament of unwanted pregnancies, I responded merely to their conscious desire to seek an abortion as the way out of a difficult situation. The fact that a woman was not legally free to make her own choice complicated the issue. I discovered that, in responding to this prior issue of enabling women to achieve the freedom to secure abortions, I was diverted from my primary task of understanding some of the psychodynamics involved in their experience.

Additional factors complicated my functioning in diagnosis. My psychodynamic training equipped me to identify and to work with feelings of guilt. The cultural and religious discussions of abortion were preoccupied with the issue of the obligation to respect the life of the fetus and with the moral guilt of anyone who terminated such a "human life." Hence, as a counselor, I was reacting against a cultural and religious value that, in my view, had subordinated the worth of individuals to a legalistic principle. I also limited myself to identifying only those psychological dynamics that impaired the individual's freedom of choice. If neurotic guilt or anxiety impeded a woman's choice to remove a hazard to her well-being, it became my responsibility as a counselor to facilitate her emotional development in such a way that she would be enabled to choose for herself.

In conversations and encounters with psychotherapeutic colleagues, I noted the same limitation. About ten years ago, in a training workshop for paraprofessional counselors, I began to raise the issue of a disturbing dimension of guilt that I had noted in post-abortion counseling. My voice was a lone one on a panel that also included a psychiatrist, an attorney, and a clergyman. I have come to identify this disturbing dimension as *existential guilt*, the guilt of unfulfilled promises or commitments that will be referred to again in the chapters on dying and bereavement. The reason for taking some pains to develop this thesis here is that I have not discovered references to the dynamics in question in the literature on counseling for unwanted pregnancies.

Existential Guilt

Existential guilt refers to a specific type of normal guilt feelings. These feelings are normal rather than neurotic in the sense that they are not the product of a distorted perception of reality. Existential guilt is a guilt experienced in relation to one's own reality or personal meanings and values, specifically including those promises and commitments to oneself that one has failed to fulfill.

The dynamics of existential guilt are complex. At the very least, they include one's personal meanings and some unfulfilled promises to oneself. In the case of abortion, this sense of unfulfilled promise appears to be related to the nature of the relationship between the persons making love. The act of coitus in a loving encounter may include the promise of procreation, even if that promise is not made explicit. Whether existential guilt develops in the event of an abortion may depend on the degree of intimacy and meaning in the lovers' relationship. To the degree that the act of coitus that results in pregnancy is devoid of personal passion, the development of existential guilt over an abortion of the pregnancy is less likely. For example, since a pregnancy resulting from rape does not involve a voluntary choice, it is unlikely that an abortion in such a case will engender any existential guilt.

A woman's disregard of the possibility of existential guilt enables her to retain her psychological defense of denial intact. The effects of such denial may not become evident until some time after the abortion. Although denial enables an individual to meet an immediate need for a way out of a difficult situation, it is a maladaptive means of coping. Any unfinished emotional business distorts a person's ability to perceive a present predicament accurately. Such maladaptive coping also results in a diminishing of coping skills.

My point is not that every woman who chooses to terminate a pregnancy will develop existential guilt but rather that it is a psychodynamic possibility that has largely been ignored. In relation to abortion, it is *neurotic guilt* that has received the most attention. Guilt is neurotic if it stems from a distorted perception of reality. In contrast, a type of *normal guilt* may be experienced by a woman who accepts a religious dogma of the absolute obligation to preserve the life of a fetus. Such guilt is normal because it is the result of a conflict of values, not a distortion of reality. Counselors need to be able to differentiate among these types of guilt if they are to intervene appropriately.

Examples of Counselor Interventions

A few case studies may help to sort out the various facets of the experience of women who consider aborting a pregnancy. As I related in the discussion of miscarriage, Jane developed neurotic guilt about her abortion. I described her guilt as *neurotic* or *distorted,* because it was primarily an expression of an *irrational* fear. Since her religious tradition had not developed definitive strictures regarding abortion, I described her guilt as a neurotic or fearful response to a generalized sense of wrongdoing. Counselor interventions included encouraging her to talk about her feelings of conflict, accepting her feelings of fear, supporting her claim of responsibility for her action, describing the meaning of forgiveness, and giving her the information that enabled her to understand the distortions of fear in her behavior.

Another illustration is the experience of Barbara. I identified Barbara's feelings as normal guilt that she specifically related to a violation of her personal set of values. Barbara was 26 years of age and was engaged to be married at the time she came in for counseling. She had sought out counseling because of periods of depression that interfered with her performance at work. She had become engaged about four weeks prior to her first consultation, and she had begun to experience conflict at the time of her engagement. In the course of three sessions with her, I discovered that she had had an abortion about a year before and that she still had guilt feelings about it. Barbara had grown up in the Roman Catholic tradition and had attended a Catholic school. Although she no longer identified with this tradition, she had retained much of its value structure, and she experienced a severe conflict and strong feelings of guilt over having violated her own set of values by obtaining an abortion. If she had remained within the Catholic tradition, she probably would have made her confession and perhaps would have sought some means of penance. Deprived of this means of coping with the violation of her own set of values, she unconsciously took it upon herself to administer punishment. She directed hostility inward upon herself, as if she had worked out her own penance. Because of this inwardly directed anger, she became depressed and unable to cope with the normal demands of her job. Counselor interventions included encouragement to talk about her earlier experience, acceptance of her feelings of guilt about the violation of her set of religious values, and a clarification of the relationship of the counselor's acceptance to the religious nature of forgiveness. This clarification included a description of the relationship between her feelings of guilt and her moods of depression and enabled her to regain some means of coping with the responsibilities of her job.

For June, the issues were different. She was 34 years old and had been married for about six years to a man with whom she was now having serious marital problems. A thematic thread of deep resentment against her husband was expressed in a variety of ways. Her resentment was based on his unwillingness to agree to have a child, even though he had agreed prior to the marriage. Now she was faced with a medical problem that necessitated a hysterectomy. She felt resentment at this denial of something of importance to her. As the consultations continued, she revealed that she and her husband had been separated for a period of several months about a year earlier. During this period, she had had an affair with a man at her office and had become pregnant. Terrified at the prospect of losing her job while being separated, she sought an easy way out. A counselor advised her to get an illegal abortion, and, without any psychological preparation whatsoever, she obtained it.

June was later reunited with her husband. Although she did not tell him about the pregnancy, her feelings about the abortion did not involve any guilt related to him or to a violation of her own values. She had neither a religious background nor any present affiliation with a religious tradition. However, in the new context of being unable even to get pregnant, she began to experience conflict about her earlier action, and she expressed a profound sense of guilt over the abortion. It was almost as if she felt guilty for having denied an implicit promise to herself; her guilt feelings appeared to be an expression of unfulfilled hopes and dreams. Counselor interventions extended over several months and included the uncovering of her existential guilt and its effect upon her. In her situation, it was not so much a matter of an immediate crisis intervention as it was a matter of working with the characteristic ways with which she coped with all of her experiences.

Lisa came for counseling simply to discover how she could secure an abortion. She was 22 years of age and was working as a secretary in a large insurance firm. To her, pregnancy was simply an embarrassment and a severe handicap. She was supporting herself, and she could not afford to keep her apartment, car, and style of life if she continued her pregnancy. She and her lover were not planning to get married, and she was frantic to find a way out of her predicament. On the surface, therefore, Lisa had no reason to want to continue her pregnancy; indeed, at the outset she resented any intervention involving a focus of her attention upon her proposal to abort the fetus. She didn't even want to talk about this decision, but she did reveal considerable anxiety and depression in the three sessions in which I counseled with her during the sixth and seventh week of her pregnancy. Despite her impatience to get it over with, I noted some ambivalence toward the abortion itself. When I was firm in relating my need to examine her decision with her, she became more relaxed. As she accepted my sincere desire to listen to her, she began to share some of her gnawing doubts about the abortion and how it affected her feelings about herself. Although she finally chose to abort her pregnancy, she had been enabled to explore her feelings about the surgical procedure itself and the personal significance of what she was doing to herself in securing the abortion. The open exploration of her motivation involved looking at feelings that she had denied and that, in turn, had resulted in her depression. Her decision was not necessarily a happy resolution of her dilemma, but at least she was at peace with herself.

In a post-abortion session two weeks later, Lisa expressed feelings akin to grieving for the loss of the fetus. The sense of loss was not related to the termination of a life, but simply to the loss of something of significance. She remarked "It's almost as if I had lost some of my future—whatever that means!" However, because she had had the opportunity to explore the meaning of this loss, she was able to say "goodbye" to this segment of her life. She would not simply forget it, but she was able to complete this segment of her personal business.

My interpretation of these data, which I have encountered in several such instances, is that an existential guilt of unfulfilled promises is very often experienced by women who choose to abort their pregnancies. Given the opportunity to explore these guilt feelings, these women have been able to accept their significant loss and to say "goodbye" to those segments of their lives without psychological impairment.

RAPE AS A TRAUMATIC LOSS

Increased attention is being given to the trauma of rape, for a variety of reasons. If, as many people believe, the incidence of rape is increasing, the increase may be due to such factors as the population shift from rural to urban areas and the rapid deterioration of the inner cities. In addition, the voluntary reporting of rape may be increasing because of the degree of anonymity available to the female urban dweller, the increased sense of freedom and autonomy of women as the result of political and social changes, and the influence of the women's liberation movement in pushing for justice for women. Nevertheless, the percentage of unreported rape is still thought to be high. Many sexual attacks on women go entirely unreported, partially because of the ways in which the crime of rape has been handled by the police and other institutions serving the rape victim.

Perhaps as a result of the increased attention being given to the problem of rape, police and hospitals are recognizing the need to provide more humane treatment for rape victims. Some police departments are employing female officers who are specifically trained to do counseling with rape victims. These victims will often talk more freely about their traumatic experiences to other women than they will to men. New York City has even set up an all-female Rape Investigation and Analysis Section within its police department. In addition, some hospitals are providing counseling resources for rape victims. An important element of such programs is the recognition that a victim of rape needs immediate treatment, because any physical damage is compounded by the psychological trauma she has suffered. Ambulance attendants and emergency-room personnel need training in preventive education and crisis-intervention techniques to ensure that a woman's trauma will not be increased by the treatment she receives in the hospital. Meanwhile, women's organizations have been formed specifically to increase public awareness of the physical and emotional needs of rape victims, especially in relation to the treatment received from police and hospital staffs. There is no excuse for the insensitive and sadistic ambulance attendant who enters the emergency room with a rape victim shouting "I got a rape for ya, Charlie."

Victim Responses to Rape

Forcible rape involves the experience of a significant loss as the result of a violent act. The psychodynamics of victim responses are complex. The suffering of such a personal violation is always a traumatic experience, and it may result in a crisis that immobilizes the victim.

Rape is criminal because it is an act of violence. In every instance of rape that I have encountered, the experience of the victim has involved an identifiable pattern of responses to a violent act. An early response is *shock* and *disbelief*. The feeling is often expressed as an exclamation: "This can't have happened to me!" Strong feelings of *anger* and *hate* are usually expressed concurrently with feelings of shock. In some instances anger is directed specifically toward the rapist, and, in others, feelings are directed against all men. Feelings of *shame* and *guilt* are expressed. The woman may feel guilty about not having resisted the rapist more vigorously, as if she were somehow responsible for the rape. Some women experience considerable guilt over having experienced some pleasure, even though the rape was clearly forcible. In some instances women experience *grief* feelings, as if they had sustained a significant loss. Indeed, the power to give and to withhold has been lost, and a woman may mourn both her loss and her humiliation. Finally, there is either a *reaching out to,* or *a defensive withdrawal from,* significant other persons. A woman who has been raped usually needs emotional support from the significant other persons in her life. At the same time, she may have strong needs to withdraw from any relationship whatsoever. The reaching out to and the withdrawal from significant other persons are psychodynamically similar. The withdrawal is an expression of the need for some psychological defense; it serves the purpose of protecting an individual from more pain than she can tolerate at that moment. The reaching out expresses her awareness of the need for emotional support.

Sutherland and Scherl, whose work is reported in a recent book by John Macdonald (1975), noted a pattern of victim responses to rape that may provide a helpful model for crisis counselors. The typical pattern of responses, they found, could be divided into three phases.

The *first* phase is one of *acute reaction.* In any counseling with victims of rape, the identification of these feelings is a helpful intervention. Helping the victim to get in touch with her intense feelings about the incident will help her in developing her coping skills. Making contact with these feelings and learning how to express them will usually help her to regain control over herself without using the mechanism of denial. The interventions of this phase include listening to and accepting the strong feelings expressed. Intervention often involves questions to direct the individual's attention to the feelings themselves, and it may include the counselor's description of them in order to assist the woman in reclaiming the experience as a whole.

The *second* phase is *outward adjustment.* It is a pseudoadjustment of a woman who appears to have coped satisfactorily with the emotional stress. However, the outward calm may be the result of defenses that mask her actual feelings. Such an adjustment may represent the resolution of an inner crisis, but it is a maladaptive one. Until the individual can make contact with her own most intense feelings, she will not be able to resolve her crisis adaptively. Counselor interventions can help the individual make contact with her own intense feelings and hence help her to discard those defenses that hinder an adaptive resolution of her crisis.

The *third* phase in the sequence of reactions is *integration and resolution.* It is usually during this period that the final resolution of the victim's feelings occurs. Macdonald indicates that this phase begins "when the victim develops an inner sense of depression and of the need to talk" (p. 101). The depression is normal, and there are usually two major themes which emerge to effect resolution. "First, the victim must integrate a new view of herself. She must accept the event. . . . Second, the victim must resolve her feelings about the assailant and her relationship to him. Her earlier attitude of 'understanding the man's problems' gives way to anger toward him for having 'used her'" (pp. 101–102).

Examples of Counselor Interventions

Joan had been raped about four weeks prior to her first consultation with me. She came in only because of her husband's concern for a developing depression and sense of apathy; her arranging of the consultation was not related to the occurrence of rape.

Joan was 36 years old, a college graduate, and had always been an outgoing person. She was the wife of a minister and had been married for more than ten years. She was an attractive and intelligent woman. Her marriage had been stable, although it seemed to be somewhat uninteresting at this juncture of her life. She expressed her love for her husband, but he seemed to have been more attentive to his work than to her, at least during the year or so prior to her violent and traumatic experience of rape.

The attack occurred in her own home. The rapist had gained access through a loose screen and open window in the rear of the house while her husband was attending a meeting. In the counseling sessions, she was not at first aware of the reason for her feelings of depression. Indeed, the fact that the rape had occurred was mentioned only in response to my questions regarding any unusual experiences during the previous few weeks. In talking about it, she expressed feelings of shame and anger. Interventions included simply accepting her intense feelings. They were the usual responses of any normal woman to the experience of forcible rape.

Strong feelings of guilt were expressed both in the first and in succeeding interviews. The guilt she initially expressed was focused around her feelings that she had not resisted the rapist as forcibly as she could have. As I accepted and helped her to clarify these feelings, describing them as the feelings of many normal women under similar circumstances, she began to cry uncontrollably. Then she began to relate her deep sense of shame over her feelings of "sinfulness." It was only in the fourth session, two weeks later, that she revealed the nature of what she had labeled her "sinfulness." She responded to my questions by acknowledging that, although the attack was real enough, and still rather frightening to her, she had to admit that she had actually enjoyed it. This fact didn't come out all at once, and some emotional support was needed before she could acknowledge it. She was shocked with herself, and she could not forgive herself for what she called this "shameful infidelity."

My interventions at this point included both accepting Joan's feelings of guilt and shame and describing the dynamics of her behavior as normal. As she explored her limited awareness and understanding of her sexual feelings, she began to expand her intellectual understanding and emotional acceptance of some of her "unacceptable" sexual feelings as normal and healthy. I also described how her feelings of guilt were related to her developing depression. Indeed, both her anger and guilt were turned in on herself, and she was punishing herself for allowing the pleasure of her sexual feelings to be directed toward an unknown rapist. The anger directed against herself was so intense that she had become both depressed and apathetic. She had given up on herself, and she was ready to abrogate any responsibility for herself. As she became more able to accept some of her own previously unacceptable feelings, she was able to part with the self-perception that would not allow for any sexual feelings whatsoever for any man other than her husband. It was almost as if she had to mourn for her lost innocence. Having become able to finish that segment of her life once and for all, she was now ready to really join her husband in the living of her life in the present without depression.

Joan's experience is not necessarily typical of rape victims. I have included her experience for the purpose of focusing on the feelings of guilt that rape victims may experience and to point up the complexity of these feelings. Although women often experience a similar pattern of feelings in response to forcible rape, they always experience them in their own idiosyncratic ways.

In some instances of rape, the primary response is not so much shock as it is anger. Eva was a 19-year-old college student who talked to me the day after she had been raped. She had gone to a park by herself and was enjoying the sunshine and her read-ing. A fellow whom she had met casually on a previous occasion stopped by to talk. Although she knew nothing about him, she went for a ride with him. When he said he wanted to pick up something at a friend's house, she accompanied him into the house. He decided to "raid the refrigerator," and they got some sandwiches and beer. As they were sitting on the couch, he tried to get her to go to bed with him; when she refused, he threatened her. She was frightened and acceded to his demand. They were in bed when his friend returned, and the friend also raped her. Her acquaintance then took her back to her dorm at the college and apologized profusely for his behavior. Still furious when she came in, she reported the incident to the police. Although she was furiously angry at her rapists, she was also angry at herself "for being such a damn fool!" She was angry at being deprived of something without her consent, but she was also angry at herself for allowing herself to be placed in such a vulnerable situation.

During both that session and the one following it, she ex-pressed feelings of loss, but her predominant response was anger. Interventions consisted of both emotional support and the anxiety-provoking approach of confronting her with her own responsibility for placing herself in such a vulnerable position with a person unknown to her. The incident became a valuable learning experience for her, and she sought appropriate punish-ment for the rapists.

Although Eva's experience included some positive results, I have counseled young women who have endured the trauma of rape or of attempted rape and who have at least temporarily lost a sense of trust and spontaneity with all men. As the result of the violence done to them, they have lost a quality of open-ness and innocence. At least for a time they have tended to be frightened of and to withdraw from any warm relationships with their male friends. The violence of rape is a serious and tragic experience that often leads to an immobilizing crisis, and every counselor needs to recognize and understand the critical nature of its consequences.

Incestuous Rape as a Special Problem

Incestuous rape poses some of the same problems present in other cases of rape. However, it raises some unique problems that can only briefly be developed here. A father's raping of his

16-year-old daughter will almost surely impair her normal development, since the meaning of the experience is inseparable from her developmental needs. Hence, the pattern of her development is likely to be affected. Incestuous rape is best viewed not only as a crisis involving a single significant loss but also as a critical incident in the total developmental process. It usually results in characterological problems that may require extensive psychotherapy by a professional therapist.

Marcia was 18 years old and had just been in college for a few months. She came in for counseling on the advice of her minister, who was evidently a strong "father image" for her. He had called me before she made the appointment, because he was concerned about her. In the beginning, Marcia did not mention anything about her minister's referring her but began to complain about the tension in her home and her feelings of hostility toward her father. Despite these hostile feelings, she expressed her desire to help her father, who drank heavily. She also resented her father because he dominated her mother, and "she depends upon me." She said that she felt close to her mother but that she was unable to tell her how she felt about "important things." Asking her to visualize her mother sitting in a chair near her, I asked her to tell her mother just how she felt. Although Marcia could visualize her mother sitting there, she could not tell her how she felt. "I couldn't tell anybody!"

Beginning with the second session, Marcia—still insisting that she couldn't tell her mother or anyone else just how she felt—related some of her dreams. In one dream, she was in archery practice. The others on the field started shooting at the target before she got her arrows out of it. She was confused. She was rushing around to get her arrows together, but she was continually anxious and frustrated. On the next night she dreamed of being in a kind of half-sleep. She saw a man sitting in a chair in her room, holding a gun. The dream was extremely frightening, "because it seemed so real." In the next dream she remembered, she saw herself in a "castle-like building." Everyone in her family was to receive a shot "which would make us immune to all feelings." She escaped from her family after trying to explain to her mother that it was wrong to take the injection. Her father finally found her, and she was trying to talk him out of taking the "shot" when the dream ended. In the next dream that she related, she and her roommate Helen were on one side in a war, and Helen's fiancé was on the other. The fiancé entered their room and plunged a knife in Helen's body. Marcia pulled the knife out and desperately tried to tell him that what he had done was very wrong. In her next dream, she saw "a man whom I knew, but I was unable to recognize him. I was afraid and woke up. It was about 2 A.M."

During the 12th session, about three months later, Marcia began by saying that she had taken a pill "to relax myself." She appeared relaxed, and she indicated that she could now talk more freely. Near the close of the session she related how, before her 17th birthday, her father had come home drunk and begun hitting her mother and brother. She had yelled that she hated him, and he had chased her into a different part of the house, torn her dress off, and beaten her. Without actually saying what happened next, she exclaimed, "I cried and screamed, but no one came to help. God, he could have been killing me. I didn't know what he was doing, but I felt guilty." The session was terminated shortly after this outburst, nothing new having been added.

Marcia called and canceled the following appointment, but her minister also called. She had talked with him two or three times after this last session and had cried considerably. She had then told him the same story and had indicated that she wanted him to call and tell me what had happened. She still had not voiced the word "rape." When I saw her about a week later, she again related the events of the scene with her father, and this time she was able to actually say that he had raped her. Her therapy continued for about five more months, focusing to some extent on her developing interest in a young man she had been dating and on how that interest might be affected by her feelings about the rape incident.

This account has been related in some detail in order to emphasize the distinctive nature of incestuous rape. Of course, Marcia had reached a maladaptive resolution of her crisis at the time of the rape incident itself. Even at the time I saw her, over a year later, she was still not able, at first, to relate the incident. Although her dreams included both sexual symbolism and the theme of fear of male figures, she was not consciously aware of their implications. She was not ready to admit her feelings about this violent and traumatic experience into conscious awareness. Some of the threat she felt was related to the ambivalence of the sexual feelings she experienced in the rape itself. When she finally admitted these feelings into her conscious awareness, including her feelings of guilt about having experienced some degree of pleasure during the incident, she still needed considerable time in therapy to clarify her fearful responses and to reach some reintegration of her life. My counseling with her represented therapeutic interventions rather than strictly crisis intervention.

Homosexual Rape as a Special Problem

The increasing incidence of homosexual rape points up still another dimension of the psychosocial problem of rape. Some of the dynamics of significant loss are similar to those experienced by any victim of rape, and the psychological scars that can result require counseling and psychotherapeutic attention.

Since my direct counseling experience with victims of homosexual rape is limited, I will not discuss this problem in detail here. It should be noted, however, that homosexual rape is a serious social problem, especially in penal institutions. The opportunity for crisis intervention with the victims of prison rapes depends entirely on the counseling resources of the penal institution. Rarely will an individual be seen in any counseling outside the jail or prison within the six- to eight-week period following a homosexual rape. In the rare instances in which the victims seek psychological help some months after the attack, they usually need the assistance of a professional psychotherapist.

Additional Sources

As I have noted, the problem of rape is extremely complex, and counselors may want to turn to some additional sources of information on this subject. Macdonald's book (1975) provides an excellent reference work on the various kinds of rape. It includes an extensive collection of case histories in the victims' own words, taken from actual police reports. Anyone who has experienced rape or who will work with rape victims should find this volume helpful in enlarging his or her understanding of the dynamics of rape and its consequences. In addition, Macdonald's report on the studies of Sutherland and Scherl, which was summarized earlier in this chapter, provides a helpful model for crisis intervention with rape victims.

Although the identification of the phases of responses to rape found in Macdonald is helpful, the book can profitably be supplemented by *Against Rape* (Medea & Thompson, 1974). These authors do not provide a balanced view of the whole problem, but they do treat the problems of rape victims and their families with skill and sensitivity. A third publication, *Rape Intervention Resource Manual* (Mills, 1977), may also be a helpful tool in counseling with rape victims.

EXPERIENTIAL TRAINING

I. Suggestions to the Instructor

The losses experienced in miscarriage, abortion, and rape are akin to those suffered in radical changes in body image, and all of these crises are contractive. Hence, the following experiential exercises are similar to those of the two preceding chapters.

II. Experiential Exercises

A. The class forms triads. Within each triad, decide who will take the initial roles of counselor, counselee, and observer.

B. Here are two suggested role-play situations:

1. A woman has consulted a counselor about securing an abortion. She had some questions about it when she was talking to her physician and decided to explore some of her feelings with a counselor. She is 25 years old and single. She does not intend to marry the man by whom she became pregnant. She had attended church as a child, but her parents had never been active in the church, and she has not attended services since her junior-high-school years. She is self-supporting and has been working as a secretary in a fairly well-paying position. She does want to get married sometime, but she learned after becoming pregnant that her lover is married, and she feels betrayed by him.

2. A woman is brought to an emergency room at the local hospital after having been raped. She had met the rapist at a party, and he had come up to her apartment to make a telephone call after taking her home. She related that he stayed after the phone call and tried to get her to go to bed with him. When she refused, he threatened her and she screamed. He quieted her screams by threats and proceeded to rape her, but neighbors who had heard her screams called the police, and the man was arrested. The police asked her to go with them to the hospital, and she is presently seated with a nurse who will talk with her before the physician examines her.

C. Choose one of these roles and tell your story to the counselor in your triad for about five minutes; then get feedback from the observer.

D. The observer should remember to secure information from both the counselor and counselee:
   1. Questions to the counselee: Did you feel heard? How could the counselor have helped you more effectively? How do you feel about the counselor now? Other questions?
   2. Questions to the counselor: Do you feel that you heard the counselee? What was left unfinished in the counseling? How do you feel about the counselee now? Other questions?
E. Switch roles and repeat the process so that each one will have the opportunity of playing each role.
F. Each observer should then share his or her own feedback on the process of the counseling.
G. Additional role-playing of crises related to miscarriage, abortion, and rape may be designed to meet special counseling needs.

The Crisis of Dying

It is a commonplace that the American way of dealing with dying is to avoid the whole issue. Evelyn Waugh's novel *The Loved One* satirized this denial of reality through a gross caricature of commercial morticians. Of course, the psychological defense of denial is not a recent phenomenon. As the 17th-century philosopher Pascal once observed, "Since men could not do away with death, they decided not to think about it." However, contemporary psychology, psychiatry, and medicine are beginning to say a great deal about death and the dying experience. I recall a group of us who were interested in relating psychology and religion gathered in my apartment with Herman Feifel to discuss some research he was then engaged in on attitudes toward death. At the time—the year was about 1955— the literature on the subject was very limited. Publication of Feifel's work and that of others in *The Meaning of Death* in 1959 was followed by the appearance of numerous articles and books that have added significantly to the literature on death and dying.

There are two basic dimensions to the problem of death within a discussion of crisis: the crisis of the dying person and the crisis of the bereaved. Although these two experiences are obviously different in nature, they do share the common element of the experience of a significant and ultimate loss.

The present interest in the subject of the dying experience is evidence of a serious problem for which our culture has not adequately provided. However, it is also a hopeful sign. At the same time that dying has become dehumanized through cultural and technological developments, the increased attention given to it by psychology and medicine is an indication of possible change.

It is ironic that the very goal of prolonging life has led to the adoption of methods that have dehumanized dying persons.

In the name of the best medical care, dying persons are often removed from familiar surroundings and placed in strange, antiseptic environments that have little resemblance to their usual milieus. Their new environments are strange both physically and psychologically. Patients not only are deprived of a familiar home and furnishings but may also be denied the presence of family and friends. The tendency of modern medical technology to strip dying persons of their dignity is compounded by dehumanizing cultural practices. Family and friends may distance themselves from or actually shun dying persons, who remind them of their own eventual death. At the very least, they may shun any talk about death, presumably to save the dying from the pain of confronting their reality. In all probability, however, the ones being protected are not the dying at all but the family members and friends, who are afraid of being left alone or of being reminded of their own mortality.

PROVIDING A SUPPORTIVE ENVIRONMENT FOR DYING PERSONS

In any work with dying persons, a primary task of counselors is the securing of emotional support from the significant other persons in the patients' environment. These interventions include preparing the families and friends of dying persons for their task of establishing a supportive environment. Support from loved ones can enable persons to cope with the awesome reality of their dying.

The first step in providing a supportive environment for the dying consists of helping the significant other persons in their lives to cope with their own feelings about the threat they are experiencing. This threat often includes fears about being left alone, or *separation anxiety.*

I recall an experience of my own that still elicits some feelings of discomfort. I have forgotten the details of the experience, but I clearly remember the impact on my feelings. On one occasion in the late stages of my first wife's terminal illness, I was in some way being overly solicitous toward her. Her mother had not been able to deal with my wife's open confronting of her own dying, and on this occasion I, too, was treating her differently. I vividly recall my wife's pained response to my denial of my own feelings: "Oh *no*, Glenn, not you too." Even though I have tried to recapture what happened just before and after her response, I have never been able to do so. The meaning of that communication, however, was, and continues to be, clear to me. Because of my denial of my own feelings about her dying, I was distancing myself from her to protect *myself*, not her. I was experiencing the anxiety of being separated from her and being left alone, and I was responding to these feelings by protecting *myself.*

The second step in establishing a supportive environment for the dying involves preparing the significant other persons for their own dying. The dying person reminds them of the threat of their own death. Consequently, interventions should include open discussions about death and the experience of dying in order to increase their ability to face their own reality. Such discussions may provide some experiential basis for the development of an attitude of openness toward death. Experiential learning can open the door to an awareness of both the potential threat and the meaning of the dying process.

The next step relates to the first two steps and includes developing an attitude of openness to talking about death. Of course, openness to talking about death does not mean simply initiating such discussions with the dying person, but it does mean being prepared to talk about death and dying when the patient shows some readiness to do so. Some terminally ill patients are at the stage of denial, and the initiation of talk about death would only become another pressure with which they would have to cope. Indeed, some dying persons may never give up the defense of denial as a means of coping. In a sense they simply choose to ignore the truth about their condition. If that strategy enables them to cope with their crisis, it becomes a coping skill that fulfills its function of enabling the human spirit to survive the indignities that accompany dying. However, contrary to the beliefs of some health professionals who work with dying patients, Elizabeth Kubler-Ross (1969) reported that, out of more than 200 dying patients, only 2% rejected an opportunity to discuss their dying, and she noted no indications of adverse reactions to her interviews with them. On the other hand, she noted many psychopathological reactions among the professional staff observing the interviews. Consequently, although an openness to talking about death may not involve initiating talk about it, it does involve allowing and, at times, encouraging dying persons to talk about themselves and their dying.

ATTITUDES TOWARD DEATH

The attitude of patients toward their own death varies with individual and cultural differences. The most prevalent attitude in our culture has involved a denial of the reality of death. Ready access to hospitals, utilization of nursing homes for the aged, and even the development of retirement homes and communities have effectively removed the reality of death from ordinary experience. Preventive-health measures such as immunization and vaccination, as well as the decreasing infant-mortality rate, have also helped to shield most families from the reality of death in their midst. The cultural denial of death's reality is even reflected in our vocabulary, in such euphemisms as "passing on" and "passing away."

These cultural influences obviously affect the experience of dying persons. However, those who are dying have the dubious advantage of being confronted with a reality they cannot easily evade. When denial is no longer a viable defense, in some ways it is easier to confront reality for what it is. Thus, people who live in ghettos know the realities of violence and of life and death in ways that most surburban, middle-class persons will never understand. In a similar way, the dying have the advantage of facing actual death now. For them, it is no longer a potential threat in the distant future.

Individual responses to the fact of death are also influenced by a variety of religious and psychological factors. In regard to religious factors, there is no evidence of any significant influence of professed religious dogma. Religious attitudes and values are potent influences only to the extent that they have been internalized and in some way related to an individual's attitudes toward life. An integrating view of life, whether religious or philosophical in origin, can significantly influence attitudes toward death. Once people can celebrate life, they are able to accept death as an inevitable experience—and sometimes as a meaningful experience as well.

Some form of anxiety is likely to be experienced by almost any dying person. The only common exceptions are aged persons, among whom a lack of anxiety is the norm rather than the exception. There is no precise differentiation between various forms of anxiety, and no descriptive statement about a person can possibly provide a discrete diagnosis. Nevertheless, different expressions of anxiety may be identified for the sake of clarity, so long as it is understood that no one person reflects a precise form of anxiety reaction.

In their attitudes toward death, some persons manifest what can only be described as *neurotic* anxiety. They have been consistently afraid of life and its possibilities. Such anxiety may be of the free-floating variety and is reflected in a generalized fearfulness of death. It may be expressed in the specific fear of punishment by God or in a more generalized anxiety about a negative sense of self-worth.

Attitudes toward death may also include what Paul Tillich (1952) has identified as *ontological* anxiety. This form of anxiety is normal for an emotionally healthy person. Indeed, only to the degree that people are able to tolerate the threat of the ambiguity and contingency of life will they be able to experience the threat of ontological anxiety. This form of anxiety is the felt threat of non-being. It is a response to the threat that death means that a person will no longer *be*. This threat relates to our awareness of our location in existence and of our bodies as filling a certain measurable space, as well as to our identification of our selves and even to a transcending of ourselves in some kind of trans-personal experience. The perception of this threat is the result of a developing sensitivity to the awesome reality of life and death.

Closely aligned to, and perhaps impossible to separate from, ontological anxiety is *existential* anxiety. Existential anxiety includes the threat of no longer being, but, more specifically, it represents the threat of no longer being in terms of personal goals. This tends to be the predominant anxiety of younger persons who are dying. Existential anxiety also includes the threat of unfulfilled commitments, especially in relation to one's small children.

Again, I recall a personal experience. Louise and I had known about the terminal status of her cancer for more than six months prior to her death. Our children were 1 and 4 years of age at the time of this discovery, nearly 13 years ago. I recall the vivid memory of crying together as we watched the screen adaptation of James Agee's tender story, *A Death in the Family*. The story captured some of the pain and anxiety of unfulfilled commitments that we experienced.

RESPONSES OF DYING PERSONS

An understanding of the feelings and conflicting emotions of dying persons is requisite for any psychological work with them. Their special vulnerability increases the importance of understanding the dynamics of their experience. Dying persons generally show similar patterns of responses to their experience, but each, of course, experiences this event in his or her own idiosyncratic way.

First of all, persons tend to respond to their dying experience differently according to age. Since needs differ in the various developmental stages of life, it is reasonable to expect that responses to dying will vary with those needs and with the intellectual and emotional ability to understand them. The developmental stages identified by Erikson (see Chapter 6) provide a focus for the differentiation of responses according to developmental or maturational needs.

Infancy and Early Childhood

Infancy. The primary relationship of infants and very young children is with their mothers. Their needs are related to the development of *trust and mistrust*—learning both how to entrust themselves to this significant other person and when to mistrust her. The discomfort of an illness may lead to the development of some mistrust; essentially, however, the response of infants to the dying experience is limited to the discomfort of the disease and the treatment procedures. The only response that mothers or mother surrogates can make is to continue to meet the basic physical and emotional needs. Continuing to satisfy infants' hunger, relieve their discomfort, and hold them with tenderness fulfills their crucial needs. Nevertheless, parents will need to be prepared for the innate physiological drive to maintain life as long as possible. At this point, parents will need emotional support as they attempt to cope with their own feelings of helplessness.

Ages 2 to 6. In the next developmental stage, a child is primarily related to both parents and is beginning to develop *self-control and a sense of autonomy*. A parent reported her experience with her 3-year-old son, who was dying of leukemia. On regaining consciousness from a coma, he looked up at his mother and said firmly "You dummy." In a gesture of independence and autonomy, he seemed to be expressing the feeling that he was in control of himself and that his mother was dumb because she was not able to take the pain away.

A debilitating illness may threaten the usual development of autonomy, since the child is unable to depend upon himself or herself or to control the course of the illness. Nevertheless, at this stage children are still responding to their dying in terms of the physical pain of the disease and the discomfort of the treatment procedures. Parental responses are limited to respecting and accepting the increasing sense of independence while realizing the strong need for dependence and reassurance. Chil-

dren in a hospital need to be reassured of their parents' love—
by their presence, as much as possible, and by their words of
reassurance that they will be taken care of. They need the security of a mother or mother surrogate to assure themselves of
feelings of safety among all the strangers in the hospital.

Preschool children have begun to relate to the family as a
whole and are beginning to develop both *initiative and a sense
of guilt.* Children dying during this stage may be threatened by
being deprived of the usual development of initiative and may
experience some guilt, seeing their illness as a punishment. If
the seriousness of their condition necessitates removal from the
home, they will suffer from the deprivation of parents and siblings and may interpret the hospitalization as punishment. A
preschool child is developing a sense of what is "me" and what
is "not me" and thus is beginning to recognize the possibility
of no longer "being." Although children normally deny the reality of this possibility, there are times when these feelings cannot
be totally denied. The normal nightmares of preschool children
may come to the surface when they are physically and psychologically exhausted by the pain and discomfort caused by their
physical condition or by the treatment procedures. Since they
are dependent upon their parents' responses, they may become
sad and depressed as they experience their parents' feelings. Although they may be unaware of why they are fearful or sad, they
will usually reflect the feelings of their parents.

Parents may feel less helpless to the degree that they can
participate in the treatment program. Hence, if parents can be
helped to cope with their own feelings and to direct their anxieties into helping their children, the children will be less anxious and more able to cope with their own feelings. Parents can
also help children to feel less anxious by verbal reassurance and
by surrounding them with familiar possessions, such as their
favorite toys. Although dying children may express anger toward
other children in the hospital, toward the hospital staff, and toward their parents, they are simply expressing the normal feelings of dying persons. Easson (1971) suggests that children who
ask "Am I going to die?" should be given a general answer to
the effect that everyone has to die sometime but that they are
not going to die today or tomorrow. Since preschool children
live in the here-and-now, they will be reassured, and the parents
or hospital staff will have been honest. If children ask whether
a treatment procedure is going to hurt, they should be given the
honest answer that it will hurt somewhat, but they should also

be reassured that the doctor will complete the treatment as soon as possible. Knowing the schedule of their medication and of their parents' visits is also helpful to children. If, in the final moments, a child asks whether he is dying, he can be answered honestly, but with the parents' reassurance that they will look after him and take care of him.

Later Childhood

Grade-school children are involved in establishing themselves in the neighborhood and school and in developing a sense of *competence.* In response to dying, these children may experience a deprivation of their relationships with peers and of their developing sense of competence. Being deprived of relationships with peers will, in all likelihood, contribute to feelings of loneliness and inferiority. With their increasing sense of independence, children at this stage are able to demonstrate a sense of individuality; nevertheless, they are still very much dependent upon parents and family. Because of their increasing sense of individuality, grade-school children can fantasize their own death, and they are more able to understand the possibility of their own dying. Hospitalized children may be frightened and lonely, and they may need reassurance that their illness is not their fault and that their parents and siblings miss them.

With their increasing ability to conceptualize, these children are also able to understand medical diagnosis and its meaning for their condition. As Easson (1971) describes it, "The young child learns the hospital routine and the significance of the different procedures very quickly. If a hospital unit is devoted to the treatment of one specific disease, the grade school child learns within a matter of hours what his situation means" (p. 47).[1] Children who reflect such understanding need to be able to turn to their families for security and comfort during their dying. In Easson's words:

> When the grade school child asks about the reality of his situation, he should be told the truth in terms that he can use. In a simple, basic fashion the meaning of his diagnosis can be explained. If he asks the prognosis for his disease, he should be given a firm but general answer. He can be told quite directly that no specific time in terms of actual days or months can be stated,

[1]From *The Dying Child,* by William M. Easson, 1971. This and all other quotations from this source are reprinted courtesy of Charles C Thomas, Publisher, Springfield, Illinois.

because each individual and each illness is different. His cooperation can be enlisted in the treatment procedures which can be explained to him. When death is near and inevitable, the child's questions should be responded to with truth. The grade school child has the emotional ability to face the prospect of his death and to reach out to his parents and his family for comfort and understanding [p. 48].

If parents share some religious tradition, religious symbols may be meaningful to the child. Since grade-school children begin to look for Someone or Something in which to believe, feelings and beliefs about God may provide some emotional support that will enable them to cope with a reality that cannot be changed. However, any religious reference is always transmitted to a child through its meaning to the parents.

Adolescence

Adolescents are busily involved in establishing peer relationships in the struggle to work out their identities. The trauma of dying frustrates adolescents' identity formation with *diffusion* and *role confusion*. They are vulnerable to losing their sense of self, and they will certainly suffer from the deprivation of peer support.

Adolescents pride themselves on the development of independence, but their dying robs them of both a present and any future independence. A terminal illness or critical accident places them once again in a dependent position, and they may react to this anxiety with anger and rage. Although they may direct their anger toward those whom they love, they also need these same persons to be with them and to stand alongside them. They may feel guilty about their feelings of anger and may feel that God is somehow administering the ultimate punishment for some unforgivable sin.

At this very time in which adolescents are separating themselves from their parents, they may also be cut off from the peer support they would normally receive. Although adolescents can express an amazing degree of compassion for injured members of their peer group, they often are severely threatened by the impending death of a friend or acquaintance. Hence, they may withdraw emotionally from any encounter with a dying friend. In this withdrawal they merely manifest the very human tendency to use denial as a way of avoiding the intensity of emotional pain precipitated by the fact of death. As Easson (1971) observed, "They are building their own strengths and solidifying their own opinions. Death, and especially the death of a friend and someone their own age, emphasizes their own basic vulnerability and fragility" (p. 54). Although there are instances of considerable peer support, dying adolescents generally tend to be very lonely. In the midst of this loneliness, they may reject their parents' expressions of love and concern, but they do so essentially because of their developmental need to become independent. Their physical dependency reminds them of the threat of the ultimate loss of control of themselves and of their independence. They are painfully affirming themselves. They may toss gifts or unopened letters aside in purposeful disdain, but they still need the concern and support of those whom they love. If they are aware of any physical disfigurement or deformity, they may reject peers because they cannot bear such a threat to their identity, but they still need others' concern.

In the actual process of dying, adolescents may become so weak physically that they allow themselves to be cared for without experiencing a loss of a sense of identity and individuality. However, at this juncture, both the family and the hospital staff need to be sensitive to providing care without threatening self-respect. The questions young persons ask about their condition will usually indicate the kinds of answers they wish. If they need to deny the ultimate truth, their need should be respected. If they ask "How long do I have to live?" there is every indication that they feel able to cope with the implications of the answer. In this case, they deserve a direct answer, but one that does not rob them of all hope of an extension of time. It is simple honesty to state that, since individuals and illnesses differ, there are no definite time limits to one's life. At the same time, the young person is shown the respect of receiving a direct answer to a painful question.

Young Adulthood

Young adults respond to their dying in ways shared by other adults, as discussed later. In terms of specific maturational tasks, their dying represents a loss of intimacy with a lover or spouse and perhaps with young children. They are at the beginning of a new stage of life in which they are now able to *affiliate* and to share life goals with another person or persons. In dying, they experience the loss of the investment of life and values. They are able to express feelings of closeness to their family, and they may allow themselves to be cared for. Their dying represents the loss of the significant and meaningful relationships they have established, especially if there is a lover or spouse involved. If there is a child, they may want to see their life somehow related to the continuing life of their child. The particular poignancy of young adults' dying is that they have just arrived completely as adult persons and may have begun forming their own families through marriage.

Middle and Late Adulthood

Those in the middle-adulthood stage are involved in the *productive contributions* they are making to their families and in their careers. Dying threatens that sense of productivity. They may become absorbed in themselves, or they may overcompensate by attempting an unrealistically high productivity. This latter response may be primarily an expression of denial, as in the case of a person in the final stages of a terminal disease who proposes undertaking a new business enterprise that would involve high expectations even of a person in excellent health.

In the later years, adults are involved in establishing a sense of *integrity* in relation to themselves and others. Dying before they are ready to renounce life may involve feelings of despair over the meaning of the totality of life. Deprived of the experiencing of the integrity of their lives, older adults may despair and may even take a hand in terminating their lives prematurely.

This analysis of the differing responses to dying according to the ages of patients consists of broad generalizations that are helpful in identifying tendencies toward particular kinds of responses. Such an analysis may provide some focus for counselor interventions, but it is not intended to indicate that everyone will respond according to a given pattern. All persons respond to their dying in their own idiosyncratic ways.

STAGES IN RESPONSES OF DYING ADULTS

After interviewing and working with more than 200 dying patients, Kubler-Ross (1969) outlined several stages of adult responses to the diagnosis of a terminal illness.

Disbelief

The first response identified by Kubler-Ross is *disbelief* or *denial:* "No, not me, it can't be true." Of course, the psychological defense of denial can be a helpful coping mechanism, especially in the early stages of awareness of a terminal disease. After all, a defense mechanism is precisely that—a defense erected purposely, if unconsciously, as a means of protection. Defenses protect individuals who are too threatened to function in a difficult situation. The psychological defense of denial may be called upon from time to time throughout the dying process and may serve a very useful purpose. In its extreme form, it can create problems both for dying persons and for their families; however, in most cases, dying persons utilize this defense sparingly. It is more likely to be used extensively by the family and the hospital staff than by the patient. The use of denial by the family and hospital staff increases the isolation of a dying person. They will avoid the dying person precisely because he or she reminds them of the reality they are attempting to deny.

Counselors of dying persons need to be sensitive to, and understanding of, the defense of denial. Dying persons have the right to know the truth, but those who need to deny the reality of their condition deserve to have their feelings respected. If counselors understand the dynamics of this defense mechanism, they will respect it.

Anger

The next stage of response is *anger*. Patients' anger may be expressed through impatience with those involved in their care; thus, the doctors and nurses are either "too attentive" or "not attentive enough." Little things may become irritating. Dying persons may show ingratitude toward their physicians and irascibility toward their families. Part of this unpleasantness may be expressive of an ambivalence experienced toward those who will survive them.

Although these expressions of anger may be difficult to understand, both family members and those professionals providing medical and counseling care need to be sensitive to the resentment dying persons may experience. Their resentment may be expressed directly toward those closest to them or toward God or Fate for allowing such a situation to occur.

Bargaining

The third stage in the responses to dying identified by Kubler-Ross is *bargaining*. In this stage, the dying bargain with God or Fate for just one more chance—or for a postponement of death so that they will have time for something that represents considerable significance to them. In her analysis of the dynamics of this stage, Kubler-Ross identified some elements of "quiet guilt" (p. 84). It is important to identify this pattern of response when it occurs, since the family or a counselor should be sensitive to the need of a patient to work out this guilt. Dying persons may experience neurotic guilt over some imagined sin or offense against some person or against God, or they may feel an existential form of guilt over unfulfilled life goals. In either instance, they need to have the opportunity to work through their guilt feelings.

The stage of bargaining is not as prevalent as some of the other stages. Although I have worked with many dying persons, I have observed it clearly in only a few instances. One instance occurred during World War II, while I was a minister of a church. One of the members of the church had been confined to her home with the diagnosis of cancer. Her son was a prisoner of war, captured at Bataan in the Philippines. As atrocity stories about the "Bataan Death March" circulated, she suffered the painful anxiety of not knowing the health or well-being of her son, in addition to her own physical pain. Her bargain took the form "If only God will let me live long enough to see my son again." Later it changed to "If only I can live long enough to know that he is well." I also recall that my wife's expressions of "bargaining" were more akin to an expression of hope that she would live long enough to see the children through early childhood.

I believe that the "bargaining stage" may be more complex than is indicated in Kubler-Ross' brief description of it. In addition to the "quiet guilt" noted by Kubler-Ross, I see elements of "quiet hope." Although the bargaining stage may involve some wishful thinking, it essentially involves all the complexity of the meaning of hope. The experience of hope integrates the intuitive act of wishing with a philosophical or religious belief system that enhances and extends the possibilities of any human situation. Furthermore, one element in bargaining may be the expression of the defense of denial with respect to the finality of the medical diagnosis. At any rate, the dynamics of this stage merit further analysis and research.

Depression

The next stage of responses is *depression*. When the defense mechanism of denial in its various forms is no longer viable, acceptance of the stark reality of impending death usually results in depressive reactions. Although depressive responses to dying are to be expected of any normal person, Kubler-Ross has made a helpful distinction between two different phases of the dying person's depression. She identified the first phase as a "reactive depression" (p. 86). In this phase, the person's depressive reactions are related to some loss *that has already been experienced.* A woman who has lost her breast in a radical mastectomy, for example, will need to develop ways of coping with this significant loss. Similarly, the loss of a man's ability to fulfill his role in the family as the result of an illness requires the development of psychological mechanisms to cope with that particular loss. For example, being assured that the family can take care of themselves in the event of his death can relieve him of this source of anxiety. The function of a counselor in this phase is to encourage the patient and to explore constructive ways of compensating for the loss. Counselors will need to identify and support those resources within patients that affirm life and its possibilities.

The second phase of depression is the reaction of the individual to the *impending* loss. In this phase, facilitating the expression of the patient's feelings is more important than any clarification of issues or offer of reassurance. At this juncture, it is appropriate simply to listen to the dying person's expression of feelings and to encourage any talking about them. Listening is an appropriate intervention precisely because it is relevant to the emotions and feelings of the dying person. Supporting the expression of feelings concerning the impending loss of self and of others is an anticipatory counselor action. This depression begins with real loss in the here-and-now but extends to that future time when the loss will be actualized.

Acceptance

The final stage of responses identified by Kubler-Ross is *acceptance.* If dying persons have had the time and opportunity to work through the feelings of the other stages, they will be able to experience some acceptance of a reality that is impossible to ignore. This acceptance is not just a tired resignation after a long struggle; nor is it a happy sense of accepting a reality in which the patient finds the joy of ultimate fulfillment. It is more an emotionless acceptance of the real situation, but one that includes a sense of peace and dignity.

I think that Kubler-Ross is correct in stating that this final stage may be the most difficult one for the families of dying persons. Despite the fact that I had observed the reality of such acceptance several times, I was totally unprepared to experience it when the dying person was my own wife. I have only recently discovered my remembrance of the three nights immediately prior to my wife's death. On the first night, Louise seemed to be somewhat uninterested in what was going on at home. On the second, she didn't seem to be as interested in the children as she had been in the past, and they, as young children do, quickly lost interest in being in her room. On the third and final night, she had just been heavily sedated when the children and I arrived, and I only looked in on her and left after a moment. I now recall that, although I felt disappointed that she was not awake, I was also somewhat relieved. The feeling of relief was a painful memory that I had successfully blocked, because she died the next morning. I now understand that my feeling of relief was at least in part related to my inability to understand some of her responses of acceptance. I think I had anticipated a kind of gradual unfolding of a mutually strengthening experience in the final days of her life. Instead, she accepted her loss of every-thing better than I could accept my loss of her. She had done her preparatory grief work better than I, and she was ready to let it all go. Whereas she had experienced some kind of closure to our life together, I had not. The need to bring a close to this part of my life remained as some of my unfinished grief work for a few years following her death.

The designation of these responses to dying as "stages" does not mean that they are clearly observed in all dying per-sons. Further, they are not discrete episodes that occur in se-quential fashion. A person can experience more than one stage at the same time, and responses may alternate between one stage and another. In addition, the feelings of a particular stage may be experienced over and over again. For example, one aspect of a person's anger may be completely expressed at one time, while another segment of anger surfaces later. The "stages" are simply common coping mechanisms that may be used in con-junction with other mechanisms. Moreover, they are used in ways that meet the unique needs of each individual. As already noted, each person approaches the experience of dying in his or her own highly idiosyncratic manner. Any attempt to delineate a pattern in responses to dying is simply an attempt to describe the possibilities utilized by the human spirit in coping with the ultimate crisis.

EXPERIENTIAL TRAINING

Counselors are threatened not only when they encounter dying persons but also when they confront powerful feelings about their own dying. To illustrate the threat posed by one's own death and dying, it may be helpful to relate an experience I had a few years ago. I had delivered a lecture on "Dying and Bereavement" at the University of California, San Diego, as one of a series of lectures on counseling with persons in crises. About 100 persons with varying degrees of involvement in mental health and paraprofessional counseling were enrolled in the course. They included teachers, ministers, nurses, probation officers, social workers, mental-health workers, and others, some of whom appeared to be primarily interested in ways to cope with their own crises. About a month after the lecture, I received a letter from the coordinator of the course that included the following comments:

> What was interesting to me was the aftermath in the next two weeks. Never in my experience has there been a response so totally divided; some people thought that your presentation was the most fantastic and stimulating discussion of the topic that they had ever heard, while others were extremely disappointed that we had "wasted the evening." When I raised the question with the class as to why there was such a division of opinion in response to your presentation, we got into some very interesting areas. Some people admitted that they had gone home and, having thought about it, admitted that they were extremely uneasy during the discussion and wished that we had not chosen to talk about it. Others were extremely belligerent in response to the issues raised the following class session. When some members of the class pointed out that belligerent spirit, they raised the question as to how well the people in the class were handling the topic of death. What was extremely interesting to me was the number of people who came up to me at break-time or at the conclusion of the class and admitted that they had done such things as not telling their spouses what the subject matter of the evening's lecture had been, or had not gone over their notes, or had refused to check any books out of the library dealing with the topic of death.[2]

I. Suggestions to the Instructor

To the degree that counselors deny the threat of their own

[2]Leslie J. Atkinson, personal communication, 1973.

dying, they are unable to counsel effectively with dying or bereaved persons. On the other hand, making contact with their feelings about their own dying may enable them to develop empathy with the dying and the bereaved. One of the guided fantasies that has been helpful in facilitating an understanding and acceptance of the idea of death is the fantasy of one's own dying experience. Each class member should make a deliberate decision whether or not to participate in this exercise.

II. Experiential Exercises

   A. Those who decide to participate should form dyads.
   1. Make yourself comfortable, relax your body, close your eyes, and open yourself to your imagination.
   2. Select the particular manner of your "dying."
   3. Use about five minutes of silence to get in touch with your feelings and to experience the fantasy of your own dying.
   4. The leader of the guided fantasy may direct questions to the participants: How do you feel right now? Where are you in your fantasy? What is it like there? What is the weather like? What time of day is it? Are you alone, or is someone with you? If someone is with you, who is it? What kind of an experience are you having now? What are you experiencing in relation to the significant persons in your life?
   5. Take ten seconds to become your normal self again, and return to this room with your class. When you are ready, open your eyes and rejoin your partner.
   B. With your partner, decide which of you is to talk first about his or her experiences and which will listen. After a few minutes, switch roles.
   C. Following the meeting of the dyads, some persons may want to share their experiences with the class as a whole. Discussion in the class may include what persons have learned about themselves that may enhance their understanding of death and dying and of the ways in which to counsel with dying and bereaved persons.

Bereavement Crises

An understanding of the dying experience provides the necessary basis for understanding and working with bereaved persons. In some ways, the experiences of the bereaved are very similar to those of dying persons. Like the dying, they must struggle to develop ways of coping with a significant loss even as they are confronted with the cultural denial of death's reality. And, like the dying, they need to prepare for their own grief work.

PREVENTIVE EDUCATION

Since cultural and technological developments have provided a context in which the stark reality of death may be denied, most people approach both the dying and grieving experiences with little preparation. From his perspective as a psychiatrist, Kurt Eissler (1955) suggested the need for "orthonasia"—preventive education for children about the nature and the reality of death. Adequate preparation for the universal experiences of bereavement and dying may prevent the development of crises and enable persons to cope adaptively with these experiences of loss.

Preventive education with children includes parents' recognition of the need to help their children face the fact of death instead of protecting them from painful grief work. A *developmental* approach to education about death includes preparing individuals to cope with grief in ways appropriate to their ages.

A gradual unfolding of the meaning of death was experienced by Peter, a young clergyman. The experiences he recalled were not all instances of human death, but they all included experiences of significant loss. Coping with these losses gave Peter an increasing awareness of the dimensions of grief work and provided him with the skills he used in adult life to cope with the death of a friend.

Peter's earliest experience of loss occurred when his dog died after being hit by a car. His pet's sudden and violent death was a shock to the 6-year-old boy, and Peter recalled the sad ritual of placing him in a box, burying him, and setting a wooden marker on the grave. Even though the death of his pet was not as serious as the loss of a human life, it did provide a significant learning experience. When such incidents occur, parents can use them to introduce children to the fact of death and the process of dying. Despite parents' good intentions, it is harmful to try to protect children from the pain associated with experiences of this kind.

Peter's next experience with death occurred when his maternal grandfather died. Peter was about 7 at the time. His grandfather had been living up the street from his home. Peter remembered how his mother told him that Grandpa had died and how it seemed to be all right, because his grandfather was old and tired. He recalled missing him, but he had been ill for several months, and his death was accepted by the family as something that was natural and not to be feared.

During his early adolescence, Peter's paternal grandparents died in a city some distance from his home, and he retained only faint recollections of attending the funerals. They were in their eighties and had both been confined to their beds for some months. Even in his early teens, Peter seems to have understood that people could be ready for death and that it could be natural and expected.

Peter's maternal grandmother died during his first year in college. She was in her nineties, but he had felt especially close to her, since she had lived in his family's home for several years. Consequently, even though her death was expected, and even though she was ready for it, it occasioned Peter's first adult grieving. A year later, he experienced his first trauma involving death when a close friend whom he had known in high school died after developing complications following an emergency appendectomy.

Peter related that these experiences, extending from childhood through young adulthood, helped to prepare him for the difficult role of pastor and counselor to dying and bereaved persons, as well as for his own future grief work. A developmental sequence of increasingly difficult grief crises enabled him to gradually deepen his understanding of dying and bereavement, and this understanding provided Peter with some resources for coping with more serious losses later in life.

The theory of the crisis-intervention approach includes the insight that developing a means of coping with one crisis increases the ability to cope with a more serious one later on. Thus, developing a coping mechanism in one experience of significant loss may increase a person's skill in coping with future losses and crisis situations.

THE GRIEF PROCESS

Work with grieving persons has traditionally been the domain of the clergy. Since they are called upon to conduct funeral or memorial services, they have direct relationships with bereaved persons beyond the confines of the particular congregations they serve. In addition, the developing field of pastoral psychology and the clinical training of chaplains have provided effective training for members of the clergy. Meanwhile, a careful study of the grief process was not made until Lindemann's pioneer study, published in 1944. As related in Chapter 2, Lindemann observed a multitude of bereaved persons and concluded that grief was a natural and necessary reaction to a significant loss. He further noted that those persons who were involved in active grief work during a *four-to-six-week period* following the death of their loved ones usually adapted successfully to their bereavement, while others developed psychiatric or psychosomatic illnesses.

Lindemann identified a series of phases of grief work, including, first, some somatic distress or complaint. The somatic symptom might be an inability to sleep or to eat, or a vague feeling of bodily discomfort. Second, the bereaved tended to become preoccupied with the image of the deceased. This reaction included reminiscences about the experiences they had shared. Third, there was evidence of guilt feelings. Everyone can recall ways in which they have failed a deceased loved one. Fourth, there were hostile reactions expressed toward God or Fate. Irrational hostile feelings were often directed against the deceased for deserting the bereaved person or for leaving him or her with the responsibility for small children or a difficult financial situation. Finally, the grieving person usually experienced a loss of his or her usual pattern of conduct. If, for example, a couple has always participated together in a bridge club or other social activity, the husband's death would change the wife's relationship to this activity, and she might well discontinue her participation in what had been a significant part of her life.

Lindemann's pioneer work has exercised a decisive influence upon the developing insight into the nature and importance of grief work. A generation of pastoral counselors have been trained to utilize the dynamics of the grief process in their pastoral work with bereaved persons. Other counselors need to recognize the importance of this process in preventive mental-health care. In my experience as a counselor, I have observed responses similar to those identified by Lindemann. The responses do not occur in any orderly sequence, and each individual experiences them in a highly idiosyncratic manner. Nevertheless, there is a pattern of responses common to persons experiencing bereavement.

In my own experience of grief as an adult, I had some time of preparation for my wife's death. I recall the anger I felt during the period of treatment for her brain tumor—anger at God for allowing anyone to suffer such terrible pain. It was an irrational kind of anger that lashed out in several directions. I also found myself talking about her in a variety of contexts, and it became evident to me only later that my preoccupation with her image provided some rehearsal of my grief feelings. I was aware of considerable energy during this time, as if my body had mobilized its resources to sustain an emotional impact. I directed considerable energy to the care of the children. I vividly recall my fierce determination to care for their physical and psychological needs and to provide for their welfare. Directing some of my energy to meet these everyday needs undoubtedly provided some relief from the continual awareness of grief.

However, despite the months of preparation for grief work, I experienced the event itself as a blow. A morning telephone call from our physician informed me of her death. Even though I cried freely at the time of his call, I continued to be close to tears whenever I thought about the fact that I had not been with her or able to say goodbye to her. For several years afterwards, whenever I thought of not being able to say goodbye to her, tears would involuntarily come to my eyes.

An additional dimension of a bereavement experience is the awareness of an anxiety that can only be termed *ontological*. A person who had been very much alive no longer *is*. Tillich identified this form of anxiety, but it is usually not understood until a person actually experiences it. Then it may evoke the kind of depth response of a painful "ah-ha!"

Bereaved persons who have had some time to prepare usually have a distinct advantage over people who experience the sudden and unexpected death of a significant other person. Even so, preparation for a death never fulfills or compensates for the actual grief work. Despite an intellectual understanding that the deceased no longer inhabits his or her body, it is often emotionally necessary for bereaved persons to actually view the body in the coffin. The integral relationship of persons to their bodies is more potent than any intellectual understanding that an individual is no longer related to his or her body. The intense motivation to view the body may be related both to the awesome reality of non-being and to the experience of separation anxiety. Since the threat of no longer being in relationship with the bereaved is so great, the viewing of the body is often necessary to alleviate some of the intensity of that anxiety.

When a death is unexpected, one of the early responses of the bereaved is shock and disbelief. An extreme expression of this response occurs when a bereaved person literally refuses to accept the reality of the death. Any such sudden news can lead to a crisis. Crises occur when individuals are confronted with situations too intense for their available coping mechanisms. If the intensity of a person's experience is combined with insufficient time in which to develop coping skills, he or she may be immobilized.

A young woman in college related the shock she experienced upon returning home from school one day and being notified of the death of her father. Although he had consistently enjoyed excellent health and had never before suffered a heart attack, he had died suddenly of a massive coronary. At first, she acted as if nothing had happened, even attending a social occasion at the school that evening. People remarked how well she was reacting to the tragedy. That night she could not get to sleep, but she did not fully recognize the reality of her father's death until the next day.

Counselor interventions with persons who have experienced a sudden death in the family consist of encouraging the bereaved to talk about the deceased, accepting and encouraging the expression of feelings of anger and guilt, and encouraging the exploration of alternative ways of establishing or reestablishing patterns of conduct that may provide stability and emotional support. Counselors may also intervene by helping bereaved persons reestablish relationships with significant other persons and open the channels of communication through which emotional support may be provided.

Some of the funeral practices in rural areas of the United

States reflect the untutored wisdom of coping mechanisms. Although these practices are largely disappearing as the rural population moves to the cities, I recall observing, some years ago, the practice of keeping the open casket in the home while family, friends, and neighbors came to pay their respects. People gathered with the family, bringing food to the home, helping out with household chores, and visiting with the bereaved. Even where the practice is to place the casket in the mortuary, the bereaved often sit for hours in the room with the open casket while family and friends come to pay their respects and to visit with them. These visits are often accompanied by laughter as pleasant memories of the deceased are shared.

These practices reflect the wisdom of recognizing death's reality and illustrate the assistance that can be given to bereaved persons as they complete their grief work. The open casket can help persons cope gradually with the anxiety of not-being and with their separation anxiety. Bringing in food and helping with household chores express both a care for the grieving persons and a recognition that the usual patterns of conduct are disrupted by the loss of a significant other person. Visiting with the bereaved fulfills a need for emotional support and provides a context in which they are free to focus upon the image of the deceased by talking about him or her and by recalling pleasant memories of the past.

THE BEREAVEMENT EXPERIENCE OF CHILDREN

Children's bereavement is a special case within the larger problem of bereavement. It may be a commonplace that children are not adults in miniature, but adults often need to be reminded of it. Although we may know better, we tend to wonder why children can't be more like us.

In *A Death in the Family,* James Agee tells the story of a mother who tried to explain to her children what had happened to their father. While driving home from a nearby town, he had been killed in an accident. The mother got the news over the phone. Since he had failed to make it home for dinner as he had promised, the mother explained to the children "Daddy didn't come home. He will never come home because God took him." The mother was shocked when her little girl then asked matter-of-factly "You mean he's dead?" The mother thought her daughter was callous because she did not seem to respond to that news with much feeling but went on to talk about her father as if he were still alive.

To the child, an announcement of a death in the family is somewhat unreal. Small children may experience a degree of separation anxiety every time a parent leaves. A mother's leaving for a day may seem to be an eternity to a child. As a result of his definitive studies of child behavior, Gesell concluded that children from 1 to 3 years of age have little or no curiosity about death. At 4 or 5 years of age, when they have extended the network of their experiences, they may ask some questions about death. However, the reality of death still has limited emotional impact. Ordinarily, young children have not come to think of death as final or irreversible. For them, there is no clear difference between the fantasies of stories or cartoons, whose characters are never dead permanently, and the real world. Children learn that the persons they love leave for the market or for the office or for a weekend trip and always come back. Children cry when they leave and laugh when they return. Similarly, to them, a person who dies can come alive again.

Nevertheless, children's grief must be taken seriously. In the first place, they deserve to know just what is happening. Children are very sensitive to the emotional climate of the home, and they know when something has gone wrong. They can tolerate considerable pain, but they cannot handle the contradiction of a parent who is obviously upset emotionally and yet reassures them verbally that everything is all right. A child will *know* that something is wrong and will tend to imagine that it is his or her fault. Children tend to equate their feelings about events with the events themselves. If a little girl hides her head, she has made *you* disappear. If she says or thinks "I wish you were dead," and you actually die, she thinks that she has magically caused your death. Hence, it is important to give children a reasonable explanation of a death in the family, precisely because they need parental reassurance at this time.

Second, children need to have the opportunity to learn about death in a way that is appropriate to their developmental stage. Helping children to take advantage of early experiences of bereavement can enable them to develop skills for coping with adult grief later in life. John Steinbeck's poignant story *The Red Pony* provides an example of such an experience. It is the story of Jody, who must learn to say goodbye to an animal he has come to love. After his red pony dies, Jody tells his neighbor that *his* horse, Blackie, is also going to die. When the neighbor replies that all living things die, Jody says that that is why he is going to get an automobile—automobiles don't die. This remark, apart from expressing Jody's grief, also illustrates the defensive maneuver of a child trying to avoid the pain of bereavement.

Helping children to understand the issues of life and death involves encouraging their participation to the extent that they are able to understand. It involves answering their questions when they are ready to ask them. It includes sharing feelings at a child's level of understanding and being aware of the tendency to overanswer a child's question as a way of coping with one's own anxiety. It means being able to share deep feelings without overloading a child with the collapse of the adult upon whom the child depends for emotional security. A child readily understands tears, especially if the adult is able to verbalize that he or she is sad about the death of grandfather or of mother. Indeed, parents who are honest about their deep feelings teach their children that they deeply care about the one who has died. Freely talking about the deceased gives children an opportunity to internalize the reality of the death and the separation from the loved one. (Edgar Jackson [1965] provides a helpful elaboration of some of the steps in talking to a child about death.)

Finally, it is important to understand children according to their developmental needs. Again, Erikson's developmental stages provide a helpful focus, but it should be emphasized that children mature at their own individual rates. The developmental stages provide a framework for understanding, but each child's development is an individual and unique experience.

The first developmental stage designated by Erikson includes the task of learning *trust versus mistrust* during approximately the first two years of life. Although Erikson stresses the development of both trust and mistrust, children predominantly need to establish a sense of trust with the significant other persons in their environment. Children up to the age of 2 have little comprehension of the meaning of death, but they do respond to the developing sense of trust.

As I related in Chapter 6, Carole was a year old when she was separated from her mother and me for a month and cared for by a relative in a town some distance away while her mother recovered from radical breast surgery. Later, when Carole was two and a half, her mother died, and Carole was placed in a day-care center. Her teachers observed that for about six months after her mother's death Carole would never turn to one of the female teachers when she was hurt. Instead, she would turn to one of her peers for sympathy and support. It was as if she could only interpret her mother's death as desertion. While in the process of developing trust in her mother, she had been separated from her twice—during the time when her mother could not care for her and then when she died.

During this time and the following year, Carole was also developing a sense of *autonomy versus doubt.* Developmentally, she included her father as a significant other person. She reactivated her developing sense of trust as I was able to provide her with warmth and reassurance, and Carole began to call Emalee "mommie" even before we married the following year. Her developing sense of autonomy also seemed to be related to her doubts about depending upon adult women. However, once she became more certain that she could exert some control over her life, she was able to allow herself to again experience some dependence upon her new mother.

During the early school years, children are in the process of developing a sense of *initiative versus guilt.* Their significant relationships now include the entire family constellation. Developmentally, they are beginning to take increased responsibility for themselves. While time has begun to take on some meaning, the idea of death is still too difficult to grasp. However, they are able to ask questions and to verbalize some of their feelings.

Elliott was 5 years old when his mother died. He was an active participant in visits to the hospital in the final two months, and he asked questions throughout the periods of his mother's hospitalization. He was included in the conversations when he chose to be included, his questions were answered when he asked them, and he indicated little curiosity about death. Since I openly shared my own tears and feelings of grief, and since Elliott attended the memorial service, he was able to express some of his feelings through his participation in these experiences. Hence, Elliott seemed to have internalized the actuality of his mother's death without undue psychological damage. His acceptance of Emalee as his mother was so wholehearted that, even before the engagement was announced, he exclaimed one day "Why don't you come and live with us, Emalee? We have plenty of room."

Between the ages of about 7 to 13, children are developing a sense of *industry versus inferiority.* Their sphere of significant relationships has expanded to include their peers in the neighborhood and school. They are involved in learning skills and in developing a sense of competence in the use of these skills. Their grief work during this stage of development may be related to some project on which they may be working. The interruption of a project may become the source of sadness and disappointment. As they move closer to puberty, they are likely to become increasingly sensitive to the feelings of others around them. They may be able to talk about their feelings both in terms of themselves and in terms of the feelings others may have. They may also show a desire to help with some physical task. At this age, engaging in physical tasks is an appropriate way of working out feelings.

In adolescence, young people are working out a sense of *identity versus identity diffusion and role confusion.* Peers become increasingly important as significant other persons, and adolescents are preoccupied with learning who they are and how to be themselves. They are developing their ability to share themselves, and they are beginning to learn about the meaning of commitment. During this time, they may need all their emotional energy just to cope with their developing sense of identity. If a crisis of bereavement occurs, adolescents may find it difficult to separate grief work from the other pressures that impinge upon their identity formation. In addition, emotional support may be sought more among peers than among their own families. In the event of the death of a parent, the remaining parent may put too great a pressure on the adolescent at the very time of his or her own greatest need. In the event of the death of a lover, the adolescent will be deprived of a basic peer support at the time of his or her own greatest need and may become a high suicide risk.

COUNSELING INTERVENTIONS WITH BEREAVED PERSONS

The concept of the generic approach to counseling is a helpful one for work with bereaved persons. As I explained in Chapter 4, counselors who are not equipped to assess the specific psychodynamics of individual behavior can be trained to focus their interventions on the course that a particular type of crisis characteristically follows. In general, these interventions include direct encouragement of adaptive behavior, general emotional support, environmental manipulation, and anticipatory guidance. Here I will outline how this general model can be applied to bereavement crises.

Counselors first need to help bereaved persons establish contact with their own highly charged emotions. The purpose of these interventions is to encourage the expression of forgotten and buried feelings. If feelings of guilt and hostility are repressed, counselors can support persons in the exploration of these threatening feelings. The expression of negative feelings does not imply blaming others for one's predicament, but it does involve facing those feelings that have in fact been experienced.

Another aim of counseling interventions is to oppose undue regression of individuals in bereavement. In a profound sense, bereaved persons are temporarily dependent. As they cope with their shock and disbelief, a measure of dependence is appropriate. Bereavement is a time in which religious believers may seek out a minister, priest, or rabbi and appropriately rely on this parental figure until they can "catch their breath" emotionally. At the same time, this moment of dependency can be unduly extended by untrained counselors. Counselors therefore need to be aware of the ambivalent feelings of any person in a crisis. Like others in crisis, bereaved persons tend to want someone to take care of them while at the same time having a healthy desire to remain autonomous. They may need the assistance of a counselor in working out this conflict between facing and evading reality. Hence, counselors can help individuals to face up to their dilemma realistically while discouraging any continuing dependence upon them.

Next, counselors can facilitate the process by which bereaved persons accept the reality of their new situation and learn about the ways in which they can regain control of their own lives. If bereaved persons can regain the self-confidence that they can make it on their own, they will have a renewed sense of power over their own destiny.

Finally, counselors can assist bereaved persons by identifying the human resources that may provide them with emotional support. Professionals within some of the helping disciplines, such as clergy and physicians, may provide the kind of support bereaved persons need at some points in a crisis. In addition, representatives of particular communities, such as clergymen, may be able to mobilize persons within the community or congregation to provide the emotional support needed by bereaved persons. Sensitive and warm individuals who have suffered through their own grief experience often can be trained to provide the kind of care and support a bereaved person needs while enabling the person to come to terms with his or her own feelings.

EXPERIENTIAL TRAINING

I. Suggestions to the Instructor

The exercise of fantasizing one's own dying, which was described in the last chapter, is the most effective preparation for counseling with either dying or bereaved persons and should precede any simulation of a bereavement crisis. If this exercise has already been completed, it may not be necessary to repeat it here. The exercises below are suggested as a continuation of this prior fantasy experience.

II. Experiential Exercises

A. Select a partner, and decide who initially will play the role of counselor and who will play the role of the bereaved person.

B. Here are suggestions for two different kinds of role-play and simulated counseling.

1. Select a particular age during childhood, and become a child at that age who has just lost his or her mother in death.

a. Using the remembrance of your own childhood and parents, take about five minutes to experience this fantasy.

b. Take ten seconds to become your present self again, and then explain the basic parts of your fantasy to your partner, including your age, the nature of your relationship with your parents, and any other data that may help the counselor understand your role.

c. Initiate the role-play, simulating your situations and feelings appropriate to the age you have chosen.

d. After about ten minutes, the role-play terminates with the counselor asking the following questions: Did you feel heard? Was there anything you wished I would have done as a counselor? How do you feel about me as your counselor?

e. Switch roles so that each student has the opportunity to play both roles.

2. In your imagination, become either a husband or wife whose spouse has just died.

a. Take about five minutes to experience this fantasy.

b. Explain the basic parts of your fantasy to your partner, including your age, the age of your spouse, the number of years married, the number and ages of the children, your occupation and basic financial position, any relationships of significance to community groups, and any other data that may help the counselor understand your role.

c. Initiate the role-play, simulating your situation and your feelings.

d. After about ten minutes, the role-play terminates with the counselor asking the following questions: Did you feel heard? Was there anything you wished I would have done as a counselor? How do you feel about me as your counselor?

e. Switch roles so that each student has the opportunity to play both roles.

Suicidal Crises

Suicidal crises present some complex and unique problems. The finality of the act of suicide, of course, places these crises in a special category. In addition, whatever stresses may lead a person to seriously consider suicide as a resolution, that consideration itself poses a new and distinctive crisis that has its own dynamics and consequently demands particular kinds of counselor interventions. A further complication is that, although suicidal behavior is usually a reaction to specific intrapersonal conflicts or interpersonal circumstances, it may result primarily from a characteristic way of responding to life. Finally, suicide raises profound philosophical and religious questions that no counselor of suicidal persons can afford to ignore.

Fortunately, suicidal behavior has been widely studied, and a specialized field of suicidology is being developed. If it is therefore difficult to say anything new about suicidal crises, it is nevertheless important to discuss them here from the standpoint of crisis intervention. In this chapter, I will focus on issues of particular relevance for both individual and community efforts in suicide prevention.

A DESCRIPTION OF THE PROBLEM

A brief review of research data may serve to put the need for suicide prevention in perspective. Suicide is known to affect more than 25,000 families in the United States each year. Medical statistician Louis I. Dublin has estimated that as many as two million individuals in the U. S. have a history of at least one unsuccessful suicide attempt (Grollman, 1966); a more recent estimate places the figure at five million (Mintz, 1970). Many of those who attempt suicide do so more than once, and Dublin estimates that, of these, 10% ultimately succeed. In addition, there is no way of determining how many of the deaths recorded each year as "accidental" are in fact suicides. A significant proportion of the approximately 50,000 fatalities resulting annually from automobile accidents in the U. S. are probably suicides, and many other "accidental" fatalities are undoubtedly suicides. The only certainties are that the number of actual suicides greatly exceeds the number of officially recognized suicides and that suicide is a social problem of some consequence.

The results of research in suicidology have provided a comprehensive analysis of the relative frequency of suicides and suicide attempts among various subgroups in the population. It has been found, for example, that sex, age, and marital status significantly affect suicidal potential. One important discovery is that the suicide rate of men is at least double that of women, while, at the same time, the *suicide-attempt* rate of women is about double that of men. Among men, the suicide rate rises consistently with age, becoming a major problem in the later years. Among women, the suicide rate at first increases with age, but falls off beginning with the age of 60, becoming negligible in the later years. In terms of marital status, the suicide rate of single men is nearly twice that of married men, and the rate for divorced and separated men is 10 times greater than the rate for married men. The suicide rate for single women is about the same as it is for married women, but the rate for divorced and separated women is nearly five times greater.

Although counselors should be aware of these data, the figures do not imply that some people need not be taken seriously if they threaten suicide. The fact that women make more unsuccessful attempts than do men does not mean that women who talk about committing suicide should not be taken seriously. *Any* talk or hints about committing suicide should be taken seriously.

PSYCHOSOCIAL DYNAMICS OF SUICIDE

Extensive research has been conducted into the psychosocial dynamics of suicide. My purpose here is simply to report some of the relevant conclusions of this research and to direct the interested reader to some additional sources of information on this topic.

Psychological analysis of the dynamics of suicide provides a basis for understanding the common emotional patterns of hostility, dependency, anguish, hopelessness, shame, paradoxical striving, and others found among suicidal individuals. An extensive discussion of the psychodynamics of suicidal behavior, as viewed from the perspectives of Freud, Jung, Adler, Sullivan, Horney, and Kelley, can be found in Farberow and Shneidman (1961). Paul Pretzel gives an excellent summary of these dynamics (Pretzel, 1972, pp. 72–86).

Some of the terms commonly used to classify suicidal behavior originated with the classic study of Emile Durkheim (1951). Durkheim's sociological analysis was originally published as *Le Suicide* in 1897, but it was not available in English until 1951, and his classification still provides some of the basic language used in the suicidology literature.

Durkheim defined three types of suicide, which he termed *altruistic, egoistic,* and *anomic. Altruistic* suicides are committed on behalf of some cause, which may be either political or religious; their victims are "overly integrated into the society" (Beall, 1969, p. 3). *Egoistic* suicides are committed by individuals who have failed to become integrated within the society, while *anomic* suicides result from radical changes in the relation of persons to their social groups—changes that produce a state of disorientation and isolation that Durkheim termed *anomie.* The loss of the support of a close-knit family could constitute the kind of change that leads to anomic suicide.

A sociological analysis such as Durkheim's stresses the relationship of human beings to the external influences upon their lives and to the groups with which they identify. Shneidman (1968) attempted to synthesize this sociological emphasis upon the "social fact" with a psychological emphasis upon conflicts *within* individuals. According to Shneidman, "A synthesis between these two lies in the area of the 'self,' especially in the ways in which social forces are incorporated within the totality of the individual. In understanding suicide, one needs to know the thoughts and feelings and ego-functionings and unconscious conflicts of an individual, as well as how he integrates with his fellow men and participates morally as a member of the groups within which he lives" (p. 2). Although he does not claim a definitive classification, Shneidman has insisted that all suicides fall into one of three principal types: *egotic, dyadic,* or *ageneratic.* I will describe this classification briefly, since it may be instructive for mental-health workers and others involved in suicide prevention.

Egotic suicides stem from inner conflicts that are psychological in nature; the effect of the environment is secondary. In egotic suicides, relationships to others are not a primary factor; rather, the suicidal person is simply responding to feelings about himself or herself, and the object of suicide becomes the annihilation of the self. This suicidal person is simply saying to the world "As far as life is concerned, I've had it." He or she wants out of life because of fears, confusion, pain, or hopelessness. In contrast, *dyadic* suicides are responses to the trauma of a radical change in a relationship with some significant other person and hence are primarily social or interpersonal in nature. Dyadic suicides are, in part, dramatic communications to another person; the suicidal act itself is usually an expression of hostility directed toward that significant other person. Finally, *ageneratic* suicides are related to the concern of one generation for the next. They result from the loss of a sense of belonging to that which is larger than life, as represented by one's history. People who have suffered this loss experience a sense of alienation from their families or from the cultural groups to which they had belonged. Hence, they experience a feeling of "interpersonal impoverishment" as the sense of familial, cultural, national, or group ties that have given meaning and value to life is lost.

THE PHILOSOPHICAL AND RELIGIOUS DIMENSION OF SUICIDE

Suicide poses profound philosophical and religious questions. Paul Pretzel (1972) has provided an excellent survey of these questions; here I want only to state some conclusions. First, it is important that counselors recognize this dimension of concern. During counseling with suicidal persons, the question of the legitimacy or value of suicide may be raised. It is therefore crucial for counselors to recognize this aspect of suicidal crises as a problem and to reach some personal conclusions about the philosophical and religious questions involved before they begin work in suicide prevention. Second, it is important that counselors understand some of the questions that may be raised, in order to increase their effectiveness as counselors and enhance their ability to cope with such questions.

My own conclusions can only be stated in paradoxical form. Suicide is a specifically human action, and, as an assertion of specifically human freedom, it is a value to be affirmed; at the same time, suicide as the ultimate "cop out" is an expression of human arrogance that I must reject. The ethical question of the right to take one's own life is a valid philosophical issue, but both my sense of values as a mental-health professional and my understanding of the dynamics of suicidal behavior compel me to simply accept the question while continuing to try in every way I know to dissuade suicidal persons from their goal.

My values as a mental-health professional include a commitment to increasing the options available to persons in effecting change in themselves and in their environments and in developing the skills requisite to coping with those circumstances that cannot be changed. My understanding of the dynamics of suicidal behavior includes two basic insights. First, suicidal impulses usually result from stress with which a person is, at least temporarily, unable to cope, and usually this situation persists for only a short period of time. Hence, counselors have both the opportunity and the obligation to assist suicidal individuals to clarify their feelings and to increase the options available to them in coping with their feelings. Second, at least in situations in which a counselor is consulted, suicidal persons usually experience ambivalence about taking their own lives and hope that something will dissuade them. Counselors therefore need to listen carefully to persons' feelings about their stressful situations and to explore with them alternative ways of coping. They should enhance the power to cope and strengthen those impulses to preserve life that prompt a suicidal person to consult a counselor in the first place. These dynamics are further elaborated in the next section.

SUICIDE PREVENTION AND THE DYNAMICS OF SUICIDAL BEHAVIOR

Some of the dynamics of suicidal behavior are implicit in the description of the psychosocial classifications of suicides given earlier in this chapter. In addition, there are specific dynamics usually present in suicidal behavior that are crucial to any approach to suicide prevention.

Ambivalence

An understanding of the dynamics of *ambivalence* is particularly important, because it is this factor that makes suicide prevention possible. It is a mistake to assume that suicidal persons have a wholehearted desire to die. Generally, they have mixed feelings about both the taking of their own lives and about anyone's interruption of their suicidal plans. Hence, one function of counselors is to relate to an individual's power to choose and to that part of the self that wants to live. Although a person's desire to take his or her own life must be taken seriously and must be heard, there is still that spark of affirmation of life and the power to act constructively that the counselor can support and strengthen.

Depression

Depression is often an important component of suicidal behavior. The psychodynamics of depression are too complex to develop adequately here; however, some observations should be made.

One of the dynamics of *process depression* is related to suicidal behavior. Some persons have learned in childhood to mobilize their psychological defenses against expressing hostility toward significant other persons. When hostile feelings were not accepted, these powerful feelings were turned inward upon the self, resulting in depression. If individuals are unable to direct hostility toward the appropriate person, they will either direct it indiscriminately toward "the whole damn world" or turn it in on themselves, resulting in depression. A good example of this is *dyadic* suicide, which consists primarily of a hostile communication to a significant other person. Thus, a 38-year-old woman addressed this note to her divorced husband before she committed suicide: "You have killed me. I hope you are happy in your heart, 'if you have one, which I doubt.'. . . You have been mean and also cruel. God doesn't forget those things, and don't forget that" (Shneidman, 1968, p. 7). This woman was striking out against her divorced husband even in death, but her hostility was turned inward, and she struck out at him by taking her own life. Indeed, the dynamics of suicide and homicide have considerable similarity, as illustrated by the case of a 35-year-old male who left a suicide note addressed to his girlfriend, whom he had just murdered. "To love you as I do and live without you is more than I can bare [sic]. . . . This is the best way. This will solve all our problems. You can't hurt me further and anyone else" (Shneidman, 1968, p. 6).

The dynamics of *egotic* suicide often include an intrapsychic conflict that stems from hostility turned inward. In her suicide note, a 21-year-old woman wrote "I can't begin to explain what goes on in my mind—it's as though there's a tension pulling in all directions. I've gotten so I despise myself for the existence I've made for myself" (Shneidman, 1968, p. 6). An additional function of counselors, then, is to assist suicidal persons in identifying their feelings of hostility toward significant other persons. Assisting them to develop skills for coping with these feelings may involve reversing the direction of their hostility so that it is directed outward toward the appropriate persons.

Another type of depressive behavior is *reactive depression,* which is a response to some external event. In reactive depression, the experience of a significant loss results in a sense of *helplessness,* or lack of power to influence the outcome of some predicament. In such cases, the function of counselors is to help persons regain some sense of power to resolve their predicaments. Interventions may include facilitating the consideration of alternative solutions and helping persons develop the skills necessary to achieve some resolution.

Some of the dynamics of *ageneratic* suicide seem to be related to reactive depression. For example, a 58-year-old widow wrote in her suicide note "I have been alone since my husband's death 14 years ago. No near relatives. I am faced with another operation similar to one I had ten years ago, after which I had many expensive treatments. My friends are gone, and I cannot afford to go through this again. I am 58, which is not a good age to find work" (Shneidman, 1968, p. 8).

Danger Signals

Related to the dynamics just discussed is the attempt of suicidal individuals to *communicate* something to someone. Suicide has been characterized as a "cry for help." I have already noted that a dyadic suicide is primarily a communication directed to a significant other person; similarly, in most instances of suicide, some "cry for help" is uttered. According to experts in suicidology, nearly every person gives a clue before actually attempting suicide. Psychological "autopsies" of suicides have been performed, consisting of interviews with persons close to the deceased and with others who had contact with the victims prior to their deaths. In examining the recent communications between the deceased persons and others, interviewers have identified some kind of "cry for help" in almost every case. Either the clue was not recognized as such at the time or it was not heeded.

Suicidal persons communicate their intention in various ways. These warning signs may be explicit statements of an intention to commit suicide, or they may be subtle hints. They may simply be physical symptoms accompanied by feelings of depression. A declared suicidal threat should always be taken seriously. People used to assume that persons who talk about committing suicide never go through with it. This assumption is absolutely false. People who threaten suicide very often do go through with it. Similarly, *suicide attempts* are often dramatic cries for help. If the significant other persons do not hear that cry, suicide will probably be attempted again, and, as noted earlier, 10% of those who attempt suicide more than once ultimately succeed. More subtle clues to suicide include comments such as "Life is no longer meaningful to me" or "I don't see anything worth living for anymore." Other clues include frequent comments about funerals or graves or a sudden interest in places such as Forest Lawn cemetary. Persons expressing themselves through *physical symptoms* may be giving nonverbal clues. A sudden loss of appetite, difficulty in sleeping, or a change in degree of alertness in physical or mental activity are all possible danger signals. *Emotional symptoms* such as sudden or chronic depression, withdrawal, and feelings of worthlessness and self-recrimination are also danger signals. Persons who experience sudden changes of circumstances, such as a serious physical illness or a significant loss, merit support from both significant other persons and professional persons such as medical doctors and clergy, as well as mental-health workers.

CRISIS INTERVENTION AND SUICIDAL CRISES

In work with persons in some kind of suicidal crisis, the methodology of crisis intervention is an important consideration. A suicide attempt is often an impulsive way of coping with stress. Although some persons are chronically suicidal, most can be helped if they are heard in the midst of their crises. There is evidence to indicate that most persons who contemplate suicide at some time or another will never again consider it seriously if they have been enabled to develop skills in coping with those feelings during a particular crisis.

Counselors or other human-services workers must listen carefully and take suicidal persons seriously. They need to be secure enough within themselves to be concerned for persons in suicidal crises. Counselors must be able to talk frankly and openly with suicidal persons about their feelings and to explore their suicidal plans with them. Discussing the way they propose to take their lives may assist suicidal persons to get in touch with their most highly charged emotions, thoughts, and goals. Such an open discussion also shows that the counselor is taking them seriously, without implying that he or she condones such action. Indeed, counselors may say very clearly that they do not want the suicidal person to take his or her own life. It is, of course, inappropriate to label suicidal plans "immoral," but it is appropriate to give a strong "I" message, saying, for example, "I don't want you to take your life." Counselors who understand persons' ambivalence about taking their own lives may be able to communicate with the life-affirming part of their personalities. Moreover, counselors can be supportive of suicidal persons and enable them to gradually accept the unfortunate aspects of their reality and to cope with them adaptively.

Related to careful listening and the communication of concern is the counselor's task of reestablishing individuals' sense of trust. Since suicidal behavior represents, in one sense, a failure of trust, it is important for individuals to reestablish their ability to trust in someone. Counselors may become models of trustworthy individuals by following through with all they promise, which implies never promising anything that cannot be delivered. A promise of an appointment or a telephone call must be kept. In a similar way, ministers, priests, or rabbis may assist individuals to reestablish a sense of trust in some community of believers. Any developing sense of trust is essentially based on the trustworthiness of the individual counselor and his or her respect for the client.

In addition, counselors should make an active effort to relate suicidal persons to significant other persons in their environment. These persons may include members of the family, friends, or representatives of communities to which the persons belong. They may include professional persons, such as ministers, or simply warm and accepting human beings who care for others. In all cases, these persons represent either significant others or a community of values that may be shared by the suicidal persons. Hence, they fulfill an important supportive role for individuals who feel cut off from others.

Shneidman's classification of suicides may provide a helpful guide for this type of crisis intervention. Considerable psychodynamic understanding is required in cases of *egotic* suicidal behavior, since this type of behavior is characterized by *intrapsychic* conflict. Counselors who encounter egotic suicidal behavior should therefore refer the person to a mental-health specialist or at least consult with such a specialist.

In cases of *dyadic* or *ageneratic* suicidal behavior, mental-health workers can provide an excellent resource in suicide prevention. Although knowledge of the psychodynamics of behavior can always be helpful, these suicidal phenomena are essentially interpersonal rather than intrapersonal. In instances of *dyadic* behavior, suicidal persons are primarily attempting to communicate something to some other person or persons, and counselors can assist them in sorting out their feelings with only a minimum of understanding of the psychodynamics of their behavior. In instances of *ageneratic* behavior, counselors (or ministers, priests, or rabbis) can help suicidal persons reestablish a sense of trust in others and a sense of relationship with members of a community whose values they share. Again, the emphasis is upon the interpersonal dimensions of trust and relationship rather than upon conflict *within* the person; hence, psychodynamic understanding is less important than the reestablishing of relationships with specific persons or with a community.

SUICIDE PREVENTION AND DEVELOPMENTAL STAGES

Suicidal behavior at any age signifies a crisis and merits the careful attention of mental-health workers and others within the community. Each age group, however, presents its own problems in both primary and secondary prevention. In this section I discuss the problems unique to persons in various developmental stages in conjunction with case histories showing some kind of suicidal behavior. Counseling interventions with suicidal persons are described with special attention to the problems related to each client's age and sex. The conviction that undergirds this counseling is that most suicides can be prevented with understanding and concern.

Suicide Prevention with Children

The psychosocial tasks of children consist of organismic efforts to establish individual identity and psychological integrity. There is no present evidence indicating that any normal childhood problem is related to suicide. Even the trauma of the battered child does not significantly contribute to the incidence of suicidal behavior in children. Indeed, the incidence of suicide among children under 10 years of age is so insignificant that little has been learned about it. The only generalization that can be made is that it is extremely important to provide children with emotionally nourishing environments that are conducive to their present and future emotional health.

Suicide Prevention with Adolescents

Although suicide among children under age 10 is extremely rare, the rate rises steadily in the preadolescent and adolescent age groups. Up to the age of 14 years, only about 1 in every 200,000 youths commits suicide. In the age group from 15 to 19 years, there are about 5 reported suicides per 100,000 population, or 10 times the number under 14 years of age. Of course, these figures need to be put into proper perspective. Although the rate of 5 suicides per 100,000 population is too high, the rate is more than four times greater among persons in the age group of 60 to 64 years. These figures simply put the problem in perspective for those who may think that the adolescent suicide rate is higher than that of adults. Needless to say, the occurrence of any adolescent suicides constitutes a problem that calls for the knowledge and skills of mental-health workers.

A confusing factor in these statistics has been the high rate of *attempted suicides.* Teenagers make more attempts at suicide in proportion to their actual suicides than do adults. Indeed, it has been estimated that the ratio of attempted to successful suicides among adolescents is about 120 to 1, while the adult ratio is only about 8 to 1. Again, these figures do not diminish the importance of suicide prevention among adolescents, and they certainly should not affect the seriousness with which anyone responds to an adolescent's threat of suicide. Indeed, the high rate of attempts indicates both the importance of taking the threat seriously and the possibility of affecting the resolution of these crises. Since a suicide attempt is a dramatic cry for help, many teenage suicides can be prevented by planned interventions. In addition, there has recently been an alarming increase in adolescent suicides, a trend that merits the attention of everyone concerned about persons and the health of their communities.

One of the critical problems in the prevention of suicide among preadolescents and adolescents is the difficulty in identifying the precipitating factors. In their study of adolescent suicide, Finch and Poznanski (1971) concluded "Efforts to delineate a presuicidal syndrome in terms of behavior changes in the three months prior to a suicide attempt have met with failure, except in those youngsters who are psychotic" (p. 3). The actual incidents that precipitate adolescent suicidal behavior often appear trivial to adults. Adolescents' suicide attempts are usually impulsive responses to stressful or crisis situations and often result from a breakup with a boyfriend or girlfriend or a quarrel with a parent or close relative. These incidents are *not* trivial, and they often cause feelings of significant loss. Furthermore, these losses are being experienced by individuals in the midst of forming their identities. Their psychosocial tasks include emancipation from dependence upon parents and the work of defining themselves as persons and in their social roles. In defining their identities, adolescents alternate between dependence and independence. Significant losses in relationships with friends or parents involve the serious loss of dependency gratification. Coping with such a loss involves identifying and accepting the seriousness of the loss and devising alternative ways of coping with the change in circumstances caused by the loss.

Occasionally, some specific behavior of preadolescents or adolescents provides a clue to suicidal intentions. The parents of a 12-year-old girl who had committed suicide indicated to me that she had given away all her toys and belongings to friends prior to her suicide. At the same time, she had spoken about not feeling loved by anyone. Although such behavior by an adult would definitely constitute a suicidal threat, it is not such a clear signal in the case of a preadolescent. In their usual mood swings, adolescents or preadolescents may often complain that no one loves them or impulsively give away all their belongings. In one study, the following model of behavioral stages in adolescent suicide attempts was proposed:

> 1) long-standing history of problems beginning in childhood; 2) a period of "escalation of a problem" which generally occurred during the adolescence period and was in excess of those "normally" associated with adolescence; 3) a chain reaction dissolution of the adolescent's meaningful social relationships [Finch & Poznanski, 1971, p. 4].

In terms of adolescent suicidology, there are some additional factors that may facilitate counselors' understanding. The sex of the suicidal person is as important a consideration among adolescents as it is among adults. Among adolescents, the number of male suicides is more than twice that of female suicides. Another factor is the method used. In the majority of attempted suicides by adolescents, some form of poisoning is used. In the successful suicides of youths in the 10-to-14 age group, hanging and strangulation occur as frequently as the use of firearms. Among adolescents 15 to 19 years old, there is a significant increase in the number of suicides accomplished with firearms. In general, males tend to use more violent means, such as guns, and females tend to use some form of poisoning.

There are some environmental factors that influence the

incidence of adolescent suicidal behavior. In relation to family influences, Sabbath (1968) pointed out that at least half of the parents of adolescents who had attempted suicide had indicated to their children that they were a burden and that they were not wanted. In reference to this parental behavior, he coined the term *the expendable child.* In general, suicidal adolescents tend to come from homes characterized by disorganization, parental disharmony, cruelty, abandonment, dependency, and delinquency. Although they tend to come from families marked by the loss of one or both parents, the stability of the remaining parent or parent surrogate is a decisive influence. There is also evidence of a larger proportion of female suicide attempts during the premenstrual and menstrual periods.

Example of an Adolescent Suicidal Crisis. Lori was 15 when she attempted suicide by swallowing about 30 aspirin tablets. She was taken to a hospital emergency room to have her stomach pumped, but there was no evidence of any permanent medical damage. (Taking a large number of aspirins is a common means of attempted suicide by adolescent girls.)

Lori was deserted by her mother at the age of 3, and her father was a periodic alcoholic. Since he could not care for her, a couple took her into their home as a foster child. The couple wanted to adopt her but were unable to do so for a number of reasons. Nevertheless, they cared for Lori and reared her as their own child, bringing her with them when they moved to California. At that time, she was about 10 years old. Meanwhile, her natural father had died. Lori referred to her foster parents as mother and father and seemed to relate well with them until she was about 13. She had matured early and had begun menstruating before she was 12. By the time she became a teenager, she had become rebellious and disobedient, and at 14 she ran away from home for a few days. In desperation, her foster parents placed her in a residential school for girls, where her life and schooling were carefully supervised. After six months in this school, she went home and transferred to a public high school.

Lori's suicide attempt occurred about six months after she returned home. She was again resisting parental supervision, and she resented interference with her dating plans. At the same time, she was having some difficulty with her boyfriend. Her foster parents asked me to see her after her suicide attempt, and I noted some sociopathic tendencies. She showed a relatively flat affect, did not seem to learn from experience, failed in a variety of circumstances, rarely followed through with her plans, lied considerably, had a low frustration tolerance, and was somewhat promiscuous sexually. Even though she felt that there had been no one available to talk to prior to her suicide attempt, she was confronted with her responsibility for cutting herself off from both parental and peer relationships.

Lori's suicide attempt was an impulsive action resulting from frustration with both her foster parents and her boyfriend. Fortunately, she did not take anything more lethal than aspirin. Although she appeared serious enough about her attempt, it was also a dramatic gesture to be heard and to exercise power over the significant other persons in her life. Counseling with her was limited to a clarification of alternative ways of coping with her frustration—a common type of counseling experience in work with adolescents.

Another example of an adolescent's contemplation of suicide is the case of Paul, which was described in the chapter on body-image crises. His contraction of polio and the loss of his normal body functions involved a serious and significant loss that engendered suicidal feelings.

Suicide Prevention with Young Adults

The psychosocial tasks of young adults include the development of a sense of *intimacy* with at least one other human being. This period of development is marked by an increased sense of self-esteem and the ability to relate to one or more other persons in a cooperative venture, as in a marriage or in a career. Each of these ventures has its own risks and opportunities. In general, however, suicide prevention with young adults follows the general pattern of interventions developed earlier in this chapter.

Joyce was a college student, 19 years of age, who had been very active in the youth program of her church. She consulted me because of some personal problems and because of the suffering she experienced in connection with her knowledge of her mother's terminal illness. Her mother died of cancer about three weeks after our initial meeting. During this time Joyce had begun to talk about some of her feelings about herself, rarely referring to her mother's imminent death in our two initial sessions together. During her subsequent bereavement, she referred to a morning shortly before her mother's death: "As she began to awaken from her coma, one of the things she said, struggling so hard to get the words out, was 'I didn't want to get well!' And she cried and cried. She felt so badly over it—that she wasn't fighting. Why do I feel guilty for her, that she didn't want to get well too? Did I want her to die?" And, in referring to a previous counseling appointment, Joyce said "The Saturday I was so awfully upset when I got there was because all the way out in the car, the only thing I could think was 'Can you *pray* for someone to die?' And violently rejecting even the question at the same time. That was the morning I had left her weeping with her head in her hands over the pain and the futility—and death seemed the only way out to me. Why did I wish for it?"

As Joyce tried to turn to her father during the month following her mother's death, she spoke of him almost as of a distant god, instead of a person with whom she had a personal relationship. "He knows all the answers. When I need to ask, he can tell me what to do. But I resent the fact that he doesn't suffer with me through my problems. He isn't really with me down here. He is always up there someplace—removed from my struggle."

Before coming to see me, Joyce had been talking to her minister, with whom she was very close. She related that she had previously counseled with him about her relationship with her father, and she described a disturbing incident involving her minister that had taken place shortly before her first consultation with me. She had been talking with him, and she related how he had "held me for a long time" and then "kissed me several times." A second incident occurred after her mother's death: "The Monday after Mom died, I spent the afternoon talking with him and again it happened. I have felt despair over it. What is happening? Why this? Why should I not trust him to be what he says he is?" She then related that her minister had explained after the first incident that he had felt she "needed the affection of a man—the kind my father had for me but wasn't expressing." What bothered her was that his wife had not been home on either occasion and that he had let go of her upon hearing his daughter come into the house. To me, she said "Am I reading things into the situation? What's the matter with me?"

In this context of mistrust of her minister, who appeared to be a father/lover surrogate, and of inability to relate to her own father, Joyce was denied the supportive resources of the significant other persons in her life. She had hidden a bottle of sleeping pills left after her mother's death, and she refused to give them up. She often referred to the pills during her sessions with me, but she never divulged where she kept them. These continuing suicidal references were threatening to me and to our relationship, but we talked about the pills and about her suicidal threats. Whenever she got close to life-threatening behavior, we talked about it openly. Ultimately, when Joyce got to the point where she felt she could look to the future without feeling fearful, she decided on her own to destroy the pills.

Suicide Prevention in Middle Adulthood

The suicide rate for both men and women continues to rise with age during the middle years. The rate of suicide among single or separated men and women is higher than it is among married persons. During these advancing years, the suicide rate of men is about three times higher than that of women.

The psychosocial tasks of the middle years include establishing one's self in terms of significant relationships within the larger community and passing on a sense of history and tradition to the next generation. These tasks involve a secure sense of belonging to a particular culture and a willingness and desire to transmit certain cultural values to others. Hence, these tasks also include developing concern for productivity and creativity in culture and in education.

Hazel was a 47-year-old married woman who had no children. She had not married until she was about 40. She was a college graduate with a Phi Beta Kappa key from a prestigious Eastern college. She had married a businessman, about 12 years her senior, who had seemed to be an established leader in the community. He was a leader in a large, conservative Protestant church and a trustee of a small college. About two years after their marriage, Hazel had begun to discover evidence of her husband's business mismanagement. By the time of her first consultation, she had tried to make some sense out of his financial mess and had accepted some responsibility for arranging payments to creditors.

During the following weeks, she became increasingly upset over the pressures from creditors, her husband's continuing financial irresponsibility, and finally with his filing of bankruptcy. Although these proceedings were humiliating enough, her husband also pressured her to lie about certain financial arrangements, and she knew that he would perjure himself. In the midst of these pressures and feelings of humiliation, she was experiencing some menopausal symptoms. She was irritable, moody, and fearful. She felt her husband did not love her and that their sexual relationship was a disruptive influence rather than a supportive one. Although she was very angry and upset with her husband, she was also fearful that he would leave her if she did not go to court and testify for him.

During these weeks she did not threaten suicide directly, but she did begin to talk about the meaninglessness of her life and to remark that nothing seemed worth living for anymore. She talked about her mother's death and about where she was buried. I followed her thoughts with active listening, occasionally identifying her implicit threats by my questions: "Do you mean that you feel that *you* don't have anything worth living for anymore?" "Are you saying that you've thought of taking your own life?" My questions were tentative but serious. Her responses were positive. Indeed, she appeared to be relieved that I had actually mentioned the possibility of her considering taking her own life. These responses enabled her to talk openly about some very threatening feelings, which in turn diminished the intensity of her impulses and gave her some feeling of competence in coping with a very difficult situation.

Suicide Prevention in Late Adulthood

The period of the "later years" is characterized by the serious problems of physical decline, health complications, loss of social contacts, loss of feelings of significance, loss of relationships through death, and change from independence to dependency. These problems are real ones for all normal aging people. Although the incidence of suicide among women begins to decline after the age of 60, it continues to increase among men. In addition, the suicide rate is highest for single or separated persons, and the rate for a divorced or separated male in the general population, including all ages, reaches the phenomenal rate of 152 per 100,000 population. Thus, the threat of suicide generally becomes increasingly serious with age, especially among separated or divorced men.

Helen was 66 years of age when she came to see me. She had been retired from her position as a teacher in public school about one year before. Her husband's death about a year prior to her retirement made retiring a very difficult step for her. Her husband had also been a teacher, and they had shared many experiences together. Although she seemed to have accepted his loss, the loss of her position was a covert blow to her feelings of self-worth. Nevertheless, the first eight months of her retirement had been enjoyable. A trip to Europe, for which she had saved her money, had been both interesting and significant to her. Even her return had been pleasant at first, since she had had so much to share with her friends. However, after about three months of visiting, she had begun to sense some of the psychological distance between herself and her friends, who were still teaching. Despite reassurances from those among her friends who were married, she also had begun to sense an increasing distance between herself and them. Meanwhile, most of her single friends were considerably younger, and they had both personal and occupational commitments that she could not share. Since she had not prepared herself adequately for retirement, she found herself in the awkward stage of letting go of that part of her life that had included meaningful work and a sense of personal significance.

Helen began our sessions by talking about her feelings of depression. Although she expressed feelings of loneliness, the chief theme of her depression seemed to be related to her loss of a feeling of significance. None of the plans that she initiated seemed to her to make any real difference to anyone. She experienced the loss of significance in everything that she did. She felt helpless to influence the outcome of anything with which she was associated.

Helen went on to express feelings of hopelessness. She questioned her sense of self-worth and began to comment that there wasn't anything worth living for anymore. In my first intervention, I began by simply listening to her. I accepted her feelings of having experienced a serious loss. I took her seriously when she began to talk about feelings of worthlessness. I both accepted these feelings and pursued the implicit question of what she had been thinking about. When she acknowledged having felt that no one would really miss her and having wondered about taking her life, we talked openly about those feelings. My interventions at this point included both an active listening to her and a demonstration that I, for one, was concerned about what happened to her. Although I did not perceive the suicidal threat as necessitating hospitalization, I took her seriously. She had experienced a serious loss, and the threat of her taking her own life was real.

My next intervention consisted of exploring with her some possibilities of involvement in constructive community work that she had mentioned in an earlier session. She was an English teacher who spoke Spanish fluently, and she had learned of a community-based program for teaching English to Spanish-speaking people. She was an alert citizen who was aware of the importance of the program, and I supported both her interest in the program and her belief in its importance. I also talked with her about her friends who shared this interest.

In my consultations with Helen, I was aware of the reality of her "regressive developmental tasks," including the acceptance of some reduction in social contact and of the loss of a sense of significance that had been occasioned by retirement from an active career. The death of her husband two years previously involved the further loss of the significant other person who could have been supportive to her. Indeed, her involvement in coping with the changes in her life-style necessitated by his death may have hindered the development of a program in preparation for her own retirement. Facilitating her discovery of alternative ways of experiencing a sense of self-worth through "compensatory developmental tasks" was therefore a crucial intervention. These interventions not only constituted suicide prevention but also demonstrated the significant function of preventive psychology and education.

EXPERIENTIAL TRAINING

I. Suggestions to the Instructor

Role-playing or simulating a suicidal crisis is difficult to do. Exercises involving such crises require careful planning and must include some precautions. These exercises are not games; they represent an expression of real feelings of normal people. Anyone may experience suicidal feelings at some time in life; hence, simulations may be very threatening and close to actual feelings. Students should be excused from the exercises if they feel uncomfortable about participating. Additional roles and simulations may be planned, especially in relationship to specific types of counseling settings.

II. Experiential Exercises

A. The class forms triads. Within each triad, select one person to be a telephone caller, another to be a counselor at a suicide-prevention hot line, and the third to be an observer.
1. The caller is a man, about 64 years of age and in poor health. He was widowed about two years earlier. He has just returned from his doctor. He feels that his doctor was impatient with him and that he did not listen to him or understand him. He has a gun on the table in front of him.

2. The caller and the counselor are each equipped with a phone, and the role-play calls for interventions that will help the man to change his mind about taking his own life.
3. Complete the role-play; then ask for the observer's observations of the phone conversation.
4. If there is sufficient class time, switch roles and play out the simulated phone call again until all students have had an opportunity to play all the roles.

B. The class forms groups of six. The roles consist of a mother and father about 45 years of age, a 15-year-old daughter, and a 14-year-old son, as well as a counselor at a family-services agency. The sixth person is an observer.

1. The parents are bringing their daughter in to see a counselor because she attempted suicide by swallowing 30 aspirin tablets. After examining her at the hospital and pumping her stomach, their doctor had recommended talking to a counselor.
2. The situation consists of the following dynamics:
   a. The daughter has been a model child and has not caused any problems to her family. She has a strong sense of responsibility for her parents and her younger brother. She had been depressed by her parents' quarreling and by her brother's beginning to smoke pot.
   b. Father is a stepfather; he and the girl's mother have been married for about four years. He also has children from a previous marriage, but they are away at college. He is a successful businessman.
   c. Mother cares for her daughter, but, since she is frightened of life, she tends to depend emotionally upon her daughter.
   d. The son cares for his sister and confides in her. He has been experimenting with pot, neglecting school, and cutting classes, but his parents have not yet learned about these things.
3. Complete the role-play in about 15–20 minutes. Take 10 minutes or more for the observer to make observations of the dynamics of the family interaction and of the function of the counselor in intervening and in working out a support system for the suicidal person. Discuss the issues raised by the observer, and evaluate the learning experience.

Drug-Related Crises

The misuse of drugs can lead to crises that disrupt the lives of both the individuals involved and their families. Although an extensive treatment of the problem of drug addiction and misuse does not come within the scope of this book, I do want to describe some of the kinds of drug-related crises that may occur and to examine briefly some of the social factors associated with these types of crises in our culture.

THE USE AND MISUSE OF DRUGS

To begin with, a distinction should be made between the *use* and *misuse* of drugs. The counterculture's misuse of drugs has received the most attention, but it is only part of the problem of drug misuse. We all are part of a drug culture. We all may use medication at one time or another to seek relief from pain or even to save our lives. The very prevalence of drugs, however, has led to "respectable" types of misuse. The dependence of many people on antidepressant drugs or sleeping pills, for example, is clearly a case of misuse. The question, therefore, is not whether a drug is legal or prescribed but how and for what purpose it is used.

I am using the idea of drug *misuse* rather than the common notion of drug *abuse*. People do not abuse drugs; drugs abuse people. I refer to drug *misuse* to emphasize that drugs can either be used or misused and to place the responsibility for being abused by a drug squarely on the individual who chooses to misuse it. Whenever drugs are used as ends in themselves rather than as a part of a total process of health and expanded awareness, there is some degree of misuse.

The misuse of drugs is usually an indication that something is radically wrong. It is a symptom that will be corrected only when the underlying problem is resolved. Neither the prescribed nor the illegal misuse of drugs solves any problems; at most, it gives relief from symptoms. In medical or psychological therapy, symptom relief through drugs can sometimes facilitate the treatment, but it does not take the place of the treatment itself.

In regard to the misuse of drugs by young people, James McFarland, a former director of the Free Clinic in our community of Redlands, has repeatedly emphasized to me that the misuse of drugs among the junior and senior high school youth with whom he has worked is a symptom of their alienation from their parents and their community. Indeed, in responding to a preliminary draft of this chapter, he suggested that these young people experience alienation from *both* the "establishment" *and* the counterculture and that many young people are presently trapped between these two cultures. They experience members of the establishment lying to them and therefore feel alienated from the community represented by parents, schools, and traditional institutions; at the same time, they experience the lies and broken promises of the counterculture and cannot trust that segment of society either. Hence, they are caught in a "schizophrenic" dilemma and may experience alienation from both worlds. In my own observation, whenever such alienation becomes too difficult to cope with, individuals tend to capitulate either to "establishment" conformity or to the rebellious and destructive patterns of the counterculture, including the misuse of drugs. Hence, a crisis may be drug related, but the misuse of drugs is primarily a symptom rather than a cause of the crises experienced by these young people.

There is an alternative to this dilemma. People who consistently "tell it like it is" will find that young people respond. Representatives of community institutions who tell the truth provide young people with an alternative to dull conformity or the personal annihilation of "dropping out." Telling the truth involves many things, but at the very least it includes telling the truth about drugs—and that means, for example, interpreting precisely what happens to the neurological structure of the brain instead of reverting to such deceiving oversimplifications as "Speed (an amphetamine) will make cottage cheese of your brain." It is both more sensible and more honest to explain just what is known and what is not known about the effects of drug misuse.

Counselors who intervene in drug-related crises therefore need to be well informed about the drugs themselves and about the vocabulary of the persons using them. Valuable references on this subject include the publication of the Drug Education Project of the National Association of Student Personnel Administrators (see Nowlis, 1969) and the *Resource Book for Drug Abuse Education* (U. S. Department of Health Education & Welfare, 1969). A brief description of the principal "street" drugs and lingo, as well as a survey of the effects of misuse, can be found in *The Drug Scene,* a paper written for the Division of Youth Services, State of Colorado (reprinted in Dugger, 1975, pp. 108–119).

COUNSELING IN DRUG-RELATED CRISES

In general, counselors of persons involved in drug-related crises need to have an understanding of the drugs and of their effects on the consciousness and physiology of persons. First-hand acquaintance with the effects of drugs can therefore be an important asset of the counselor. Young adults who have experimented with drugs and experienced their dangers may be especially effective in relating to and counseling with young people in drug-related crises. Whatever the extent of a counselor's experiential acquaintance with drugs, however, it is imperative that he or she avoid faking experience with drugs, or with a particular drug, in order to establish rapport.

Of course, personal acquaintance does not by itself qualify a person to be a counselor in drug-related crises. Moreover, counselors who have had little or no experience with drugs can nevertheless be equipped to counsel effectively in these types of crises. In essence, a "bad trip" consists of unusual subjective experiences. Perceptions are altered, and the person may feel that others perceive him or her differently as well. Since basic emotions such as fear are intensified, and since time distortion makes it appear that the "trip" will last forever, the experience can become unbearable, and a severe anxiety attack may ensue.

Counselors who understand these dynamics are usually able to talk persons down from such trips. The first intervention is to prevent the individuals from harming themselves or others, which may involve holding them firmly. The calmness and self-confidence of a counselor who knows that the "trip" will end and who shows care for the person will provide the basis of crisis resolution. Accepting the feelings of this frightened person is a beginning, but it has also been suggested that "the major task is to redefine the drug experience so that it is no longer anxiety arousing," much as parents do with children at amusement parks (Colorado Youth Workers Training Center publication, quoted in Dugger, 1975, p. 118). Obviously, any moralistic rejection of the person or of the drug experience will usually result in disaster. Such confrontation may simply intensify the terror of the experience and increase the possibility that the person will harm himself or herself in the process.

Further helpful interventions include pointing out that the ill effects of the drug are temporary and that what the person is experiencing is not uncommon. Both the content of this information and the calmness of the counselor can be reassuring. Calm acceptance by a therapist helps to counteract the fear of going insane and ultimately provides a basis for the person's increased flexibility and potentiality throughout the therapy.

Intrapsychic Crises

Some drug-related crises may be identified as *intrapsychic* in the sense that the problems are primarily within the individual and only secondarily related to other persons in the environment. Some drug users become dependent on the use of drugs to cope with reality. The use of any drug that alters a person's relationship to reality, and that makes reality more acceptable, may lead to a dependence on the drug. In addition, in the use of a mind-altering drug such as LSD, a "bad trip" may become a crisis either because of the dissociation from reality that occurs or because of the way the experience is interpreted. Drug-induced dissociation from reality is akin to psychotic experience, and persons may lose some control of their thinking processes and engage in socially inappropriate behavior. Such behavior may be difficult to understand, and persons surrounding the user may be threatened. This lack of understanding by the user and by those in the environment may be combined with a heightened intensity of emotion and some distortion of time. The resulting feelings can be extremely frightening. The role of counselors in such crises is to establish a relationship of trust and support that will enable frightened persons to calm down. Once the immediate crisis is over, the individuals may be able to begin working on accepting the actualities of the real world with the acceptance, care, and understanding of a counselor.

The nature and intensity of drug-related crises vary with individuals and with the circumstances surrounding them. Hugh came into a crisis-intervention clinic in a state of fear and confusion. He was 22 years old and a recently returned Vietnam veteran. His immediate reason for coming into the clinic was his frightening experience of confusion. He was occasionally unable to distinguish between reality and hallucinations, and he was in a panic after experiencing hallucinations at a time when he had ceased using drugs.

Hugh had experimented extensively with LSD. Since his last two trips had been bad ones, he had stopped using the drug about two months prior to our first session. However, he had experienced several trips in the past few weeks that he insisted had occurred spontaneously, without his having taken any LSD. These trips, he said, "scared the hell out of me."

Hugh had begun smoking marijuana and using heroin while in Vietnam. He had not become addicted to heroin, although he had used it several times after returning to the United States about six months prior to our first session. His experience in Vietnam was marked by feelings of meaninglessness and boredom, as well as a sense of guilt over the killing that had occurred in a small village. After several in his group had been killed, they all had started shooting indiscriminately—"shooting at everything that moved," as Hugh put it. Although it had seemed to be a matter of survival at the time, he knew that they had "killed first and asked questions afterward." Following that experience, he had begun smoking marijuana regularly, and had continued to do so after his return from Vietnam.

Hugh was not working at the time that he came to the clinic. He had been painting and using LSD in his experimentation with expansion of consciousness. While on LSD he had painted what had seemed at the time to be very creative work, but after he had come down from a trip, the work "just didn't look that good." It was after about three months of this experimentation that he had experienced the severe reactions he referred to as his "bad trips." Having become disillusioned with the effects of LSD on the expansion of his consciousness and disturbed by his severe reactions to the drug, he had discontinued using it.

Although Hugh's relationship with his family had some effect upon his immediate situation, it did not seem to be a predominant influence. He had an authoritarian father who had wanted his son to enter the family business. This issue had been basically resolved, and he only worked occasionally for his father. His mother was overprotective and still wanted to have her son at home, but, since he had taken his own apartment, this issue had also been basically resolved. Thus, although Hugh reflected some characterological problems related to his childhood and family, the basic issue disturbing him was his drug-related panic about his sanity.

My first intervention consisted of listening to Hugh's story and providing emotional support. He was confused and frightened, and he needed a stabilizing influence upon which he could depend temporarily. A second intervention consisted of reassuring him that reactions to LSD have occurred to others for a time after they have stopped using it and that, in all likelihood, his reactions would soon cease. I also recommended a medical consultation. Since there is usually no quality control of LSD, there is always a danger either of an unusually high concentration or of impurities in the drug that can result in severe reactions. Knowledge of such facts can be helpful to an individual who is confused and frightened; in Hugh's case, this information enabled him to exercise increased power to cope with his feelings of threat. A third intervention, concurrent with the second, consisted of helping him to make contact with his own fearful feelings about loss of control and with what he was saying to himself through these feelings. A fourth and final intervention consisted of opening up the possibility of group therapy, which he could initiate when he was ready to work with his characteristic pattern of denying unpleasant and traumatic experiences. Hugh's relationships with both his family and his friends were such that they were not available to provide either the emotional support or the confrontation he needed to cope with himself and his environment. Hence, a therapy group was proposed in order to provide the climate of emotional support and confrontation needed to establish his connection with the here-and-now of his life.

In summary, counseling in this drug-related crisis consisted of demonstrating concern for Hugh, listening to his expressions of fear about his sanity, and providing support, information, and an encouragement to seek out further help. The crisis counseling facilitated Hugh's rediscovery of his power over his own actions and the resolution of the immediate inner experiences that had temporarily immobilized him. The final step was to refer Hugh to resources he could use to further improve his ways of coping, given that existing relationships did not seem to be appropriate sources of support at the time.

About two months after our last session at the crisis clinic, Hugh began his work in group psychotherapy. Although his initial need was to cope with his panic, participation in the group facilitated his personal growth and helped him to take increased responsibility for himself. While he was still in our group, he married, and, at the time of my last contact with him, he and his wife had a baby boy.

Interpersonal Crises

Drug-related crises are sometimes primarily interpersonal, particularly when drug misuse is related to situations in which young people and their parents are no longer able to communicate. This breakdown in communication may be related to distortions inherent either in the individual personalities involved or in the social environment. My first professional encounter with the problems of young people consisted of work with high school youth in my job as a Youth Director on the staff of a community church. Since then I have worked with college students in a large metropolitan university as a University Pastor and as a Faculty Fellow in the experimental Johnston College. Despite all the cultural changes that have occurred during these past twenty-odd years—including the recent complication of widespread misuse of drugs—my work with the problem of what we now call the "generation gap" has all along consisted of respecting young people, listening carefully to their problems, and intervening with confrontations appropriate to their particular reality.

A recent expression of conflict between generations is provided by Jon's experience. Jon was 21 and a former member of a communal group. At the time I first saw him, he had decided to try college a second time but seemed to be relatively passive about it. He had grown up in a middle-class White family. His parents had been active members of a Protestant church in a small community, and Jon had been involved in the youth program at the church. After graduation from high school, he had entered college for the first time. Then, as he related it, "I was busted for sharing my grass with a guy."

Jon's arrest had led to increased tension between himself and his parents. Their eldest son had graduated from college a few years previously, and, since he was now a successful high school teacher, they could not understand Jon's attitudes or behavior. He was not interested in any conventional way of doing things but instead became interested in Eastern philosophies and different forms of mysticism. He studied I Ching and Tarot cards and became involved in astrology and experimentation with various kinds of drugs. Ultimately, he dropped out of college to join a commune. At this point, his alienation from his parents was decisive. They resented his leaving college, and they simply could not understand or accept the style of life he had adopted. Experimentation—with drugs, mystical experiences, various forms of music, sexual freedom, and a vegetarian diet —marked his year and a half in the commune. When the commune broke up as the result of interpersonal conflict, he came to see me at the urging of a friend.

Jon appeared somewhat disoriented, and at first I simply listened to him as he talked about himself. It was soon apparent that, although his disorientation was drug related, he was also shaken up by the conflict that had disrupted his utopian dream. He was immobilized by his inner turmoil. His source of security within his communal "family" had been rudely interrupted by interpersonal conflict. Moreover, the interpersonal conflict that had erupted within the commune was directly contrary to his philosophical and religious values, and at the same time he was unprepared for a return to his earlier value structure. Caught on the horns of this dilemma, he was immobilized by his crisis in values.

After intervening with the emotional support Jon needed at this point, I described to him what I had heard him say. The intervention consisted of enabling him to look squarely at his dilemma and to do so with a sense of security sufficient to move himself off the "dead center" of his conflict. Any move on his part inevitably involved making contact with the feelings of grief that had been aroused by the loss of significant relationships and of a measure of innocence. The *danger* of this crisis was that Jon would resolve his conflict by either reverting to the cynicism of disillusionment or settling for a capitulation and returning to the conventional perspective against which he had rebelled. The *opportunity* of this crisis was the possibility that he would come to grips with his disillusionment without losing the aliveness and potency he had discovered in his new life-style.

After Jon had made contact with his feelings of loss, he was also able to make contact with the feelings of potentiality that he had discovered in the course of his uncertain pilgrimage. He was then able to explore the alternative of reestablishing some relationship with his parents without forfeiting what he had gained in his own search for meaning. Having reestablished his relationship with these significant other persons, he was able to work out his own priorities. He returned to college and, at this time of writing, is involved in a program of study of his own choice.

In interpersonal drug-related crises, the role of counselors is to listen with caring concern and to identify the primary basis of alienation. Identification of the interpersonal conflict, emotional support in the experience of loss or change in relationship, and an opening of new opportunities in relating to others may enable persons to establish or reestablish some significant relationships in which life's options may be increased and their potentialities enhanced.

SPECIAL NEEDS OF YOUNG PEOPLE IN DRUG-RELATED CRISES

Some of the individual and group work in free clinics exemplifies the kind of supportive network that can meet the special needs of young people in drug-related crises. Often, these clinics provide a place where alienated youths can "rap" with someone within the establishment who will listen to them. Most of the problems of junior or senior high school youths are both developmental and cultural in nature, and these young people desperately need someone with whom to talk things out. They need to explore both the personal and cultural issues that relate to the problem of authority and their consequent sense of alienation.

Those who undertake work in programs and agencies concerned with drug misuse should consider using and consulting young adults who have had experience in the drug culture. In addition, it should be remembered that misuse of alcohol still remains the number-one problem of drug misuse among young people and, indeed, continues to be one of the most serious health problems of all age groups. Although crisis intervention can be utilized in various kinds of situations involving drug use and misuse, it is usually ineffective with chronic alcoholics or drug-dependent persons. Since their use of drugs as an escape is an expression of the characteristic way in which they respond to reality, some form of long-term psychotherapy, medical treatment, or involvement in therapeutic communities such as Alcoholics Anonymous or Synanon may be necessary for effective treatment.

In addition to their understanding of drugs and their effects, effective counselors in the drug-related crises of young people should be motivated by an empathetic understanding of both the unique nature of these crises and the individuals who are caught in a conflict between two cultures. Such counselors can facilitate young people's development of skills with which to adapt to their environment. This effort may be characterized as *rehabilitation* in the sense that it enables persons to cope with the situations in which they are involved. A somewhat different function of counselors may be to facilitate the kind of personal growth in which individuals become, to some degree, different persons. This type of effort can be characterized as *habilitation.* It involves an emphasis upon changes within individuals that may give them the power to change their situations rather than simply adapt to them.

Although adolescents may need the presence of young-adult counselors, there are some occupational hazards to such work. In particular, there is a tendency to develop some self-deception, including the attitude that parents and authorities in the establishment are somehow seriously limited people. Young adults, in the role of counselors being sought out by alienated young people, may seem to know the answers and may find it difficult to understand why parents are so inept and so much out of touch with their children. They may begin to perceive themselves as gurus with some esoteric knowledge or capability not available to all persons.

The description of this "messianic syndrome" is not intended to undermine the position of young-adult counselors but only to emphasize an occupational hazard. After all, there is considerable evidence to provide a basis for this self-deception. Parents and authority figures often *have* filled their roles with an abysmal lack of competence. However, there are several additional factors that contribute to the development of counselors' self-deception. First, there are the personality dynamics of their youthful clients. A high school boy, for example, is in the midst of his maturational development. He is experiencing important changes both within himself and in relation to his parents that signify the beginning of his declaration of independence from authority. The psychosocial tasks during this period of development include the beginning of a critical evaluation of authority and the development of a sense of autonomy. To the degree that counselors have not completed their own struggle for autonomy, they will tend to *identify* rather than *empathize* with the young people they counsel. The very dynamics that motivate them to work with alienated youth and that facilitate their success in relating to them may be the ones they have not yet fully resolved within themselves. Hence, the *opportunity* provided by their identification with youth is, at the same time, a potential *danger*.

There is another dimension of the developmental needs of young people that is crucial for counselors to understand. Developmentally, a young man needs to identify with his father, and a young woman needs to identify with her mother. To the degree parents lack some of the qualities crucial for their children's needs, teachers, scout leaders, ministers, and others can meet some of these needs. In rural areas and small towns, these needs are often met in subtle ways that are not available in larger, more impersonal urban environments. Thus, counselors who "rap" with young people may meet some of these developmental needs. Parents must therefore accept the fact that they may not be able to respond to all of the developmental or emotional needs of their children, while counselors must learn that they can value their own charisma in their work without deceiving themselves into thinking that they alone can understand and relate to alienated youths.

POSTSCRIPT

One of the important functions of crisis intervention is to provide information about alternative ways of coping with crisis situations and to explore these alternatives. In some instances, a referral to some supportive network is a crucial intervention. Counselors in drug-related crises should therefore familiarize themselves with the various kinds of rehabilitative and habilitative programs available to persons involved in drug misuse, including both out-patient facilities and residential communities. Free clinics staffed by supportive counselors exist in many communities, and therapeutic communities such as Synanon provide residential environments specifically designed for work with drug addicts. In addition, counselors and therapists have developed various methodologies appropriate for particular cases, including individual and group counseling, encounter and confrontation therapy, gestalt therapy, psychosynthesis, and various kinds of spiritual practices.

Both highly skilled professional specialists and specially trained mental-health workers have counseled effectively with persons in drug-related crises. As is true of any counseling, the primary requisites for effective counseling in drug-related crises include a sincere concern for the individuals involved and an empathetic understanding of the specific nature of these crises and of the circumstances surrounding them.

EXPERIENTIAL TRAINING

I. Suggestions to the Instructor

These exercises will be most effective if used in class sessions, but they may also be useful in encouraging out-of-class assignments where that is possible. The exercises are designed for triads and small groups, but it is often helpful for all members of the class to gather together afterwards in order to share what happened in their various groups.

II. Experiential Exercises

A. The class forms triads. Within each triad, decide who will play the role of counselor and who will be the drug user who is on a "bad trip" from LSD. The third person will be the observer.
   1. The function of the counselor is to talk the person down, using whatever methods seem to be effective.
   2. The person on the "bad trip" is to play the role convincingly, but in keeping with the dynamics of the drug user described in the chapter.
   3. The role of the observer is to make observations following a period of about ten minutes of the role-play and to discuss the counselor's effectiveness.
   4. The class may come back together and discuss what happened in the triads.

B. Divide the class into groups of about six to eight persons. All but two members of each group form a family. The members of each group decide on the family's composition—that is, whether one or both parents will be included, how many children there are in the family, and what the ages of the family members are. They also decide about the type of family, its sociocultural class, and its specific problems. Finally, they decide who is to play the role of the drug user within the family and assign the remaining roles.
   1. The drug user is a 15-year-old boy who is psychologically dependent upon some sort of drug (or drugs) and who wants to continue using the drug(s) despite the destructive effects on his goals and the relationships within the family.
   2. The father is alienated from his son, while the mother is attempting to understand the problem.
   3. One person in the group is designated as a counselor and another as the observer.

4. The family comes to talk with the counselor as they attempt to cope with their crisis of an adolescent drug user within the family. The simulation will take at least 30 minutes to develop and another 20 minutes or so to discuss following its completion.
5. It is usually helpful for the groups to gather back together and discuss what happened in each of their simulations.

Crises Related to
Ethnic Discrimination and Sexism

An appreciation of the special problems faced by women and members of ethnic minorities in our culture is necessary if counselors are to work effectively in crises that are related to, or complicated by, discrimination and sexism. Moreover, both types of discrimination can lead to specific behavioral dynamics when their victims experience crises. Crisis counselors should therefore be sensitive to these dynamics and to their relation to the predicaments often faced by women and minority-group members. In addition, crisis intervention can be an effective strategy of preventive psychology in dealing with the special problems of these segments of the population.

SPECIAL PROBLEMS OF ETHNIC MINORITIES

There is no question that the issue of simple justice for persons of ethnic minorities is a political one. The extension of the concepts of preventive and community psychology to include community development and the end of discrimination are crucial concerns, but they lie beyond the purview of this book. However, applying crisis intervention to the problems of ethnic minorities does not imply defusing the emotional tensions within a community in order to prevent political confrontations. Applied psychology often offers psychological explanations of political issues in a way that implies possible solutions to these issues, but a failure to differentiate between the political and psychological aspects of social problems and their solutions is a tragic mistake. Both White and Black psychologists have often committed the blunder identified by Black psychologist Charles W. Thomas in an interview published in *Psychology Today* (1970). Thomas indicated that the traditional counseling of Blacks is usually conducted in a context of social control rather than social change. Too often Blacks go into counseling to learn how to accommodate themselves to the pathology of their environment.

In contrast, the goal of crisis intervention is not to work out an adaptation of individuals to the pathology of the majority culture but rather to facilitate the understanding and acceptance of the feelings that result from their predicament and to assist them in expanding their alternatives for coping. Crisis intervention provides a means by which individuals can utilize their own coping skills without adapting to the cultural mores of the counselor.

Developmental Deprivation

One dimension of stressful or crisis situations may be traced to *developmental deprivation.* Basic trust is first developed during infancy and is related to the gratification of oral needs. Erikson has suggested that the way in which Black children move, laugh, talk, and sing demonstrates that they have received ample oral and sensory satisfactions. However, the tendency of Black mothers has been to interrupt at least their male children's development of autonomy and initiative for the sake of survival within the majority, White-dominated culture. From the time of slavery, and extending in some cases into the present day, Black mothers have known that, to survive the realities of their world, their sons would need to be trained to show the "proper respect" toward White people and the demands of the majority culture.

An example of the disruption of the developmental work of non-White youngsters can be found in the disruption of their fantasies. The psychosocial tasks of childhood include beginning to develop self-esteem through the exercise of freedom and self-expression, as well as developing initiative in working out a sense of direction and purpose. Play and fantasy are an important part of this development. However, non-White children who watch TV see a White Lone Ranger, a White Superman, a White Batman. At first, when Black children begin to fantasize themselves as Batman rescuing a city, they see Batman as Black, but when they realize the discrepancy between the TV image and their own fantasies, they often abandon the fantasy and hence interrupt their development. In many such ways, non-White children may find themselves unable to develop a self-concept that includes being capable of undertaking risky ventures, and they may consequently develop guilt about even dreaming of trying out new ideas.

Until recently, minority children have had considerable difficulty in discovering a variety of images with which to identify. Prior to our marriage, my wife had an experience that illustrates this psychological need for identification. In the early 1960s, before the time of the Watts riot in south Los Angeles, she was teaching second-graders in a school in south Los Angeles that consisted entirely of Black children. On one occasion, she asked the children to draw their teacher as they saw her. They drew pictures of a darkly colored woman, in some cases showing her with outstretched arms. In the midst of this exercise, one of the youngsters suddenly asked "Miss Rogers, are you White?" Emalee experienced a sinking feeling that the children were separating themselves over against "Whitey," but before she could reply, another child blurted out "'course not! She just looks that way!" Although this was a beautiful expression of the acceptance of a child who felt accepted and loved by her teacher, it was also an expression of the child's need for an image with which she could identify. Some improvements in commercial TV, including programs such as *Sesame Street,* offer some hope that the cultural sources of identification for minority children will increase.

The development of a healthy sense of identity is crucial not only for individuals but for the very fabric of any society. The disruption of such identity formation is bound to have serious consequences both for particular persons and for society at large. Certainly, the deprivation experienced by many minority persons during the years of childhood development has had serious consequences in later life.

Situational Discrimination

Discrimination in specific situations may result in stressful or crisis experiences having their own unique dynamics. For example, a Black man in the ghetto who loses his job may not experience a loss of self-esteem in the same way as would a middle-class White man in the suburb. A White aerospace engineer might react to the termination of his position with panic due to a loss of self-esteem. The Black man might react with explosive anger against the established institutions of society or might express a low sense of self-esteem by turning his anger in on himself, resulting in depression or psychosomatic disorders.

Many of the persons from the poorer socioeconomic classes with whom I have counseled have been in prison. In the 1950s, I was struck by the large proportion of people convicted of felonies within the state of California who were Black. It was not difficult to discover a relationship between the low self-esteem engendered by discrimination and the resulting anger and anti-social behavior that led to imprisonment. The number of Blacks addicted to drugs seemed to be related to the same dynamics. I recall the intensity of the feelings expressed by a Black woman in regard to the tragic experience of her younger brother. Elsie had struggled to make her way with varying degrees of success. Although she was a capable actress with several film credits, it was difficult for a Black woman in the 1950s to obtain a role other than that of a maid or a servant. She was a beautiful and interesting person who had a sensitive appreciation of youth and their struggles and who contributed her time and talent to a variety of youth programs, perhaps as a way of exercising some influence over what happened to the youth in her own community.

Elsie's younger brother, Matt, had graduated from UCLA in the mid-1940s with an engineering major. But he was continually passed over by employers and only found employment in menial jobs. Increasingly he turned his anger in on himself, resulting in depression, apathy, and finally in addiction to hard drugs.

The crisis that destroyed Matt was the direct result of discrimination. The deprivation he experienced because of racial discrimination frustrated any of his efforts to exercise some control over his own destiny. The solution to this type of problem lies first of all in the sphere of political and community development. The primary level of prevention in preventive psychology involves providing a socioeconomic environment in which the mental health of the community is enhanced, thus preventing the occurrence of a crisis like Matt's. The secondary level of prevention involves providing crisis support and intervention to persons in the midst of crises in order to enable them to develop the necessary coping mechanisms.

In working with persons from backgrounds other than their own, crisis counselors can relate to them in ways that do not threaten their identity and integrity. Interventions provide support and understanding without robbing individuals of their own power to cope. Because the duration of crisis counseling is brief, and because the counseling contract is clear-cut, accepting this type of aid does not involve an extensive risk of confronting sociocultural attitudes and behavior significantly different from one's own. Interventions focus upon the ways in which present coping skills have already failed and on the discovery of alternative means of coping. This focus on the here-and-now can facilitate the development of skills to cope with the present situation instead of dissipating energy on past injustices.

SPECIAL PROBLEMS OF WOMEN

Women are presently struggling to realize their own rights and identities in a male-dominated culture. Although their crises are, in a profound sense, the crises of all human beings, sociocultural pressures, combined with their own biological nature, have created some special stresses for women in our society. Some appreciation of the unique stresses and crises experienced by women is necessary if counselors are to facilitate rather than hinder the development of their potential.

Women are a numerical majority in the United States, but, like minority groups, they have suffered discrimination. Indeed, sexism is so deeply embedded in the culture that women are frequently brainwashed by other women as well as by the male-dominated power structure.

In 1966, my wife and I participated in a week-long workshop with Betty Friedan that helped me to see for the first time some of the dire results of discrimination against women. Since that time, I have become increasingly sensitive to some of the culturally derived problems of women. For example, I have been struck by the seemingly disproportionate percentage of my counseling and psychotherapeutic time that has been spent with women clients. Certainly the reason is not that women have more feelings or that they are more unstable than men. Even the coinage of the word *hysteria* to describe a peculiarly female disorder is evidence of male myopia. It may be that more women than men tend to utilize psychotherapeutic resources because our culture grants them permission to more freely acknowledge and accept their affective development. However, it seems to me that women need to utilize these resources largely because of some unique cultural pressures that they experience.

Developmental Deprivation

There seems to me to be a similarity between the problems of identity formation experienced by women and by Blacks of both sexes in our culture. White mothers have often interrupted the development of their daughters' sense of autonomy and initiative for the sake of survival in a male-dominated society. Little girls are taught to limit their expectations to those careers that will not place them in competitive roles with men. They are taught to deny their normal anger and aggressiveness. When anger is denied its normal expression, it is displaced and often turned in on the self. The high incidence of depression that I have noted among women may be related to these dynamics. Another result of the denial of normal aggressiveness is the use by some women of covert means of controlling males. There is a remarkable resemblance between the self-abnegating and in-gratiating means of controlling others used by some Blacks and by some women. There is considerable similarity between the "Black laughter" that "Whitey" doesn't understand and the co-vert laughter of a woman in actual control of a man who retains the illusion of being the boss.

In the past, little girls have grown up in our culture with a limited number of careers from which to choose and a limited number of heroines with whom to identify. Upon being asked what she wants to be when she grows up, the little girl often replies "a mother." When the little boy is asked the same ques-tion, he usually refers to some career, such as that of policeman, race-car driver, or pilot. He rarely replies "a father." Part of the reason for this difference may be the intensity of meaning as-sociated with the bearing of a child and the emotional meaning of this expression of creativity for the mother with whom the child identifies. However, part of the reason seems to be the lack of heroines with whom little girls can identify in their fantasies. The women and older girls they see aren't playing baseball, rac-ing cars, or flying airplanes. Rather, in both the neighborhood and on TV, little girls see women and older girls working around the home and taking care of children. Although the characteri-zations in TV commercials of both men and women tend to be inane, the prevailing image of women is well characterized by the question in one commercial, "What's a mother to do?" She is always busily doing housework or hovering over her chil-dren's and her husband's life and health. Although this analysis has not overstated the issue, there are some hopeful signs that our society is beginning to break out of some of these disastrous limitations on female sources of identification.

One of the results in adult life of cultural deprivation has been the prevalence of a specific kind of anxiety in women. The psychiatrist Viktor Frankl provided the term *noogenic neuroses* to describe the kind of impairment of emotional life resulting from an existential experience of meaninglessness. Human beings are by nature "directed toward meaning," Frankl insists; to be a person is to be involved in the "search for meaning." Thus any person "must accomplish concrete, personal tasks and fulfill concrete personal demands"; any person "must realize that unique meaning which each of us has to fulfill" (Frankl, 1959, p. 100).

Paul Tillich made a similar diagnosis of the nature of the person from a philosophical and theological perspective. He developed the concept of an anxiety that expresses emptiness and meaninglessness. "The anxiety of meaninglessness is anxiety about the loss of an ultimate concern, of a meaning which gives meaning to all meanings. This anxiety is aroused by the loss of a spiritual center, of an answer, however symbolic and indirect, to the question of the meaning of existence" (Tillich, 1952, p. 47). Hence, for Tillich, emptiness and meaninglessness are expressions of the nonbeing of the spiritual life. Although Tillich insisted that the threat of spiritual nonbeing must be distinguished from the threat of nonbeing in death, it is difficult to see how they can be separated. As Tillich himself declared, "Man's being includes his relation to meanings. He is human by understanding and shaping reality, both his world and himself, according to meanings and values" (p. 50).

Prior to modern times, women at least had essential roles that were clearly defined. These roles were more highly specialized than they are now, and, as is the fate of all specialists, women have frequently experienced crises both in prolonging an unneeded specialty and in finally effecting the necessary change. The development of factories to manufacture clothes and household appliances to do the household work has both freed women from the constrictions of their roles and stripped them of some of the meaning with which those roles had endowed them. Until very recently, these problems, heightened by the insecurity of men who feared the economic competition of women, made it impossible for women to develop alternative ways of coping with the opportunities and dangers of their new reality.

Situational Discrimination

The concept of *decidophobia* has been developed by Walter Kaufmann in a recent book (Kaufmann, 1973). In essence, *decidophobia* means "the fear of making decisions." Although decidophobia is certainly not limited to women, the combination of circumstances confronting them in our society has added considerably to the risks involved in their decision making. Kaufmann points out that the word *decidophobia* traces its origin to the Latin *decidio*, which may mean both "decide," its primary meaning, and "fall off." Hence, decidophobia also refers to the fear of falling.

The etymological circumstance may help to clarify a basic problem confronting women. First, the complexity of women's decision making increases the risks involved. Because of a combination of biological and cultural factors, a woman's decision about a career is more complex than a man's. She may be compelled to choose both the career of bearing and rearing one or more children and a career outside the home that provides a broader sense of meaning and fulfillment. It is no wonder, then, that women may deny one or the other dimension of their personal fulfillment in order to be able to tolerate the dizziness of decision making that they must endure. The ambiguity of their position involves the threat of "falling." Many women almost seem to be saying "Stop the world—I'm afraid of falling off." A woman may run the risk of having to decide which of the two careers she will choose. If she chooses one, the other may not be available. If she chooses a career in business, for example, her possibilities of marrying and raising a family are diminished, and vice versa. A further risk is involved in preparing for a specific career—she may not have the opportunity to pursue it because of economic competition and cultural discrimination.

All of these factors complicate the decision making of women and thus explain why they may utilize the strategies for avoiding decision making more readily than do men. One strategy for avoiding decisions is drifting, covertly refusing to make decisions that challenge the status quo of political or religious beliefs, or simply the status quo of a meaningless existence. The high frequency of depression and ennui evidenced by women in psychotherapy is simply not coincidental. Similarly, the increasing incidence of alcoholism in women may be similar to the high incidence of narcotic addiction among Blacks in the 1940s and 1950s.

The women who have most successfully "used the system" for their own enhancement have been the "beautiful women" in the worlds of business, sex, and entertainment. But the beautiful women have learned that their strategy for coping works only as long as they hold the high card of their physical desirability. Having accepted the status quo of their culturally derived desirability, they have never decided to develop skills with which to cope with their environment. The status quo has enabled beautiful girls to become desirable accessories, but like any accessory, they are disposable. Since the beautiful girl becomes an object, she is interchangeable with other objects.

My wife once observed with some interest the number of beautiful women who were in individual and group psychotherapy with me. After discounting any unique animal magnetism on my part, I observed that they often experienced the most critical problems precisely because their physical beauty constituted a handicap as well as an advantage. Whenever anyone's life situation is such that there is no requirement to develop coping skills, he or she is at a disadvantage. The fact that coping mechanisms have not been developed in previous stressful situations means that the person is vulnerable when faced with a new and stressful situation. The fat boy or girl who becomes a comedian in order to cope with the ridicule of peers responds to the pressure of a handicap by developing coping skills that enable him or her to psychologically survive in the environment. Without the pressure to cope with some handicap, the "beautiful woman" is not sufficiently motivated to decide to develop other strengths with which to cope adaptively with her environment.

In crisis therapy with one of the most beautiful women I have ever seen, I noted this lack of coping skills. Elise was 19 years old and beautiful by any cultural standard of physical beauty. Although she had considerable sensitivity to herself and to others, it took some time to discover it. Working with her was like mining for gold. When you discovered some of her inner beauty, it was worth it, but it took a lot of chipping away to get there. It was as if she had never had to develop any depth encounter either with herself or with any other person.

Elise was the youngest of three girls in a family of five children. Her two sisters were about two and four years older than she. Within the family constellation, she was always the sweet, pretty little sister. She never had to do anything to get attention. While her sisters and brothers had some conflict with their father, Elise usually got what she wanted just by being her quiet, sweet self. Since I had seen the entire family in some family-therapy sessions, I had observed these dynamics first-hand. Indeed, some members of the family were aware of the problem and concerned about Elise because of it. It was obvious that she got what she wanted from her father without any hassle but that there was conflict between her father and her sisters. An interesting sidelight here was that her two sisters were also very attractive, but not as beautiful as Elise. While writing this section,

I recalled that I was much more attracted as a man to one of the older sisters. Although she was not as physically beautiful, she had learned the skill of interacting with herself and with others in a way that made her a more interesting and attractive woman.

Elise had originally come in for counseling because she could not decide what to do about her marriage of about four months. Indeed, she had married Jim without actually making any autonomous decision. Jim was about two years older than Elise. He was a handsome man, and somewhat passive and dependent. He and Elise had "gone steady" for about two years. After proposing, he had continued to pressure her to marry him, saying that he needed her. Elise had never actually decided so much as she had continued the status quo until, ultimately, they were married. Two months before our first session, Jim had been drafted. While he was away, Elise was confronted with herself in a new relationship for which she was totally unprepared. Jim was in a nearby training center and came home nearly every weekend, but Elise discovered that she was uneasy and bored with him and with herself. One of my early counseling interventions involved confronting her with her responsibility for herself.

Since she was still unable to develop the skills necessary for coping with her decision making, family-therapy sessions were arranged that included her parents and siblings. A combination of the family network and separate conjoint therapy with Elise and Jim finally enabled her to face her reality head-on and to divorce him. She did not experience any separation anxiety, precisely because she had never actually committed herself to the relationship.

Ruth's situation illustrates some of the problems that are specifically related to cultural deprivation. She was 27 years old, a college graduate, and a registered nurse. She was experiencing considerable inner turmoil in relation to her decision about marriage. She and Tom had been engaged for about six months, and he was pressuring her to set the date for their wedding.

Ruth was a highly successful nurse who worked for a medical specialist. She was outgoing and friendly. She enjoyed meeting people and being with them. Tom was a young engineer, and he was quiet and reserved. Although I never met him, he evidently was a well-trained professional who was very involved in his work. He did not like his present job in a large aerospace firm, and he had just been offered a position in a small company that specialized in a particular product. This firm was located in a nearby suburb of Los Angeles. Tom planned to accept this position, and he wanted to get married and to move to this community with Ruth.

Although Ruth insisted that she loved Tom and did not want to lose him, she experienced considerable personal conflict. Tom was asking her to give up her job and to move away from the excitement of the city to a quiet, suburban, family community. The move itself was not absolutely necessary, but it would enable Tom to avoid commuting on the freeways; besides, he wanted to begin his family. Ruth, meanwhile, had invested considerable emotional energy in both her career and her social values. She wasn't ready to settle down in the suburbs. She also felt that Tom was somewhat threatened by her. When she had expressed some of her needs in relation to both her career and her social life, he had withdrawn from her. She began to see ways in which he seemed to avoid competition, and she felt that his interest in moving to the smaller firm was related to this fear of competing. She also began to see ways in which he sought comfort from her when he was faced with any situation of tension. While she continued to experience some conflict within herself because of her own desire or need to be comforting, she was also disturbed about the kinds of demands that Tom placed upon her. When he reminded her that, because of her age, they should begin having children immediately, she felt some guilt that she did not want children for several more years. Hence, she experienced some guilt both about not wanting to give up her career for the sake of marriage and about not wanting to have children until some time in the future.

By the time of the third session, she had decided to marry Tom, despite some lingering doubts. During this session she showed some ambivalence in that, although she kept the appointment, she still was unwilling to consider any options other than her decision to marry, give up her job, and move to the suburbs.

I did not see Ruth again until about four years later, when she returned to the same counseling service. She had married Tom but had now separated from him. She returned for counseling not because of any specific crisis but rather to sort out her priorities. She had already moved back to an apartment in the city. She related that she had tried to live her life the way Tom had planned it. Her mother had been happy about her marriage and delighted with the birth of a son about a year later. She had remained fairly close to home while caring for her son, but now she was restless and depressed. About two years earlier, she had had an affair with a neighbor that had continued for several months before his wife had discovered it, with the result that they had moved away. Tom had learned about the affair, but, after a period of angry quarreling, he had wanted to "just forget the whole thing." Through this experience Ruth had become consciously aware of some of the anger and depression she felt as a result of having denied her own emotional needs and career goals. When she had begun to explore the option of returning to work and arranging for day care for her son, she had once again met resistance from Tom. This time she listened to her own needs and goals, and her decision to separate provided the basis for exploring the alternatives open to her.

During her second session, she finalized her decision to divorce Tom and to seek a nursing position. She understood how she had struck out covertly at her husband through an affair, and she knew that he would not change his life-style. In some ways, she seemed to be correcting her decision of four years before. Although the expectations of women had changed somewhat during these years, the real change had taken place in Ruth. She was now able to accept responsibility for her own needs and goals, even though it caused some emotional pain for herself, her son, and her husband.

Anne's situation specifically included some career decisions as well as some of the complications resulting from cultural deprivation. She was 34 years old at the time she came to the counseling center, and, although she was not a college graduate, she had completed training as a legal secretary and had worked with an attorney both before and after her marriage. She had been married for nearly 10 years. She and her husband had two sons, 8 and 9 years of age. Her husband was a high school science and math teacher and was a fairly passive man.

Anne came to the counseling center because she was experiencing considerable conflict within herself, and she had read about the center in a recent newspaper account of its work. After not working as a legal secretary for over eight years, she had taken a part-time position six months previously to supplement the family's income. She had become involved in an affair with a recently divorced member of the law firm, but the affair did not seem to be a critical matter to her. Although she had experienced some conflict about it, she had terminated the affair, and she had no intention of leaving her husband or of telling him about it. However, her work schedule had created some tension within the family, and she had now been offered a full-time position with the firm. Although she knew that working full-time would increase the tension within the family, she was also responding to guilt feelings within herself about the kind of demands the position would make upon her. The offer had been made over a week before, but she had still not discussed it with her husband. She had to make her decision by the end of the month, which allowed her another three weeks. The more she thought about it, the more tense she became, both at home and at the office.

After we explored some of her fears about the job offer, she decided to talk with her husband. Although it was important for her to talk with her husband about the offer, talking with him also increased her conflict. Her beginning salary would be equal to her husband's income at that time, and a promised increase and bonus would mean that her salary would exceed that of her husband in less than a year. The opposition he expressed was ostensibly based on concern for the children's welfare, but it seemed that the salary question constituted a point of tension for both of them. Although it gave Anne's ego a boost, the fact that she would be making more than her husband bothered her somehow. In addition, her conflict was augmented by her feelings about not being a good mother if she spent that much time away from her family.

By the time of the third session she had decided to refuse the full-time position, even though that meant looking for a new part-time position in another law office. Although her decision may have been adaptive to her particular circumstances, it meant that she denied some of her own aggressiveness in order to maintain a stable position in relation to her family. Ordinarily, a man faced with the same alternatives would have had a different basis upon which to make his decision.

POSTSCRIPT

There are, of course, other stressful or crisis situations that are unique to women. Some of the questions raised by pregnancy, prematurity, menopause, miscarriages, and so on have been discussed elsewhere in this book. Moreover, members of minority groups may of course experience any of the other crises that have been discussed, as well as other special problems. The purpose of this chapter has been simply to alert counselors to some of the unique dynamics of crises that either stem from, or are complicated by, the sociocultural status of women and minorities.

EXPERIENTIAL TRAINING

I. Suggestions to the Instructor

Role-reversal fantasy is a useful exercise for general training in counseling but is especially important for learning to counsel with those whose sexual identification or sociocultural background differs from one's own.

II. Experiential Exercises

A. Divide the class into groups of six. Each group gathers in a circle, and the instructor directs the following fantasy experience (adapted from Stevens, 1971).

1. Find a comfortable position, and close your eyes. Relax and let go of your tension. Focus upon your breathing and continue to relax as I share these thoughts with you.

We all tend to build up an image of how things "really are," and an image of who and what we are. This image of ourselves might be somewhat true, but it is a fantasy. There are always aspects of ourselves that don't fit this image. If we hang onto this image tightly, we restrict and deaden ourselves, and we prevent ourselves from discovering the parts of our experience that are unknown and alienated. If you can let go, even a little, of your *idea* of what you think you are, you have a chance to discover more of what you actually experience at this moment. What I want to do next is to give you some experience in reversing the way you experience parts of your world and how you experience yourself. It's a simple way of loosening some of your binding prejudices about reality. It can even be a way of finding new ways of functioning, and discovering new things about yourself that you usually are not aware of [p. 55].

2. Now, focus your attention on your breathing (pause). Become aware of your inhaling and exhaling (pause).

Now imagine that your skin color is reversed: If you are black or dark-skinned, you are now white. If you are white-skinned, you are now black or dark-skinned. . . . Become really aware of your new body. . . . How is your body different now? . . . And how do you feel in this body? . . . How will your life be different, now that your skin color is changed? . . . And how do you feel about these changes? . . . Continue to explore your new existence for awhile. . . .

Now change back to your own skin color and your

own body. . . . Silently compare the experience of being yourself with the experience of having a different skin color (pp. 56–57).

3. Continue with your eyes closed.

> Now I'd like you to imagine that your sex is reversed. If you are a male, you are now a female; if you are a female, you are now a male. . . . How is your body different now? . . . Become really aware of this new body, particularly the parts that have changed. . . . If you don't want to do this, that's OK. But don't say to yourself, "I *can't* do this." Say "I *won't* do this," and then add whatever words come to you next. By doing this you may get some idea of what it is that you are avoiding by refusing to do this reversal. . . . How do you feel in this new body? . . . And how will your life be different now? . . . What will you do differently, now that your sex has changed? . . . And how do you feel about all these changes? . . . Continue to explore your experience of being the opposite sex for awhile. . . .
>
> Now change back again and get in touch with your real body and your real sex. . . . Silently compare the experience of being yourself with being the other sex. . . . What did you experience as the other sex that you don't experience now? . . . Were these experiences pleasant or unpleasant? . . . Continue to explore your experience for a little while [p. 56].[1]

4. When you are ready, open your eyes and rejoin your group. Share some of your experience with the others in your group.

B. Divide your group into two triads, and simulate two different counseling situations, utilizing one person as a counselor, another as a counselee, and the third as an observer.
1. The first role-play involves a woman from one of the ethnic minorities in the community in which you work. She is new to the community, having recently moved from another part of the country. Her husband deserted her and their three small children five days ago. She has been in a panic over the desertion and has felt too threatened to get out of her apartment and make the necessary arrangements for welfare assis-

[1]From *Awareness*, by John O. Stevens. © 1971 by Real People Press. Reprinted by permission.

tance to purchase food and clothing for herself and her children. She has been living on the food that was in her kitchen at the time her husband left, but the food is running out. Now she is seeking help at a family-services agency. Complete the role-play in about ten minutes, and take time to discuss the observer's comments about the counseling. Switch roles and repeat the process until each person has had the opportunity to play all three roles.

2. In the second role-play, each person in turn plays the role of a woman facing some difficult problem. Each person should select a problem and have it well in mind before beginning the simulated counseling situation. Include at least one of the basic conflicts that result from sex discrimination. Complete the role-play in about ten minutes, and take time to discuss the observer's comments about the counseling. Switch roles until each person has had the opportunity to play all three roles.

PART 3

Crisis Intervention and Community Mental Health

Part 3 includes a discussion of the work of mental-health workers in relation to the broader issue of community mental health. Crisis intervention is viewed as constituting one important level of preventive psychology and as providing the context for a working relationship among the various persons involved in maintaining and improving the mental health of the community. Professional consultation is proposed as the primary means of increasing the effectiveness of mental-health workers and of coordinating the efforts of specialists and nonspecialists in the field of community mental health.

17

Crisis Intervention
and Preventive Psychology

The development of skills for coping with emotionally hazardous situations is only part of the larger task of utilizing preventive psychology to enhance community mental health. The provision of a sound basis for emotional health in the community involves interdisciplinary and interprofessional collaboration.

In my last book, I developed a model of the working relationship between clergy and mental-health specialists (Whitlock, 1973). The conceptual basis of this model applies as well to the collaborative venture of mental-health specialists and mental-health workers. The possible modes of interaction between these two groups can be characterized in terms of the *goals* each seeks to achieve, the *values* they attempt to preserve, and the *means* they utilize to achieve their goals.

Equal Partnership

Interaction as equal partners increases the sense of interdependence of specialists and mental-health workers. Each profession becomes a resource for the other, even though each fulfills its function within its own context. Participation as equal partners does not mean that specialists and new professionals do precisely the same things. In terms of crisis intervention, they share the *goal* of helping persons confront their crises and develop coping skills, the *value* of being responsible for oneself in a crisis, and the *means* of counselor interventions.

244

Consultative Collaboration

Consultation is another form of interaction between specialists and mental-health workers. Consultation can be a two-way process in which each party benefits from the other's expertise. Mental-health specialists are specifically equipped to provide consultation in the areas of intrapersonal and interpersonal dynamics. Professional help in diagnosis can assist counselors to identify emotional problems in their early stages.

For their part, mental-health workers are often able to identify community needs and to provide insight about the persons being served. In a consultative collaboration, the *goal* of the specialist is to assist mental-health workers in understanding specific dynamics of human behavior. The goal of the mental-health worker is to assist an individual in facing a specific reality and in developing the skills necessary to cope with a specific crisis. The *values* of persons being responsible for themselves in crises and the *means* of crisis intervention may be shared by both the specialists and the mental-health workers.

Social Collaboration

Involvement of all the service professions is crucial to the development of an effective social strategy for the enhancement of a community's emotional well-being. The establishment of comprehensive mental-health facilities is the responsibility of all those involved in promoting community mental health. In particular, mental-health workers are often in a position to be helpful in developing strategies for shortening the duration of emotional disturbance and mitigating its ill effects—for example, by establishing after-care facilities in the community.

In social collaboration, the specific *goal* of the specialist may be to develop a model of mental-health services to be made available to the community, while the *goal* of mental-health workers may be to provide a network of mental-health services, such as crisis counseling centers. The primary *values* of the specialist may be focused on research or on the long-range goals of a comprehensive mental-health plan, whereas the *values* of mental-health workers may be focused on providing counseling services to meet immediate needs. Both specialists and mental-health workers continue to share the *means* of crisis intervention.

In all three types of collaboration just described, the specialist and the mental-health worker are engaged in a cooperative venture in which each supplements the work of the other. In instances of *professional compartmentalization* there is no interaction, and the beneficial results of collaborative effort are lost.

INTERACTIVE RELATIONSHIPS AND RESULTING TENSIONS

As those concerned with the mental health of the community move toward a more contemporary view of their roles, their interdependence upon each other increases, and tensions between them may also increase. In the case of extreme *compartmentalization,* there is no interaction, except on a nonprofessional level. As long as mental-health specialists and workers remain entirely separate, they remain alienated from each other. Both their values and the way they perceive their roles preclude any functional interaction. Since they see no basis for interaction, they simply ignore each other. In the area of *social collaboration,* any one of the persons involved may initiate the interaction and interchange when areas involving specific or expert knowledge is involved. For example, the social-work profession may be the best equipped to initiate action regarding the need for day-care facilities for patients discharged from mental hospitals. In *consultative collaboration,* the various workers who are aware of the need for consultation may initiate interaction with the specialists at the level of work with particular persons. A probation officer, for example, may become aware of a need to understand some specific dynamics of intrapersonal or interpersonal behavior and therefore of a need for professional consultation in this area. Interaction and interchange as *equal partners* offer both the greatest potential and the greatest tension. In this mode of interaction, there is the danger that this same probation officer, for example, might attempt to be an amateur psychiatrist, and the mental-health specialist pretend to be an expert in probation work. However, to the degree that each person is aware of the need to learn from and contribute to the common dialogue, the interaction can make a significant contribution to the unique functions of both.

This area of interchange as equal partners holds the most promise in meeting the need for community mental health. Increasing specialization without cooperation, on the other hand, limits our approach to the complex problem of the sanity and health of the total community.

Until there is a way to join the *knowlege* of mental-health specialists with the service provided by mental-health workers, communities will be unable to meet the needs of preventive mental health. A mental-health specialist in private practice directly affects, at best, only a fraction of a percent of the total population of a community. A mental-health worker may affect the lives of more persons every year than the average psychiatrist or clinical psychologist in private practice. In addition, the professionals involved in teaching, social work, law enforcement, the ministry, medicine, and so on relate to and significantly affect nearly 100% of the population. In varying degrees, these persons lack the specialized knowledge of mental-health professionals, and hence their effect upon the emotional development of the persons with whom they work is limited. Bringing specialized *knowledge* and *community function* together is a crucial social strategy.

CONSULTATION FOR MENTAL-HEALTH WORKERS

One of the ways in which the effectiveness of mental-health workers may be enhanced in the community is through their use of consultation. Consultation consists of a contract between a specialist in a particular field and a consultee who seeks assistance in understanding some particular problem. The purpose of the consultation is to assist the consultee in fulfilling his or her responsibilities more effectively. Thus, a minister might consult a mental-health specialist in regard to counseling with a person in a suicidal crisis. The mental-health consultant will not tell the minister how to do his or her pastoral work, but he or she can assist the minister to counsel more effectively with a person experiencing a kind of crisis with which the minister may be unfamiliar.

Consultation may be needed by any counselor or mental-health worker in specific instances, and it is critical to the development of counseling skills. The concept of consultation is based on an awareness of the limitation of any one individual. The knowledge that any professional or paraprofessional may need consultation at some time or another may free some individuals from the tyranny of the thought that they *ought* to know what to do in every instance, without assistance from anyone else. Specifically, mental-health consultation represents the additional understanding that no single family of professions or institutions can resolve all the mental-health problems of a community. Mental health is everyone's business, and no branch of the mental-health profession has the competence to manage all the concerns involved.

Consultation is the tool by which human effectiveness can be increased throughout the community. M. Brewster Smith (1968) has stated the case well:

> Consultation is essential. People interact with their social environment; to change aspects of that environment can make great differences in the mental health of whole groups. The people and institutions that in large part influence or determine that environment—government agencies, churches, schools, business, industry—are amateurs when it comes to the psychological effects of their policies or decisions, and they are preoccupied with other matters. This does not mean that the mental health professionals know best how the community should operate— such a claim is presumptuous and foolish. Rather, they contribute a special perspective that can help the agencies and institutions perform their functions better. Through consultation, at all levels, mental health people can improve the quality of community and family life for all citizens [p. 22].

This approach to increasing the human effectiveness of the entire community is relevant to crisis support and intervention as one of the levels of preventive psychology. The training and equipping of persons in various helping professions as crisis-intervention counselors, as well as the training of mental-health workers, is an important function of the specialist, and consultation is an important tool in that training.

The Function of Consultation

A clear understanding of the function of consultation may increase its usefulness to mental-health workers who are unacquainted with it. Although consultation is an effective educational tool, its primary purpose is not to teach the conceptual nature of a specific work. Discussion of the theory and practice of crisis intervention is a way of learning the conceptual framework of such counseling skills. In contrast, the primary function of consultation is to assist persons in using themselves, their skills, and their training in a more effective and efficient manner.

Although mental-health workers may gain considerable insight about their own behavior through consultation, its primary function is not therapeutic. The self-awareness that occurs as the result of skillful consultation is a secondary rather than a primary benefit. In a doctor-patient relationship there is an implicit contract in which the patient agrees to suffer the indignities of exposure, and the doctor agrees not to take advantage of that situation. In consultation, the consultees do not agree to self-disclosure. The consultation contract is limited to the consultant's agreement to provide the data the consultees request in order to do their work more effectively.

Consultation is often confused with supervision. Although there are some similarities between the two functions, there is also a significant difference between them. Supervision involves an experienced person in one profession supervising and training an inexperienced worker in the same profession. Consultation involves consultees in one profession seeking the assistance of a specialist in a different profession. The consultant's function is not to tell the consultees how to do their job but to assist them in that part of their tasks with which they are unfamiliar. In addition, in supervision, the responsibility for a client or program remains with the supervisor. In consultation, the responsibility remains with the consultees. While the consultant may clarify issues, offer diagnostic interpretations, or advise regarding specific treatment, the consultees choose to accept or reject such counsel, precisely because the responsibility remains with them.

The Types of Consultation

There are various types of consultation appropriate to different circumstances. Gerald Caplan (1964) has described in detail four different types of mental-health consultation. In a previous book I have discussed these types of consultation as they relate to the needs of ministers, priests, and rabbis as mental-health counselors (Whitlock, 1973, pp. 62–76). Two of these forms of consultation are relevant to the equipping of mental-health workers for crisis intervention.

1. Client-Centered Case Consultation. Client-centered case consultation focuses upon the client to be helped. Since mental-health workers often have had only a minimum of training in the fundamentals of personality psychodynamics, abnormal psychology, and counseling techniques, they may need professional assistance both in identifying problems and in knowing what to do to help a particular individual in crisis. In psychiatric or psychological terms, they may need assistance in the *diagnosis* and *treatment* of particular cases. Caplan (1964) describes the purpose of this type of consultation as follows:

> The problems encountered by the consultee in a professional case are the focus of interest; the immediate goal is to help the consultee find the most effective treatment for his client. Educating the consultee so that he may in the future be better able to deal unaided with this client or class of clients is a subsidiary goal. Since the primary goal is to improve the client, the consultant's fundamental responsibility is to make a specialized assessment of the client's condition, and to recommend an effective disposition or method of treatment to be undertaken by the consultee. The consultant's attention is centered on the client, whom he will probably examine with whatever methods of investigation his specialized judgment indicates are necessary in order to arrive at an adequate appraisal of his difficulty [p. 214].

Thus, the primary purpose of client-centered consultation is to help the individual client, but to do so through the counselor who has already established a relationship with him or her. Such consultation is an efficient use of the time of both the counselor and the specialist. The counselor, having already established a relationship with the client, already has the kind of rapport with the client that the specialist would probably have to spend hours developing. In addition, since the counselor is seeing the individual in the midst of a crisis situation, time is of the essence.

In any consultation there is a problem of communication. Specialists in any field inevitably develop their own vocabulary and frame of reference. Hence, both the consultant and the counselor need to be sure that they understand each other.

2. Consultee-Centered Case Consultation. Consultee-centered case consultation may be the most important type of consultation for mental-health workers. Caplan's description is a helpful one:

> The focus of the consultant in this type of consultation is on the consultee, rather than on the particular client with whom the consultee is currently having difficulties. True, the problems of this client were the direct stimulus for the consultation request and will form the main content area of the consultation discussion, and a successful consultation will usually lead to an improvement in the consultee's handling of the current

case, with consequent benefit for the client. But, in contrast to client-centered case consultation, in which the consultant's main interest is diagnosing the difficulties of the client, his primary endeavor in the present instance is to assess the nature of the consultee's work difficulty and to help him overcome it [Caplan, 1964, p. 219].

Consultation and Counselor Limitations

Caplan has described several types of difficulties that interfere with a counselor's effectiveness—namely, lack of professional objectivity, lack of understanding of the psychological factors involved, lack of skill or resources to deal with the problem, and lack of professional confidence and self-esteem. These difficulties account for distortions and omissions in a consultee's report on a client. The mental-health consultant must be able to identify the internal inconsistencies and the verbal and nonverbal clues the counselor gives in discussing the client.

Lack of Professional Objectivity. The implications of a lack of objectivity are related to the use of the self of a counselor in crisis intervention. Counselors need to approach their self-understanding with some sense of objectivity in order to be open to their own feelings and emotions. They need to be relatively free from the tendency to project their own insecurities or aggressive needs onto other persons. To the degree that they are emotionally unsure of their own psychological needs, they will tend to exploit their clients for the sake of their own unmet needs rather than help them.

A loss of objectivity occurs when counselors' own emotional needs enter into their relationships with their clients. Caplan has called this difficulty a *theme interference.* Its source is some long-standing personality difficulty that a counselor has not yet resolved. The difficulty is usually unconscious, and the subjective involvement of the counselor results in a change from *empathy* to *identification* with the client. There is a fine line between empathetic understanding of a person's problem and identification with him or her, but the difference is crucial. Empathy enables counselors to establish rapport and to assist in the resolution of personal problems. Identification with a client confuses the counseling relationship. It involves a loss of objectivity that leads to a "distortion of perception and judgment and a lowered effectiveness in utilizing professional knowledge and skills" (Caplan, 1964, p. 223).

In the event that counselors lose their sense of objectivity in counseling, they will need mental-health consultants to describe to them the nature of the "theme interference" in such a way that it will be understood and resolved. Otherwise, they will be unsuccessful in their counseling, and they will continue to project their own unmet needs upon persons in similar situations in the future.

Caplan's approach to this problem of a loss of objectivity involves separating the consultee's personal life from any work difficulty. Hence, the consultant does not try to work with the *causes* of the theme interference but only to define it in relation to the counseling context in which it occurred. Dealing with the causes of the interference draws a consultant away from his or her primary function; moreover, since the counselor may be using clients to work out personal problems vicariously, he or she may be defensive about dealing with the causes of the theme interference. However, if the consultant simply describes *how* the counselor's emotional involvement interferes with his or her ability to see a client objectively, the counselor's perception may be improved and corrected.

Lack of Psychodynamic Understanding. Another type of difficulty experienced by counselors is a lack of understanding of a situation, especially in terms of the psychodynamics involved. Mental-health workers may not have had sufficient training in the psychodynamics of behavior or psychopathology to understand the factors involved in some intrapsychic or interpersonal problems. Consultants can help these counselors by adding to their knowledge in these specialized areas and relating pertinent data to particular individuals and their crises.

Such consultation should not be confused with teaching courses in the various areas of human behavior, especially if the consultation is on an individual basis. If the consultation is conducted with a group, such teaching may be included, but even then it would be a subsidiary goal.

Lack of Professional Skill. Although some counselors may understand the psychodynamics of a particular behavior, they may lack the specialized skill necessary to resolve the crisis. Mental-health consultants can assist counselors in choosing a specific course of action. The consultation may focus on ways in which the counselors can intervene more effectively themselves, or it may focus on the appropriate community resources to which a person may be referred. Consultation on referral resources may be accomplished through group instruction and the compilation of a list of community resources.

An additional form of mental-health assistance is the suggestion of a specialized plan for therapy for a particular client. In a crisis situation, for example, there may be specialized ways in which interventions can be planned to meet a particular need.

Lack of Self-Confidence and Self-Esteem. In some situations, counselors may feel frustrated, frightened, or powerless to deal with a problem posed by a person in crisis. The function of a consultant in such a case may simply be to provide encouragement and support. Young or inexperienced counselors, especially, may feel more capable to deal with a problem once they have talked it over with a mental-health specialist. The first time counselors encounter a suicidal threat, for example, they may become so frightened that they are immobilized. A consultant may help such a counselor to discover the most skillful way of working with the suicidal person, but the most important assistance may simply be the support the consultant gives. Such support can enable counselors to do what they are uniquely able to do in such a situation.

Endings and Beginnings

Every ending is also a beginning. An ending involves bringing something to a close—facing the reality of a significant loss, accepting it as final, and moving on. If a loss is never accepted realistically, the experience is never terminated, and an individual will live with the illusion that the loss has not really been sustained. When a significant loss has been genuinely accepted, that segment of life can be ended and a new segment begun.

When a person sustains the loss of a significant other person or a part of himself or herself, a crisis may occur. Coping adaptively with the crisis involves accepting its reality and bringing the experience to a close. Saying "goodbye" to the loss provides the basis of an adaptive resolution of the crisis and of the beginning of a new segment of life. People can learn how to cope adaptively either through the achievement of an understanding of their own crises or through the interventions of a counselor or of some other caring person who facilitates the development of their coping skills.

CONCLUDING UNSCIENTIFIC POSTSCRIPT

Crisis intervention is one expression of a larger concern for the emotional health of the community. I conclude as I began, with an emphasis upon a psychology *of* community that includes supportive interpersonal relations and crisis intervention. Indeed, we need to move beyond this level of concern to the entire area of preventive mental-health care. Prevention is everybody's business. It is the job of the entire community to provide an environment that is conducive to the development of emotional health and to prevent the development of a toxic environment that erodes personal autonomy and responsibility. We need to enhance the nurturance potential of schools, churches, and community-service agencies in order to help all persons learn how to cope with that reality which cannot be changed and how to develop their potential to change that which can be changed. The learning of coping skills enables persons to make adaptive responses to change. Such responses, in turn, make possible the flexibility and creativity needed to celebrate human existence rather than merely to endure it.

In an address to a division of the American Psychological Association several years ago, Carl Rogers directed what he called "some new challenges" to his fellow psychologists. His critical analysis of his profession led him to raise questions about credentialing that challenged a "sacred cow" of psychologists. "As soon as we set up criteria for certification," Rogers insisted, ". . . the first and greatest effect is to freeze the profession in a past image." His answer to the credentialing problem was to use the energy and money expended on certifying and licensing to concentrate on "developing and giving outstanding personal help." He indicated, "In my estimation we must face the fact that in dealing with human beings, a certificate does not give much assurance of real qualifications. If we were less arrogant, we might also learn much from the 'uncertified' individual who is sometimes unusually adept in the area of human relationships" (American Psychological Association, 1972, p. 14).

Indeed, the question raised by Rogers opens up not only the area of interdisciplinary and interprofessional collaboration but also the training of mental-health workers and interpersonal facilitators who will be able to provide both a caring concern and crisis intervention for normal persons with temporary needs. Warm, caring persons can often be most effective in real-life crises simply because they have the capacity for helping others. A good example was provided by Rogers in a recent book:

> He [Clyde] was simply inwardly with her in her isolation, jealousy, and self-hate. It makes no difference that she did not respond. She [Libby] simply "recognized" his deep companionship in her private isolation. I know from long experience as a therapist that this is definitely the most helpful attitude he could possibly have held. Where did he learn it? How did he know? It simply confirms my belief that many, many people have an intuitive capacity for helping—a capacity which equals that of the best trained therapist—and can release it in a climate in which they feel freedom to act spontaneously [Rogers, 1972, pp. 149–150].

In raising questions about the relevance of psychology as a profession to new social priorities, M. Brewster Smith observed that community psychology has thrust the psychologist into an area beyond the one-to-one consultation. The emerging focus on social problems, Smith wrote, may thrust psychologists into working relationships with various professionals: "If psychology is to make its potential contribution to coping with these problems, psychologists will have to learn to work with specialists in these widely different domains, and even to take the initiative in establishing such interdisciplinary relationships" (Smith, 1973, p. 466). He went on to point out that in 1969 George Miller had observed that the most important contribution of professional psychology to human welfare may be what it "gives away" to the general public. The ideas that are given away through writing and teaching, and the attitudes represented in these efforts, may in the final analysis be the chief contribution that the profession of psychology can make to the common good.

This kind of openness to utilizing the helping capacities of persons in the community at large can provide for the development of a psychology *of* community relevant to the needs of all persons in our society. Although not everyone will experience all the emotionally hazardous situations described in this book, everyone will experience some potential crises in a lifetime. Persons can be trained in the understanding of human crises and of crisis support and intervention. These interpersonal facilitators can then help persons in a variety of ways and in many different situations. Community-based "Help Lines" and "Crisis Lines" are examples of this kind of human assistance. For their part, mental-health specialists can become "translators" of specialized psychological knowledge. They can translate the data of psychological expertise into training programs in the community. This translation includes the training of mental-health workers to help persons develop the skills they need to cope with life's usual and unusual crises.

References

Adams, E. Barbiturates. *Scientific American,* February 1958.

Aguilera, Donna C., & Messick, Janice M. *Crisis intervention* (2nd ed.). St. Louis: C. V. Mosby, 1974.

Aguilera, Donna C., Messick, Janice M., & Farrell, Marlene S. *Crisis Intervention Theory and Practice.* Saint Louis: C. V. Mosby, 1970.

American Psychological Association. APA *Monitor,* November 1972.

Bach, George, & Wyden, Peter. *The intimate enemy.* New York: Avon Books, 1964.

Bandura, A. *Principles of behavior modification.* New York: Holt, Rinehart & Winston, 1969.

Barrett, James H. Group psychotherapy in old age. *Geriatric Focus,* November 1972, p. 4.

Beall, Lynnette. The dynamics of suicide: A review of the literature, 1897–1965. *Bulletin of Suicidology,* March 1969.

Berne, Eric. *Transactional analysis in psychotherapy.* New York: Grove Press, 1961.

Bing, Elizabeth. *Six practical lessons for an easier childbirth.* New York: Bantam, 1969.

Bradley, Robert A. *Husband-coached childbirth.* New York: Harper & Row, 1965.

Brammer, T., & Shostrom, E. *Therapeutic psychology.* Englewood Cliffs, N.J.: Prentice-Hall, 1968.

Caplan, Gerald. *An approach to community mental health.* New York: Grune & Stratton, 1961.

Caplan, Gerald. *Principles of preventive psychiatry.* New York: Basic Books, 1964.

Carkhuff, R. R. *The art of helping.* Amherst, Mass.: Human Resource Development Press, 1972.

Carkhuff, R. R. *The art of problem-solving.* Amherst, Mass.: Human Resource Development Press, 1973.

Dick-Read, Grantly. *Childbirth without fear.* New York: Harper & Row, 1944.

Dugger, James G. *The new professional: Introduction for the human services/mental health worker.* Monterey, Calif.: Brooks/Cole, 1975.

257

Durkheim, Emile. [*Suicide*] John A. Spaulding and George Simpson, trans. Glencoe, Ill.: The Free Press, 1951.

Easson, William M. *The dying child*. Springfield, Ill.: Charles C Thomas, 1971.

Egan, Gerald. *The skilled helper*. Monterey, Calif.: Brooks/Cole, 1975.

Eissler, K. R. *The psychiatrist and the dying patient*. New York: International Universities Press, 1955.

Erikson, Erik. *Childhood and society* (2nd ed.). New York: Norton, 1963.

Farberow, Norman J., & Shneidman, Edwin S. (Eds.). *The cry for help*. New York: McGraw-Hill, 1961.

Feifel, Herman (Ed). *The meaning of death*. New York: McGraw-Hill, 1959.

Finch, Stuart M., & Poznanski, Elva O. *Adolescent suicide*. Springfield, Ill.: Charles C Thomas, 1971.

Fort, J. Comparison chart of major substances used for mind alteration. Paper presented at the NASPA Drug Education Conference, Washington, D. C., 1966.

Frank, Jerome D. *Persuasion and healing*. New York: Schocken, 1963.

Frankl, Viktor E. *The doctor and the soul*. New York: Knopf, 1955.

Frankl, Viktor. *From death camp to existentialism*. Boston: Beacon Press, 1959.

Fromm, Erich. *The dogma of Christ*. London: Routledge & Kegan Paul, 1963.

Glass, A. J. Psychotherapy in the combat zone. *American Journal of Psychiatry, 110* (1954), 725–731.

Glasser, William. *Reality therapy*. New York: Harper & Row, 1965.

Grollman, Earl A. (Ed.). *Rabbinical counseling*. New York: Bloch, 1966.

Hartman, Heinz. *Essays on ego psychology*. New York: International Universities Press, 1964.

Holmes, Thomas H., & Rahe, Richard H. The social readjustment rating scale. *Journal of Psychosomatic Research, 11*(1967), 213–218.

Ivey, Allen E. *Microcounseling*. Springfield, Ill.: Charles C Thomas, 1971.

Jackson, Edgar N. *Telling a child about death*. New York: Channel Press, 1965.

Jacobson, Gerald F. Crisis theory and treatment strategy: Some sociocultural and psychodynamic considerations. *Journal of Nervous and Mental Disorders*, August 1965, pp. 209–217.

Jacobson, Gerald F., Strickler, Martin, & Morley, Wilbur E. Generic and individual approaches to crisis intervention. Paper presented before the Mental Health Section at the 94th Annual Meeting of the American Public Health Association, San Francisco, 1968.

Jacobson, G. F., Wilner, D. M., Morley, W. E., Strickler, M., Schneider, S., & Sommer, G. J. The scope and practice of an early-access brief treatment psychiatric center. *The American Journal of Psychiatry*, June 1965.

Kaufman, Walter. *Without guilt and justice: From decidophobia to autonomy*. New York: Wyden, 1973.

Kempler, Walter. Experiential psychotherapy with families. In Fagan, Joen, & Shepherd, Irma Lee (Eds.), *Gestalt therapy now*. Palo Alto, Calif.: Science and Behavior Books, 1970.

Kubler-Ross, Elizabeth. *On death and dying*. New York: Macmillan, 1969.

Lester, David, & Brockopp, Gene W. *Crisis intervention and counseling by telephone*. Springfield, Ill.: Charles C Thomas, 1976.

Levitsky, Abraham, & Perls, Frederick S. The rules and games of gestalt therapy. In Fagan, Joen, & Shepherd, Irma Lee (Eds.), *Gestalt therapy now*. Palo Alto, Calif.: Science and Behavior Books, 1970.

Lindemann, Erich. Symptomatology and management of acute grief. *The American Journal of Psychiatry*, September 1944.

Macdonald, John M. *Rape: Offenders and their victims*. Springfield, Ill.: Charles C Thomas, 1975.

Medea, Andrea, & Thompson, Kathleen. *Against rape*. New York: Farrar, Straus, & Giroux, 1974.

Menninger, W. C. *Psychiatry in a troubled world*. New York: Macmillan, 1948.

Miller, Donell. Psychodramatic techniques in academic settings. *Group Psychotherapy*, September-December 1967, pp. 212–217.

Mills, Patrick. *Rape intervention resource manual*. Springfield, Ill.: Charles C Thomas, 1977.

Mintz, R. S. Prevalence of persons in the city of Los Angeles who have attempted suicide. *Bulletin of Suicidology*, July, 1970.

Morley, Wilbur E. Treatment of the patient in crisis. *Western Medicine*, March 1965.

Nowlis, Helen H. *Drugs on the college campus*. New York: Anchor Books, 1969.

Parad, H. J. (Ed.). *Crisis intervention: Selected readings*. New York: Family Service Association of America, 1965.

Perls, Frederick S. *Gestalt therapy verbatim*. Lafayette, Calif.: Real People Press, 1969.

Pretzel, Paul W. *Understanding and counseling the suicidal person*. New York: Abingdon Press, 1972.

Psychology Today. Different strokes for different folks: George Harris' conversation with Dr. Charles Thomas and Joann Garner. September 1970.

Rogers, Carl R. *Client-centered therapy*. New York: Houghton Mifflin, 1951.

Rogers, Carl R. *Becoming partners*. New York: Delacorte, 1972.

Sabbath, Joseph C. The suicidal adolescent—The expendable child. *Journal of American Academy of Child Psychiatry*, 7 (1968).

Shneidman, Edwin S. Classification of suicidal phenomena. *Bulletin of Suicidology*, July 1968.

Sifneos, Peter E. *Short-term psychotherapy and emotional crisis*. Cambridge, Mass.: Harvard University Press, 1972.

Smith, M. Brewster. The revolution in mental-health care—A "bold new approach?" *Transaction*, April 1968.

Smith, M. Brewster. Is psychology relevant to new priorities? *American Psychologist*, June 1973.

Stevens, John O. *Awareness*. Lafayette, Calif.: Real People Press, 1971.

Tanzer, Deborah, with Block, Jean Libman. *Why natural childbirth?* Garden City, N.Y.: Doubleday, 1972.

Tillich, Paul. *The courage to be*. New Haven: Yale University Press, 1952.

Whitlock, Glenn E. Emotional crises of those facing the draft. *Pastoral Psychology*, April 1968, p. 183.

Whitlock, Glenn E. *From call to service: The making of a minister*. Philadelphia: Westminster Press, 1968.

Whitlock, Glenn E. The pastor's use of crisis intervention. *Pastoral Psychology*, April 1970, p. 203.

Whitlock, Glenn E. *Preventive psychology and the church*. Philadelphia: Westminster Press, 1973.

Name Index

Subject Index